About the Author

Elizabeth Rakoczy is a Professor of Molecular Ophthalmology at The University of Western Australia. She holds several patents, is the author of more than 160 scientific papers and recipient of the prestigious Florey Medal. She is an enthusiastic skier, somewhat of a runner and a passionate reader. Since their first date, she and her husband Steve have been sailing the world's oceans with great enthusiasm and a keen eye for history.

Elizabeth Rakoczy

KEEP ON SAILING
THE WINE-DARK SEA

A JOURNEY IN SPACE, TIME
AND THE HUMAN MIND

AUSTIN MACAULEY PUBLISHERS™

LONDON • CAMBRIDGE • NEW YORK • SHARJAH

A CIP catalogue record for this title is available from the British Library.

ISBN 9781786290779 (Paperback)
ISBN 9781786290786 (Hardback)
ISBN 9781786290793 (E-Book)
www.austinmacauley.com

First Published (2018)
Austin Macauley Publishers ™ Ltd
25 Canada Square
Canary Wharf
London
E14 5LQ

DEDICATION

For my father, who travelled to a place of no return

ACKNOWLEDGEMENTS

The idea for this book first occurred to me in around 2002. I remember the first time I tentatively walked into the library and made handwritten notes on Socrates' defiant speech. By the time I had begun my research on Ancient Greece in earnest in 2006, everything had changed. The Internet and Wikipedia became my number one research tools and Amazon the supplier of the majority of the books I refer to. I am eternally indebted to the wonderful writers who gave us those unforgettable works, and all those anonymous contributors who make the Internet an endless fountain of knowledge. Without your selfless work, I could never have finished this overly ambitious work. I have tried to take great care to acknowledge all my sources; nevertheless, my sincere apologies if I have overlooked some.

The book that inspired me most was *The Consolations of Philosophy* by Alain de Botton. For me, de Botton was the first author who cared to explain to us mere mortals how ancient philosophical thoughts weave themselves into our ordinary lives and can help us to understand our everyday struggles. *Odysseus Unbound* by Robert Bittlestone is the best crime story I have ever read and gave me the courage to venture into something that could not have been further from my own profession.

I sincerely thank Steve, an irreplaceable partner in all my adventures in life. Without you nothing is possible!

I'd also like to thank my children Gavin and Anna for their unwavering encouragement. I know that it has been a long time coming, but at least I've made an honest attempt to answer your questions put to me all those years ago.

I am eternally grateful to graphic artist Sophie Szepessy for the beautiful artworks and to Steve Rakoczy for the photographic recording of our adventures. Thanks also to my dear friend Miranda Grounds for your kind, wise words and our endless discussions.

In Defence of the Rational Mind

John Keats: Ode on a Grecian Urn

"Beauty is truth, truth beauty –
that is all Ye know on Earth, and all ye need to know."

CONTENTS

INTRODUCTION

The origins of this book go back to our decision to "call Australia home", our love of sailing and our resolve to do some extensive cruising in the Mediterranean. As with all travellers, I felt an urge to learn more about the countries we planned to visit, and starting with Greece, I ventured into the world of ancient literary works. The more reading I did, the more I recognised the similarity between my view of the world and that of the Ancient Greeks. Somehow, living halfway across the world from this small ancient country, this did not seem to make sense.

We came to Australia for a year, but when I breathed the fresh air blowing from the Indian Ocean and stared mesmerised at the colourful sails criss-crossing on the Swan River I knew that I was destined to stay. After a year, of hesitation, we settled in Perth, Western Australia. Our children grew up in that beautiful, windy city. They became wild, freethinking, imaginative little rascals, equipped with a wonderful, though sometimes narrowly focused, education. It was no surprise then that an endless number of questions followed our announcement that Dad (Steve) and I were to go on a sailing holiday in Greece.

"Where is Greece? How old is Greece? Who are the Greeks? Is Athena Greek?"

"Darlings, Ancient Greece is the cradle of civilization," came my measured answer, followed immediately by their next question: "*Why Greece?*"

I am a scientist. I don't know whether doctors see a world full of sick people, whether the teacher always notices naughty children, whether for a plumber the world is full of leaky, unruly pipes. For us scientists, the world is a series of deconstructable, testable propositions that ultimately must and can be proven. This old proverb gives something of the idea:

"The isness of things is well worth studying but it is their whyness that makes life worth living" – William James Durant

Our minds, full of "Whys", make the scientists of the world an overarching force, crossing racial, ethnic, religious and political barriers and forming a United Nations of Scientists. I always thought that I had more in common with a scientist from Timbuktu than my next-door neighbour, a financial advisor. This book, in search of "Why Greece?", took me out of my comfort zone of medical science into the field of humanities. And it did not take long for me realise that combining the deep understanding of Ancient Greek scholars with the finesse of writers is a challenging task. I often felt that my own powers of descriptions were inadequate. Fortunately, over the last 3,000 years, plenty of talented writers have visited the region, giving us sublime descriptions of its landscape, people and ideas. This book is a strange combination of quotations from the masters of literature intertwined with a personal journey initiated by a sailing adventure.

My involvement with sailing goes back to my first date with my future husband. I recall the warm summer night, the dreamy walk on the Chain Bridge in Budapest while searching for a topic that would make my new friend unveil something about himself. I asked the irresistible question that makes even the most reserved boy talkative: "Do you do any sport?"

His body language changed, his eyes lit up and without delay came the unexpected answer, "I sail!"

In the mind of any self-respecting female, sailing is associated with gin and tonic, romantic sunsets and gentle breezes. So, not very tactfully, I declared, "Sailing is not a sport!" With these inept words my sailing adventure had begun.

The Viking 30s are legendary in Perth, and there is a bit of a story behind them. It all started in 1983 when John Bertrand made the unlikely leap from competitive yachtsman to national hero when he skippered *Australia II* to victory in the America's Cup against *Liberty*, skippered by Dennis Conner, thus ending 132 years of American supremacy. In true Aussie spirit, the jubilant Prime Minister Bob Hawke enthusiastically participated in the celebrations and memorably stated, "Any boss who sacks a worker for not turning up today is a bum."

The little-known Royal Perth Yacht Club became the challenger, and for the next couple of years Fremantle became the centre of the yachting world. In a typically understated Perth manner, the international crews tested West Australian winds and waters in a fleet of humble Viking 30s. Dennis Conner himself handled the tiller of a Viking 30!

Fifteen years on, we raced our Viking, *Balaton*, through three pretty hopeless seasons at the Royal Perth Yacht Club and started to make regular visits to the Indian Ocean. I discovered my love for long-distance ocean sailing and we both became extremely fond of the yearly 140 nautical mile Christmas Cruise to Quindalup, hidden in the southern corner of Western Australia. Unable to resist the call of the ocean, we moved to the Fremantle Sailing Club, of which we are still members to this day.

Towards the middle of the 1990s, we also started bare boat chartering on the Mediterranean. We enjoyed the relatively calm waters and the history of the

Mediterranean so much that after a couple of seasons we decided to look for a sailing boat, with the intention of keeping it on the "Med".

In 2002, we chartered in Palma de Mallorca. As we walked out from the marina for a late dinner, I spotted a brokerage that was still open. With not too many customers around, we received an enthusiastic demonstration of all the available yachts. We did not like any of them and, feeling a little embarrassed about taking up so much of the salesman's time, as an excuse I blurted out, "We would need a blue-water yacht that is capable of sailing back to Australia."

"Oh, why didn't you say so?" exclaimed the agent, and pulled out a file from which an extended Hallberg Rassy 42 gently smiled at us, as graceful as a queen. It was love at first sight! Without a second thought, we changed our plans, sailed our chartered boat to Barcelona (not allowed by our contract), arranged a test sail and right then and there said: "Yes!"

This is the story of *Fenix* and its crew in search of an answer to the question:

"Why Greece?"

THE
JOURNEY

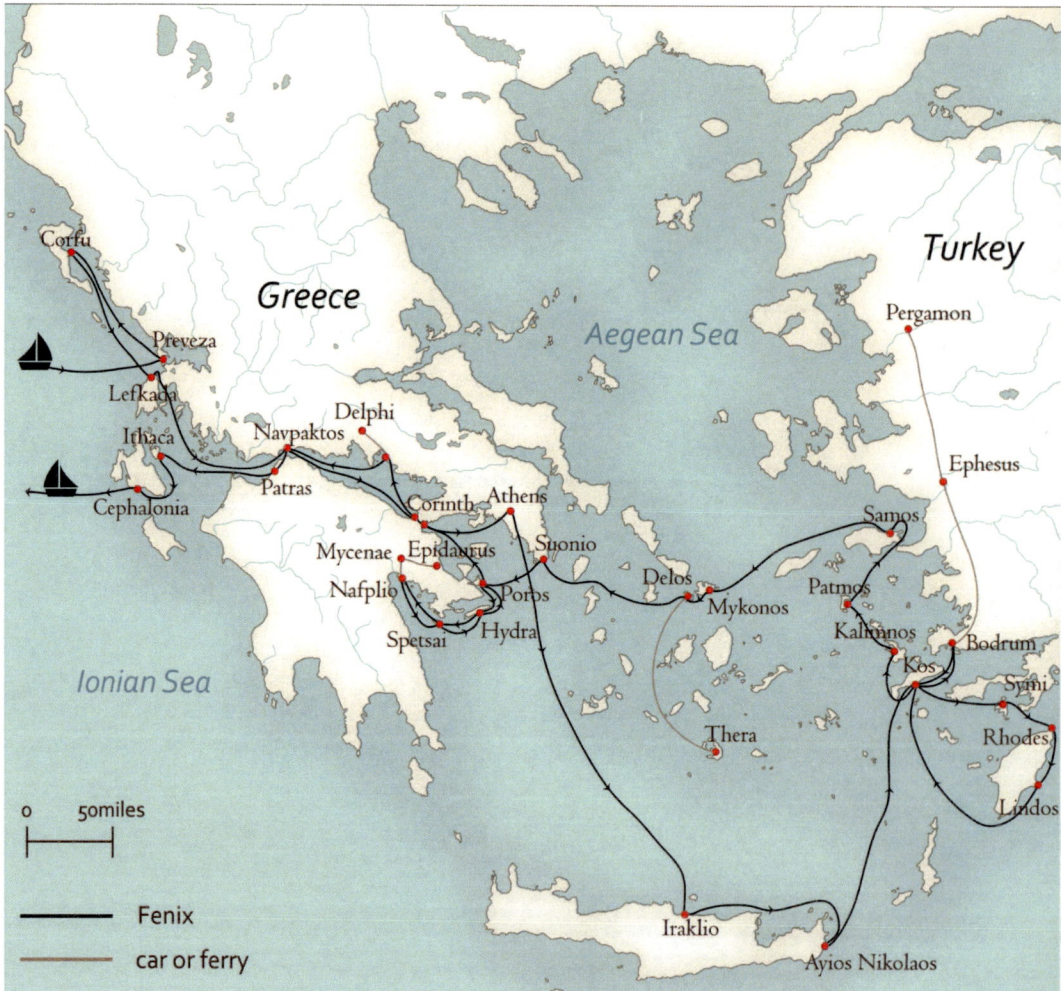

Corfu

Greece

Turkey

Preveza

Pergamon

Aegean Sea

Lefkada

Delphi

Ithaca

Navpaktos

Ephesus

Patras

Cephalonia

Corinth

Athens

Samos

Mycenae

Epidaurus

Sunio

Patmos

Nafplio

Poros

Delos

Kalimnos

Spetsai

Hydra

Mykonos

Kos

Bodrum

Ionian Sea

Symi

Rhodes

Thera

Lindos

o   50miles

Iraklio

Ayios Nikolaos

Fenix

car or ferry

The Battle
of Actium

September, 2005

The Passage

*"Other countries may offer you discoveries in manners or lore or landscape;
Greece offers you something harder – the discovery of yourself."*

(Durrell 1975)

Around 2 am a faint flashing light appeared on the horizon signalling the presence of something human in the middle of the darkness. The flashing single LED was clearly visible one minute, then it disappeared to appear again, and again. We knew it was an LED from the dry whiteness of its glow and its strong luminosity. The "now-you-see-it, now-you-don't" game suggested that the source of the light was close to sea level. The flashes were screaming:

HELP!

A flashing white light in the middle of the sea means that someone is in trouble. So, having watched it for couple of minutes with our VHF radio switched to channel 16, we were preparing to turn around and find the source – to rescue passengers of a sinking ship or to pick up an unknown sailor who had fallen overboard without anyone noticing and was now floating alone with only his flashing strobe light to keep him company. But our radio remained silent. No mayday or pan-pan call disrupted the monotonous sound of the waves and the steady humming of the 15-knot wind. And no one answered my call either.

"Vessel at 39°10′; 18°05′ flashing light, Vessel at 39°10′; 18°05′ flashing light, Vessel at 39°10′; 18°05′ flashing light. This is *Fenix, Fenix, Fenix*. Do you copy?"

"Vessel at 39°10′; 18°05′ flashing light, Vessel at 39°10′; 18°05′ flashing light, Vessel at 39°10′; 18°05′ flashing light. This is *Fenix, Fenix, Fenix*. Do you copy?"

"Vessel at 39°10′; 18°05′ flashing light, Vessel at 39°10′; 18°05′ flashing light, Vessel at 39°10′; 18°05′ flashing light. This is *Fenix, Fenix, Fenix*. Do you copy?"

Then, suddenly, an eagerly awaited cracking noise signalled that somewhere nearby a radio had come alive.

"*Fenix*, this is *Pandora, Pandora, Pandora*, Channel 73."

"*Pandora*, this is *Fenix*, switching to Channel 73."

"*Pandora*, this is *Fenix*. Do you see a flashing LED light? Over."

"Fenix, this is *Pandora.* Yes, it is me. I am sailing alone from Greece to Italy on a 28-foot sailing boat and I keep a flashing LED on the mast to make myself more visible. Where are you heading? Over."

"Glad to hear that you are OK. We thought you were in strife. We are heading to Corfu on a sailing boat. Two people, enjoying the passage. Over."

"Thank you, *Fenix.* Do you have a weather update?"

"Pandora, there is a Sirocco warning but it is not expected to reach us for another day or two. We should be safely in port by that time. Have a good trip."

"Thank you, *Fenix.* Fair winds. Over and out," and he started to whistle a well-known tune happily to himself into the dark night.

The tune was from the latest hit movie, *Kill Bill,* directed by Quentin Tarantino. *Kill Bill* was a very popular movie in 2004, with catchy tunes, lots of blood and fights with all sorts of deadly weapons. This blood-soaked movie, in a bizarre way, had many fairytale qualities. I left the radio on and listened to his joyful whistling, which, enhanced by the hull and bouncing between the low clouds and the waves, surrounded me like the music of the best concert hall. But the whistling became fainter and fainter and the flashing light slowly disappeared over the horizon. Soon I was alone in the cockpit, continuing my watch under the starless sky.

Those of us who live in crowded cities yearn to be alone. I remember that some time ago when we were in the middle of building our careers, establishing a new life in Australia, bringing up children and renovating a house, all I wanted was a week of solitary confinement in a prison cell. I simply did not want to see a single human being for a week!

How quickly things can change! Just spending half a night alone in the cockpit of a small yacht under a dreary sky in the middle of the seemingly endless oceans of Planet Earth – we tend to forget that 75% of the surface of the Earth is covered by water – I was feeling sad as the sometimes-off key notes of the movie song whistled by an unknown man slowly vanished.

We had to make the crossing to catch our flight from Athens, although this meant taking a considerable but calculated risk. We were running in front of a storm. During the passage, the sky was covered with black clouds, and for most of the trip, I watched the horizon with some trepidation. But for now, the barometer was only falling slowly and the mighty Sirocco remained trapped somewhere along the African coast. The Sirocco, a hot, dry wind that sweeps across the Mediterranean for days with ferocious force, is known to be responsible for the loss of many lives on these waters. Although, its first tentative rumblings had been just born somewhere along the African coast, fear and respect already appeared to be keeping the busy passageway between Italy and Greece empty. The route plied by ancient and modern sailors for more than five millennia appeared to have been abandoned by the people of the Internet age. For two and a half days, we saw no vessels other than the lonely sailor of questionable musical talent – no container or cargo vessels, fishing or sailing boats or cruise ships. Even the small, overloaded motorboats of people smugglers remained in port or were concealed by the starless sky.

We continued our trip with determination while the already large and ever-building swell slowed our progress. Perhaps, it was this huge swell that caused our autopilot to fail. I woke up Steve and he managed to put together something that relieved us from continuous steering for the next 12–15 hrs.

Sailing is a slow mode of transport, but the relentless motion of your vessel propelled by the wind eventually takes you to your destination. After two days and nights of sailing, we were approaching the land of Homer. The land appeared as a soft line gently floating on the grey horizon at dawn.

"Land!" I called out, just as I heard a big sigh from the autopilot, which finally and irreversibly died on us. Neither of us cared, we were so excited! Caressed by the morning sun, we gently steered Fenix into the Gulf of Ambracia, the site of the greatest ancient maritime battle.

The year of the battle was 31 BC, the apex of the Roman Empire that ruled the "known world". Julius Caesar had been dead for 13 years, assassinated. According to Nicolaus of Damascus, who wrote his account of the murder of Caesar a few years after the event:

> "All quickly unsheathed their daggers and rushed at him. First, Servilius Casca struck him with the point of the blade on the left shoulder a little above the collar-bone. He had been aiming for that, but in the excitement he missed. Caesar rose to defend himself, and in the uproar Casca shouted out in Greek to his brother. The latter heard him and drove his sword into the ribs. After a moment, Cassius made a slash at his face, and Decimus Brutus pierced him in the side. While Cassius Longinus was trying to give him another blow, he missed and struck Marcus Brutus (his adopted son) on the hand. Minucius also hit out at Caesar and hit Rubrius in the thigh. They were just like men doing battle against him."

I guess that in comparison to this, the movie *Kill Bill* really was a fairytale. We all remember the Caesar's last words from Shakespeare's *Julius Caesar*:

> "Et tu, Brute."

Octavian, Lepidus and Anthony defeated the armies of Caesar's assassins Brutus and Cassius at Philippi in 42 BC. The winners divided up the land around the Mediterranean Sea. Octavian ruled the west, Anthony the east and Lepidus the north of Africa. Anthony's part covered present-day Macedonia, Albania, Greece, some parts of modern Turkey and all of the Middle East. It was not long, therefore, before he met the Queen of Queens: Cleopatra.

Cleopatra, a descendant of Alexander the Great, was beautiful and intelligent. A quick-witted woman, blessed with a charismatic personality and fluent in nine languages, she was known not to take "no" for an answer. She was one of the first women we know of to have used her wit, intelligence, beauty and charm to get what she wanted: to rule Egypt. She had no hesitation in seducing Julius Caesar, who helped her to become the Pharaoh. One could consider her clever moves to be like a modern-day hostile corporate takeover. Perhaps one day we will re-evaluate her and she will become a 21st-century feminist icon.

The first meeting between Anthony and Cleopatra took place on a luxurious cruiser. It was love at first sight! Their meeting and what followed were chronicled in great detail by ancient historians and remains part of our folklore and culture.

The most memorable dramatisation of this fatal relationship is given by Shakespeare in *Anthony and Cleopatra*.

DOMITIUS ENOBARBUS
The barge she sat in, like a burnish'd throne,
Burn'd on the water: the poop was beaten gold;
Purple the sails, and so perfumed that
The winds were love-sick with them; the oars were silver,
Which to the tune of flutes kept stroke, and made
The water which they beat to follow faster,
As amorous of their strokes. For her own person,
It beggar'd all description: she did lie
In her pavilion—cloth-of-gold of tissue—
O'er-picturing that Venus where we see
The fancy outwork nature: on each side her
Stood pretty dimpled boys, like smiling Cupids,
With divers-colour'd fans, whose wind did seem
To glow the delicate cheeks which they did cool,
And what they undid did.

AGRIPPA
O, rare for Antony!

DOMITIUS ENOBARBUS
Her gentlewomen, like the Néréides,
So many mermaids, tended her i' the eyes,

8

And made their bends adorning: at the helm
A seeming mermaid steers: the silken tackle
Swell with the touches of those flower-soft hands,
That yarely frame the office. From the barge
A strange invisible perfume hits the sense
Of the adjacent wharfs. The city cast
Her people out upon her; and Antony,
Enthroned i' the market-place, did sit alone,
Whistling to the air; which, but for vacancy,
Had gone to gaze on Cleopatra too,
And made a gap in nature.

AGRIPPA
Rare Egyptian!

DOMITIUS ENOBARBUS
Upon her landing, Antony sent to her,
Invited her to supper: she replied,
It should be better he became her guest;
Which she entreated: our courteous Antony,
Whom ne'er the word of 'No' woman heard speak,
Being barber'd ten times o'er, goes to the feast,
And for his ordinary pays his heart
For what his eyes eat only.

AGRIPPA
Royal wench!
She made great Caesar lay his sword to bed:
He plough'd her, and she cropp'd.

DOMITIUS ENOBARBUS
I saw her once
Hop forty paces through the public street;
And having lost her breath, she spoke, and panted,
That she did make defect perfection,
And, breathless, power breathe forth.

MAECENAS
Now Antony must leave her utterly.

DOMITIUS ENOBARBUS
Never; he will not:
Age cannot wither her, nor custom stale
Her infinite variety: other women cloy
The appetites they feed: but she makes hungry
Where most she satisfies; for vilest things
Become themselves in her: that the holy priests
Bless her when she is riggish.

Approaching Preveza, the fateful coast for the ancient lovers, I felt like the Desert Queen herself, reassured that even girls of the ancient past had great affection for water, boats, discovery and all the pleasures they may offer!

Following their historic meeting, the besotted Anthony married Cleopatra. This union was not popular with the Romans and the situation steadily deteriorated. Eventually, the Senate declared war on Anthony and Cleopatra. The battle took place at Actium, in the Gulf of Ambracia, near where the Preveza/Levkas international airport now stands, exactly at the site of our landfall. Today, there is not much to see for the few enthusiasts who climb the promontory and venture north to the site of Octavian's camp. However, more than 2,000 years ago the site was occupied by thousands of soldiers and sailors who were preparing to fight the strangest battle in history, fuelled by jealousy, greed, fear and revenge.

Ships gathered from all over the known world. Anthony occupied the promontories. They offered an excellent view of the Gulf of Ambracia, filled with his fleet, and the Ionian Sea. Then, on 2 September, 31 BC, 220 of Anthony's ships, mostly quinqueremes, and 60 Egyptian warships fought the forces of Octavian. The bows of the quinqueremes were armoured with bronze plates and square-cut timbers, making them powerful for ramming. Ramming was a standard battle strategy at the time, aiming to inflict holes large enough to sink the enemy boat. Anthony's forces met Octavian's 260 lighter liburnian vessels at the entrance of the Gulf of Ambracia.

The battle was a stalemate – and then suddenly, powered by the afternoon northerlies, Cleopatra's fleet turned to the open seas and sailed towards the Peloponnesian peninsula. Seeing this, Anthony, to the astonishment of his fellow soldiers, broke out and followed his lover.

DOMITIUS ENOBARBUS
Naught, naught all, naught! I can behold no longer:
The Antoniad, the Egyptian admiral,
With all their sixty, fly and turn the rudder:
To see't mine eyes are blasted.

SCARUS
Gods and goddesses,
All the whole synod of them!

DOMITIUS ENOBARBUS
What's thy passion!

SCARUS
The greater cantle of the world is lost
With very ignorance; we have kiss'd away
Kingdoms and provinces.

DOMITIUS ENOBARBUS
How appears the fight?

SCARUS
On our side like the token'd pestilence,
Where death is sure. Yon ribaudred nag of Egypt,—
Whom leprosy o'ertake!—i' the midst o' the fight,
When vantage like a pair of twins appear'd,
Both as the same, or rather ours the elder,
The breese upon her, like a cow in June,
Hoists sails and flies.

DOMITIUS ENOBARBUS
That I beheld:
Mine eyes did sicken at the sight, and could not
Endure a further view.

SCARUS
She once being loof'd,
The noble ruin of her magic, Antony,
Claps on his sea-wing, and, like a doting mallard,
Leaving the fight in height, flies after her:
I never saw an action of such shame;
Experience, manhood, honour, ne'er before
Did violate so itself.

DOMITIUS ENOBARBUS
Alack, alack!

CANIDIUS
Our fortune on the sea is out of breath,
And sinks most lamentably. Had our general
Been what he knew himself, it had gone well:
O, he has given example for our flight,
Most grossly, by his own!

DOMITIUS ENOBARBUS
Ay, are you thereabouts?
Why, then, good night indeed.

CANIDIUS
Toward Peloponnesus are they fled.

SCARUS
'Tis easy to't; and there I will attend
What further comes.

CANIDIUS
To Caesar will I render
My legions and my horse: six kings already
Show me the way of yielding.

DOMITIUS ENOBARBUS
I'll yet follow
The wounded chance of Antony, though my reason
Sits in the wind against me".

    Without their leader, Anthony's forces suffered a decisive defeat. By the end of the day they'd lost 5,000 lives and all their ships. Anthony and Cleopatra fled to Alexandria, where they were forced to commit suicide. The consequences of this loss were significant, as the battle marked the end of the Roman Republic and the beginning of the Roman Empire, with Octavian becoming the first Roman Emperor under the name of Augustus.

Preveza/Levkas

L evkas, the closest town to the battlefield, is the most unlikely place for a thriving boating life. The town is practically landlocked, surrounded by salt marshes. From the south you have to wade through a narrow dredged canal cutting across the salt marshes. From the north its waterways can be reached through a bridge opening on the hour. If you approach from the north, you are greeted with a mirage of the Venetian castle glowing in the summer sunshine from early morning until late in the evening. During summer it is only after 9 pm that the sun, encircled by red flames, dips into the Ionian Sea, marking the end of the day by painting the town and the surrounding hills to the colour of glowing embers. Day or night, for the sailor without a chart plotter, it is very difficult to find the opening in the wall surrounding the Venetian harbour. With careful navigation, you eventually notice the green starboard entrance mark. Then you have to make a decision against all your natural instincts to take the mark with a sharp turn and sail into a very shallow inner harbour. Boats are required to wait in the tiny inner harbour until the bridge on the other side of the castle opens. Yachts and motorboats are forced to loiter for 10–20 minutes manoeuvring back and forth, testing the maritime skills of their crews. The bridge is kept open as long as there is a boat in the line of vision of the operator. Boats pass through in an orderly fashion and disperse along the 2 km-long town quay or find shelter in the marina. In spite of the difficult approach, Levkas is visited by a large number of yachts from Italy, France and further afield.

The town seems to be on the point of transforming from a typical Greek town of tavernas with checkered tablecloths and uncomfortable straight-backed chairs, serving excellent but somewhat limited choice of Greek food, into a more sophisticated destination. The Ionian Islands were ruled by Venice from 1200 to 1797, and after centuries of absence, Italian influence in style and architecture is again evident. Everywhere, there are signs of the famous Italian flair. During the two seasons we spent there, stylish Italian restaurants, cafés and clubs popped up all over the town. The shops became better stocked with fashion items and Italian designer gear. Clearly, the whole place was thriving!

Perhaps as a recognition of all this, the Greek cabinet met in Levkas during our stay. To our surprise, without any fanfare or visible security staff, they dined alongside the tourists in one of the town's best fish restaurants. The owners and staff of the restaurant – fully aware that the future of Levkas (a new road, a new bridge, dredging of the marshes) might depend on the quality of food and service they provided – were stressed out of their minds, frequently apologising to the other guests for mixing up or forgetting their orders. Fortunately, the busy statesmen left after a quick dinner and the restaurant soon returned to its normal routine.

I personally liked the Levkians' enthusiastic and imaginative approach to mixing mass tourism with local flavour. Generally, Greece has managed to avoid the emergence of monstrosities like the Spanish and French holiday villages. In those places, tourists live in something like a reservation, separated from the real world. A Club Med-type holiday village provides everything. You do not have to think, do not have to ask, and mostly you do not mix with the locals: it is all there for you to grab, whatever it might be. Levkas, with its thriving tourist industry, remains a genuine and exciting place to visit, and it does not take long to get to know some of the locals.

In Greece, family business remains entrenched. We noticed that most businesses in Levkas remain family affairs, as has always been customary in that part of the world. The whole family participates in the business, as do friends. Parents do not worry about how to entertain their children during school holidays: the children simply hang around the family business, be it a restaurant, petrol station, travel agency or a fishing boat. Children as young as one are around from morning until late at night. From the tender age of seven, as soon as they learn to count and read, they man the cashiers and serve the customers. I suppose this arrangement contributes to the low crime rate and the lack of rowdiness on the narrow streets of Levkas, making it a most pleasant place to visit.

Skorpios

We left Levkas to sail south by passing through the canal. The salt marshes sparkled in the sun and the most exquisite scenery of high mountains covered with green vegetation surrounded us. There is not too much time to admire nature, as navigating the sometimes badly marked channel requires continuous attention. After we left the marshes, the scenery quickly changed and we arrived in one of the best sailing grounds in Greece, with the fresh breeze rolling down the mountains. With the early afternoon winds powering our sails, we soon reached the island of Skorpios.

Skorpios is a beautiful island covered with lush, cultivated greenery that carefully hides the personal retreat of the Onassis family. Aristotle Onassis was one of the first shipping magnates of Greece and accumulated a vast personal fortune. In a bizarre twist, Aristotle met Jacqueline Lee Bouvier, the widow of the assassinated American president John Fitzgerald Kennedy, and to the shock of the world the beautiful Jackie married the old and seriously ill Onassis. Jackie loved spending time on the island. One can speculate that, she was perhaps following in the footsteps of Cleopatra, that it was a well-thought-out transaction and that it was not Onassis but the island she fell in love with. The island remains beautiful and it continues to be maintained with great care and lots of money. There is also a beautiful harbour that used to shelter the family's favourite yacht *Christina* and provided a safe landing for boats carrying the rich and famous to the memorable parties. The mundane present could not be further from the glorious past. During the time of Onassis, the nearby villages were prevented from developing their tourism potential, so as not to disturb his private paradise. Perhaps he could see into the future: today, the island is the major attraction for visitors of the nearby Levkian town of Nidri. The tourist boats, weighed down by their human cargo, slowly approach the island while loudspeakers tell the story of "Jackie and Ari". The boats heel to one side as everyone strains to catch a glimpse of a fairytale life long-since passed. However, they all leave disappointed, as only the routinely patrolling guards, the gardeners and, from time to time, some old members of the clan are ever visible. At sunrise and sunset, a couple of four-wheel drives arrive by the sea and matrons in black dresses emerge. Under the watchful eyes of the driver and the guards, they peel off their clothes and without too much fanfare immerse themselves in the sea. Although setting foot on the island is not permitted, there are several delightful, fairly busy anchorages nearby that are excellent for a day-trip or even an overnight stay.

The white cliffs of Levkas where Sappho jumped to her death

To further investigate the spirit of love, we sailed around the island of Levkas to visit its southernmost part where Sappho, the famous female poet of Ancient Greece, yearning for her lover Phaon the ferryman, jumped from the 70m-high white cliffs of Cape Levkas to her death, where reunited forever she continues to whisper beautiful words into the ears of her lover.

The Ionian Islands are blessed with regular rain, ample sunshine and good soil. No wonder then that their history goes back to Mycenaean times, 1500 BC and beyond. With this in mind, we finished cruising for 2005 and left the boat in the Levkas Marina with the firm determination to come back knowing much more about Ancient Greece.

BACK
TO THE
FUTURE

Old Wanderings

During our previous trips to Greece in the early 1980s, I became fascinated with Ancient Greece, although at the time I did not truly appreciate the richness and enormous influence of its culture on the world. The first trip was done on a shoestring budget: hitchhiking and sleeping on the sometimes hard surfaces of the Mediterranean shores.

"Oh, yes my dear! You can sleep on the ground, just that you have to get up from time to time and have a rest," quipped my late father-in-law.

Regardless of the difficulties, we travelled from the monasteries of Meteora across the Peloponnesian peninsula to the majestic site of the Acropolis in Athens. I remember the bittersweet taste of the retzina wine, a cheap national drink of the Greeks that actually becomes drinkable after some training. As with all cheap wines, it becomes better and better glass after glass.

"The practice of adding resin to wine is thousands of years old. The discovery of wine is attributed to the god Dionysus, the place generally held to be Eleutherae, on the slopes of Mount Cithaeron. The story of the god's strange wanderings and the later mystic rites of the Dionysian cult were presumed to symbolise the spread of the wine cult, in supercession to the Thracian beer cult, across Europe, Asia and North Africa. In fact more likely that wine was first made in Crete – the Cretan grapes and wines are still famous – and exported to Greece in wine jars around the beginning of the second millennium before Christ. Lacking the knowledge of maturing and preserving wine in wooden casks, these early wine makers added pine resin as a way to keep the wine fresh aboard ships. Theseus sailing to Crete or Jason taking the Argo to Colchis in search of the Golden Fleece, would have drunk retzina probably no different from the retzina we drink today. It was the drink of Odysseus, of the men tho sacked Troy, of the victors at Salamis. Wine jars 2,600 years old have been brought up from beneath the sea still bearing traces of the resin with which they had been impregnated.

The practice of resination has another value also. The characteristic astringency it imparts to the wine counteracts the oily heaviness of most Greek food. Moreover, there is a particular significance attached to the drinking of retzina which applies to no other beverage." (Clift 1956)

I also recall seeing a disproportionate number of women in the countryside dressed in long black dresses. I thought they were old matrons, but it turned out that they were not old, but married, young women. There was almost a Middle Eastern-style segregation of women and men, and I remain disturbed by the memory of seeing men masturbating in public places. During one of our rides, we were slowly approaching a truck carrying watermelons. As we got closer, it became clear that the man sitting on a pile of watermelons was absentmindedly masturbating. He was not disturbed by the sharp turns made by the truck on the winding road or by the fact that it was a busy road with trucks, buses and sedans passing him every minute!

But it was also during this trip that we saw the Hippolytus at the ancient theatre of Epidaurus (built in 380 BC) – and the image of Phaedra – is one that will stay with me forever. The architecture is such that it creates perfect acoustics. In an age when loudspeakers were unknown, the actors' voices could be clearly heard by all 14,000 people. Even today, in its damaged form, the drop of a coin on the stage can be clearly heard anywhere in the theatre. Today, Epidaurus continues to bring the magic of the Greek theatre to the sometimes-rowdy crowds of the modern age. School children, backpackers, package tour groups and visitors from luxury cruisers and private yachts fill the carved stone seats. They all experience the unique sunset that slowly brings on a special darkness layered with anticipation. Slowly the red sky darkens, the crowds become quiet, and the viewer is transported to 400 BC.

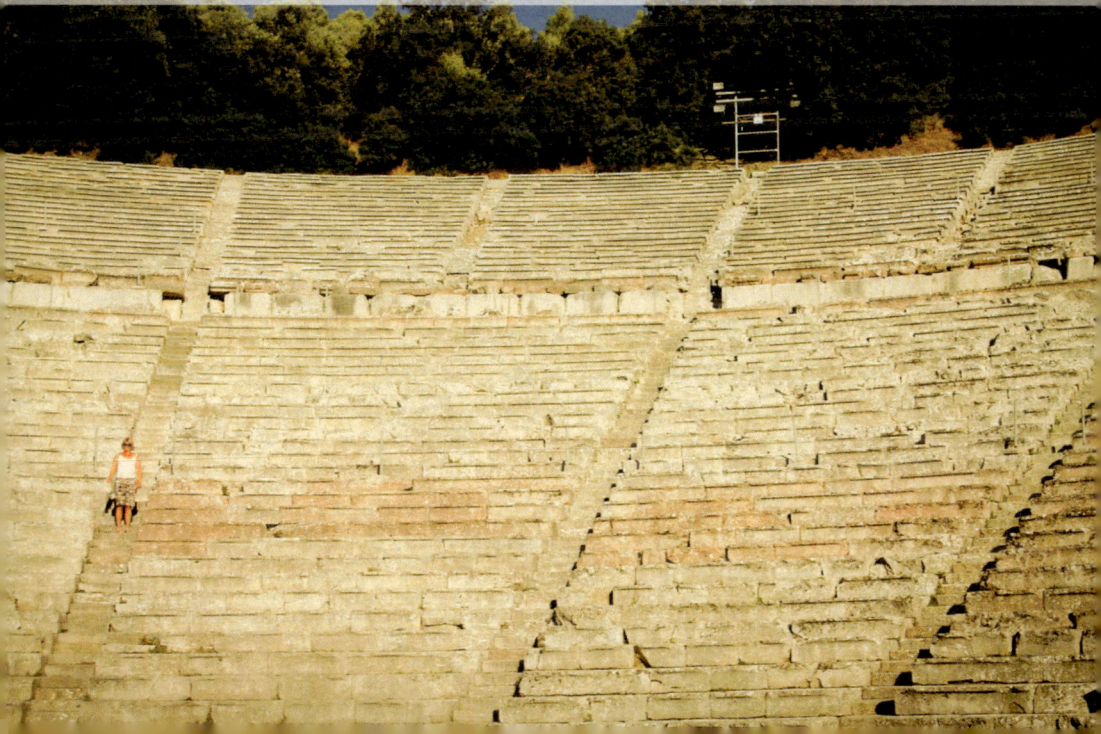

The theatre of Epidaurus

The sad, disturbing tale of the ancient queen Phaedra, which I first heard from my boyfriend at the age of 15, is about the power of love and all the things – both good and bad – we do in its name.

"Phaedra is best known for her role in Euripides' play, *Hippolytus.* The plot follows a pattern of sexual intrigue and betrayal that has parallels in ancient Mediterranean myths, mostly notably, the Biblical account of Joseph and Potiphar's wife.

Phaedra married Theseus, who had a son, Hippolytus, from a previous marriage. The young Hippolytus, however, angers Aphrodite by shunning her worship and devoting himself entirely to Artemis, the virgin goddess of the hunt. To punish him, Aphrodite compels Phaedra to begin lusting after the young man. At first, she resists and seeks magic cures for her passions, or at least a noble death. Hippolytus learns of Phaedra's desire for him through Phaedra's nurse and launches into a fierce denunciation of women – a locus classicus for misogyny.

Out of shame and guilt, Phaedra hangs herself, but not until she has a letter accusing Hippolytus of trying to rape her. Hippolytus is trapped into silence because he had promised that he would never repeat what Phaedra's nurse told him. Therefore, when confronted by his father he is defenseless. Out of anger Theseus asks Poseidon to punish Hippolytus, which he does. Hippolytus dies as Poseidon's bull emerges from the sea and frightens his horses. Then, Artemis reveals the truth to Theseus but unfortunately, it is too late for Hippolytus.

In a typical Euripidean *deus ex machina*, the goddess Artemis is questioned as to why she stood by and allowed her devoted follower to be destroyed. She reminds the chorus that there is an agreement among the gods that the favourites of one divinity can be destroyed by another divinity at will. It is a scant consolation that she promises that someday she will similarly destroy a mortal favourite of Aphrodite in revenge. And so, 'as flies are to wanton boys, are we to the gods. They kill us for their sport.' – *King Lear.*" (Encyclopedia Mythica 2012).

Hitchhiking was an interesting, exciting experience. We met many people, and had endless adventures, but it could become tiresome to rely on the generosity of others all the time. We were over the moon when after three weeks of hitchhiking we rewarded ourselves by hiring a motorbike for three days. After the tedious formalities, we happily rode out into the fragrant Cretan countryside, admiring the olive groves, the vine plantations and the incredibly blue sky.

Our pleasure did not last long as, only 20 km out of Iraklion, a car, obviously annoyed by our slow speed, ignored the sharp turn in front of us and swung into the opposite lane – only to be confronted with a small truck. Without too much hesitation, the car started to come back into our lane and pushed us off the road. Steve bravely manoeuvred our little scooter onto the gravel but the wheels skidded and losing its balance, our motorbike slowly toppled over onto its side.

They say your whole life flashes in front of you before you die, but the opposite happened: the world came to a standstill. The clock slowed down in my mind and all I could feel was how slowly, almost imperceptibly, my upright body came closer and closer to the bitumen, hitting it with a soft thud.

Our bodies provided an excellent soft landing for the bike and, driven by our speed the motorbike continued to slide forwards over our legs. It seemed like an eternity, but everything has to come to an end, and after a couple of seconds, the sliding stopped. At a snail's pace, we took account of our body parts, then gradually noticed that we were conscious and started to crawl back to life from the house of Hades. We were covered with blood – but alive!

The traffic stopped, except for the offending car; people were shouting and, after some hesitation, they tentatively approached us. They were delighted that the two bodies lying under a motorbike were able to move without their help. No one knew what to do with two bodies showing raw flesh and covered with blood-soaked clothes. The creatures were too much alive to be left unaided but, apparently, too injured to be touched.

Finally, the bravest offered some help to the lady of the gory scene – me. We were lucky, as our injuries appeared to be more serious than they actually were. To the great relief of our rescuers, the other piece of flesh, Steve, had also moved, crawling out from underneath the bike, and started to talk. After a quick, tense discussion, someone agreed to take us to the closest village doctor. Steve, by this time, was in full control and insisted that they bring the motorbike too! Who can argue with a half-dead man?

So the procession to the next village started, one car carrying two human-looking creatures, and another small truck transporting the totally intact bike. We interrupted the Sunday slumber of the local doctor, who was quite ready to deal with my minor injuries but found Steve's blood-soaked, dirt-covered body totally revolting. He was particularly worried about the cleanliness of his surgery and simply prevented us from entering his rooms. After some hesitation, he instructed me to clean Steve with the garden hose at the front of the house.

The afternoon sun was creating an immense heat and the cicadas were protesting against the burning rays at the top of their voices. My love slowly lowered himself onto a rickety chair in the middle of a cabbage patch. I opened the tap and gently lifted the hose to his left shoulder, watching his reaction closely. Other than the tap oozing a slow flow of water over his battered body, nothing moved, as if our moment of unconsciousness had suddenly extended itself into the very texture of this dreary afternoon. The water slowly flowed from his shoulder to his arms, reaching his legs, which were covered with a mixture of soil, bitumen and flesh. In the course of its journey, the water colour changed from clear to light pink, then to ruby and finally turned into wine-dark red. To begin with, the flow was thirstily swallowed by the dry soil. Then, the steady flow of water turned into a small red stream, finding its way among the cabbages and cutting red streaks into the dirt. My husband gradually began to look like someone skinned alive, but human. Once finished, the doctor, still wearing a disgusted expression, handed me some bandages to soak up the blood and we finally gained entry to his sanctuary. He found no broken bones, and the bleeding, although over a large surface, was only superficial. Probably using up his yearly supply, the doctor bandaged all our wounds and looked at the end result with some satisfaction. He was looking at two weird creatures with white bandages all the way up their left arms and legs. We had two glasses of water and, with nothing else to do, Steve declared us fit to restart our ride, this time back to Iraklion. For the first time, the doctor felt it necessary to offer his opinion and said, "You might feel fine as a patient, but as your doctor I do not feel fine about you riding to Iraklion."

First I tried to drive, and although I have been riding scooters since the age of 15, with Steve's weight behind me, I found it hard to balance the motorbike. Stopping became a particularly hazardous activity, and Steve therefore took the driving seat. We must have been a bizarre sight – like something I saw years later in the pretty bad movie *The Mummy* – two bodies covered with bandages from head to toe apparently out for a Sunday afternoon ride.

I was constantly worried that either of us would faint and we would end up seriously hurting ourselves. So, every three minutes I asked, "Is anyone fainting?" Eventually the unwanted answer came, "Yes."

We stopped immediately and luckily found ourselves in front of a taverna. After setting down the motorbike and finding that we were still able to stand and walk, we approached the taverna and ordered two coffees, one Coke and some water. The coffees and the Coke ended up in our stomach, but to the astonishment of the locals we poured the glasses of water over our heads. The water flowed down to our shoulders, arms and waist and gently soaked through the already bloodstained bandages, creating a surreal scene. Then, the two aliens stood up, paid, got back onto the bike and rode off into the sunset. In Iraklion, we successfully returned the bike and recovered our money!

Since we had to wait a couple of days for our flight, we badly needed some type of accommodation other than the roadside. With the trick of not presenting my husband at the hotel reception, I managed to secure a small room and we spent three anxious days in Iraklion. Even sick people get bored, so eventually we ventured out from the security of our room and visited the archaeological museum. As we slowly approached the entrance, with every move optimised to cause the least movement of our wounded limbs, we gingerly walked past a group of youngsters, who started to laugh and pointed to our injuries, enquiring, "*Vespa?*"

"Mind your own business," I was just about to say – when I noticed that several people in the group also had bandages and plasters around their limbs. We perched next to them on the fence to tell our story. The youngsters who surrounded us were from all over Europe and were bearing their injuries with good humour. Apparently, due to the lack of experience of both riders and motorists, with the introduction of bike rentals, the number of accidents on the island had soared.

When we made it to Athens, the overwhelming beauty of the majestic marble of the Acropolis soothed my soul and some of my injuries, but I was terribly worried about Steve, who was in a lot of pain and had developed a high temperature. For the most part the medical care was Third World, and hospital care remained a distant dream. Finally, we secured two seats on the plane to Budapest and at last he received proper medical care at the burns unit. His injuries were the equivalent of having burnt 25% of his body's surface. It took another six weeks, but eventually he did get better.

Mediterranean Mooring

W**here are you going?"** asked my children when I told them we were going on a sailing holiday.

"To Greece?"

"Where is Greece?"

"In Europe, along the shores of the Mediterranean Sea."

"What will you do there?"

"Sail, visit islands and look at all sorts of old ruins."

"What sort of ruins? Like castles?"

"No, more like majestic ruins of an old civilisation. The way we see the world around us, the way we think, the way I work as a scientist, what we consider beautiful, important and good is all because of the Ancient Greeks. Greece is the cradle of civilisation."

"Why Greece? Why not China or India? Why not the Aborigines?"

Indeed: Why not?

It was the mid 1990s and the Greek political system had changed. The remnants of military dictatorship and the violent demonstrations in opposition were gone. Greece became a democracy in 1974, and a member of the European Union in 1981. These changes fast-tracked the nation into modern Europe. Men and women became cosmopolitan, short skirts and bikinis ruled, and the restoration of ancient ruins restarted. Like so many times before, Europe rediscovered its roots in Ancient Greece. Money and tourists started to pour in, and archaeological restoration projects popped up everywhere. Little by little, the foundations of houses, temples, market places and gymnasia materialised from the ankle-deep rubble. By this time, visualising the glory of these places was not confined to the privileged few scholars. The heritage of the Ancient Greeks became accessible to the masses. Anyone with a little bit of imagination looking at the now knee-high walls, could picture how these places looked two millennia before. With increasing prosperity around the world, the combination of balmy weather and an interesting history turned Greece into the busiest tourist destination in Europe, bringing all the benefits and disadvantages of mass tourism to the country. Among archaeologists, there is great debate about the form and quality of the restoration that should be carried out on ancient ruins. One argument is that the sites should not be destroyed or changed by restoration in order to let future generations of archaeologists explore them. On the other hand, there is the need of the average person to get an insight into the life of those who created those monuments. After all, what are knowledge and culture worth if they are only owned by a few? Today, there are careful restoration projects to correct the mistakes of previous efforts. Depending on the amount of money available, the monuments are built from "ankle to knee to shoulder high", and sometimes to their full glorious splendour.

The science of Mediterranean mooring

As part of our cruising agenda, we had to learn the basic rules of long-distance cruising and the intricate details of Mediterranean mooring (see drawing). Executing a Mediterranean mooring with a short-handed crew consisting of a skipper (husband) and a first mate (wife) is a challenge at the best of times; at worst it can wreck your holiday. Several dream trips ended in bitter disputes due to the skipper's inability to correctly estimate the distance between the point of dropping anchor and the length of the attached chain. Of course, in this modern age of equality, the skipper and the first mate are equally responsible for the skipper's wrong decision.

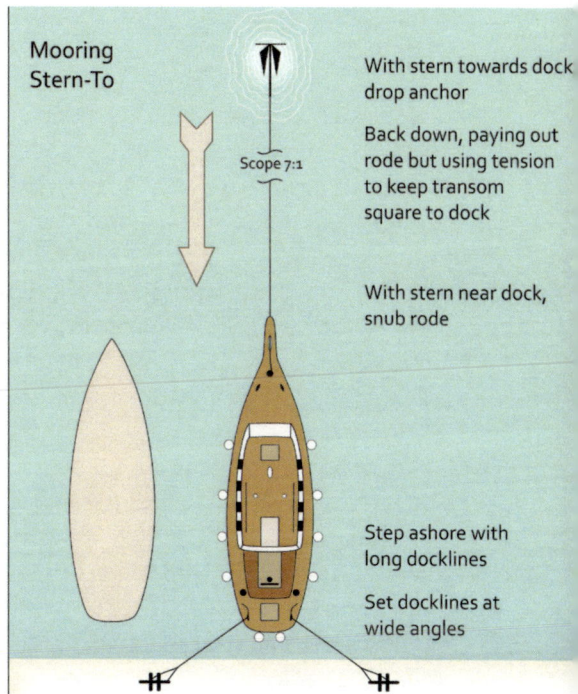

Mooring Stern-To

Scope 7:1

With stern towards dock drop anchor

Back down, paying out rode but using tension to keep transom square to dock

With stern near dock, snub rode

Step ashore with long docklines

Set docklines at wide angles

As my husband, the skipper, pointed out, "Even when you are on another hemisphere, a stuffed-up mooring is your fault. I can hear your protestations across the ether confusing me to the point of making the wrong decision."

After a busy day of sailing, you arrive at a minuscule, picturesque medieaval harbour surrounded by a sometimes run-down, but nevertheless charming, town. The harbour is jam-packed with every sea-going vessel invented by man. All jostle for position: the slow, bulky ferries; the fast, sleek hydrofoils; the million-dollar floating palaces; the ever-present hyperactive local fishermen in their cute blue and white caiques; and your fellow sailors. You would love to take in the scenery but, being aware of the Mediterranean temperament, you know better. Tired or not, you manoeuvre frantically to avoid running into anything that floats while trying to get your boat into a location where the distance to the shore equals the length of your anchor chain. If you succeed, you launch your anchor. In the midst of the noise generated by the fast running anchor chain, the skipper steers astern at an angle exactly perpendicular to the town quay.

As you get closer and closer to the shore, your nerves are more and more on edge. Around five metres from the shore, the show that everyone – the crews of already secured yachts, the promenading townsfolk, the harbour staff, the children on their bikes, even the birds on the wire – has been waiting for begins.

Action!

The skipper slows down the boat. The first mate secures the anchor chain. This action, depending on the size and age of your boat, can be as easy as putting the anchor switch into neutral position or be the most frightening experience of your life. On older boats, it requires putting your hand frighteningly close to the chain, which is running at full speed into the depth of the water with a horrid noise, preventing any communication between the skipper and the crew. Having overcome your fear, you grab the windlass handle and, making an educated guess, you push it either forward or backward. Then you hope and pray that the chain slows down and eventually stops.

Knowing that there is a high probability that the anchor will not hold, the skipper, the first mate and all the spectators anxiously wait for the boat to stop. If the boat stops, the first mate quickly lets out another two or three metres of chain. Then the skipper makes an honest attempt to keep the boat hovering one metre from the town quay while the first mate rushes aft, grabs the mooring rope, collects it into a perfect coil and attempts to throw the coil in one clean motion to someone on land. If all of the above is carried out successfully, the boat is secured to a bollard or, in the absence of one, to anything that appears to be strong enough to hold your "pride and joy" in place.

Bollards of all sorts of shapes and sizes are generously provided by the local town councils. To enhance everyone's entertainment, they are usually cleverly positioned in carefully chosen, inaccessible locations. Sometimes the council also provides a person outfitted in a crisp uniform exuding an aura of importance. The uniform has a nautical theme and is suggestive of nautical knowledge and competence. These assumptions are all wrong, as more often than not the helpers lack any nautical skills. They regularly secure the mooring rope incorrectly, leaving the boat to slowly but irreversibly collide with neighbouring yachts. Alerted by the noise, "all hands" appear on the deck, desperately squeezing fenders between the hull of their beloved craft and the newcomer.

Sometimes the chain is short, delaying this entertaining conclusion of the show until the distance between the point of dropping anchor and the shore is perfected. On these occasions, the anchor is collected and the manoeuvre starts again. While you are doing all this, the whole town in the middle of their afternoon stroll watches and never fails to provide shouted advice. This obviously embarrasses all sailors, and after numerous failed attempts the blame game starts up and the couple heads for divorce. A lucrative Las Vegas-style divorce industry could be set up along the shores of the Mediterranean. With the fast increase in the number of short-handed cruisers on the Mediterranean, these courts could make a significant contribution to the local economies, particularly in windy locations.

In our case, the skipper and first mate were ready to sacrifice their dignity by sometimes allowing themselves to be towed to shore. Sometimes one of us would simplify the procedure by swimming with an extended mooring line to the town quay. But we prevailed and eventually mastered the procedure. Having survived the challenges of Mediterranean mooring, we cheerfully spent the next decade sailing around this big, interesting pond, where the signs of at least 5,000 years of human civilisation are visible everywhere.

Successful Mediterranean mooring of Fenix (the grey ghost at the back is our motorbike)

Prehistoric Times

We were rewarded for our persistence in learning to moor by visiting one of the most exquisite groups of islands on Earth, with one of the longest histories of human civilisation: the Cycladic Islands. The islands take their name from their geographical arrangement: they form a circle in the middle of the windy eastern corner of the Mediterranean Sea close enough to each other that their inhabitants could be in frequent contact.

All of the Cycladic Islands are speckled with ruins. If one knows ancient history, this is not surprising, as the islands of Syros, Paros, Antiparos, Naxos, Sifnos, Melos and Amorgos are close to the region known as the Fertile Crescent: the cradle of agriculture. This region, which covers much of the modern Middle East, including Turkey, Iraq and Syria, was where plants were first cultivated in around 8500 BC.

Agriculture was gradually introduced to the Stone Age inhabitants of the Mediterranean region and settlements were formed along its coastlines. Nevertheless, it took up to 5,000 years to develop a significant enough agriculture that people could be involved in other activities and could begin trading. This is when the Cycladic civilisation really took off. The islands were rich in raw material: silver in Sifnos, marble in Paros and Naxos, obsidian in Melos. The presence of obsidian was particularly important, as it enabled the islanders to manufacture superior-quality tools, particularly blades. Obsidian is a type of naturally occurring glass produced by volcanoes when the lava cools rapidly and solidifies without sufficient time for crystal growth. It is commonly found within the margins of felsic lava flows, where cooling is more rapid. Because of the lack of crystal structure, obsidian blade edges can reach almost molecular thinness, leading to its ancient use for arrowheads and its modern use in surgical scalpel blades.

Cycladic culture was dominated by fine sculptures. Cycladic statuettes are made from delicate white marble, which is almost transparent. With their heads turned towards the sky, these statuettes are called stargazers and resemble modern sculptures. They are precious reminders of the skills and imagination of the ancient island dwellers. The exact date of the decline of the Cycladic civilisation is unknown, but it has been established that the eruption of the volcano on the island of Thera (Santorini) in around 1500 BC wrought havoc on the whole eastern Mediterranean and the Middle East. It not only potentially destroyed the Cycladic way of life and weakened the gentle Minoan civilisation of Crete (more about these beautiful people later), it is also thought to have helped the miraculous escape of the Israelites from Egypt. Some scholars have proposed that the the volcanic eruption was followed by a tsunami that was felt even along the Red Sea. As we learnt from the 2004 tsunami, before the wave hits, the sea levels recede. According to the Old Testament, the receding sea enabled Moses to lead his people across the Red Sea to the Promised Land. Volcanic eruption or not, the Cycladic Islands managed to survive and continued to play some role in the development of Ancient Greece for the next 2,000 years – and we saw signs of this continuity all around the islands.

With the weakening of Cycladic and Minoan societies, the history of civilisation in the Mediterranean changed forever. When one civilisation disappears, another will take charge, and from 1600–1100 BC, the Mycenaean civilisation (named after the most important city of the time, Mycenae) ruled the land and the sea from the Ionian Sea to the shores of the Eastern Mediterranean.

Thanks to the discoveries of Erich Schliemann, who in 1876 discovered the city of Mycenae, and to Michael Ventris and John Chadwick who deciphered their writing, Linear B, we know a lot about the Mycenaeans. They built huge stone structures surrounded by enormous walls and buried their kings in large cone-shaped chambers.

The area of the Fertile Crescent in the eastern corner of the Great (Mediterranean) Sea.

The Lion Gate of Mycenae, 1300 BC

The Mycenaeans had highly developed agriculture, trade and manufacturing, and generally lived in a sophisticated society. Linear B is the unique writing system of the Mycenaeans and is an early version of the Greek language.

Little clay tablets and vases carrying Linear B inscriptions of the Mycenaean period were found scattered across the Mediterranean. These have given us a large amount of information about the size of the economy and the history, commercial activities, diplomacy, administration and generally the nature of the Mycenaean world. Of course, the best-known and most complete description of this society comes from Homer, whose epic poems *The Iliad* and *The Odyssey* have become immortal.

During the 13th century BC, the Mycenaean civilisation reached its peak. It was a wealthy empire of restless and enterprising people who colonised the shores of the Mediterranean and fought many battles for trading routes. This was also the time of the emergence of epic poems, which were told and kept alive by generations of illiterate bards.

It might be surprising that, although Linear B was widely used for the governance of the empire, there are no signs that it was ever used to preserve the epic poems. There are two reasons for this, one technical, the other social. The first is that writing in Linear B is cumbersome: it is not readily suited conveying complex words or to depict complicated situations or emotions. It was based on no more than 90 syllabic signs and a number of logograms. Syllabic signs are signs for a combination of a consonant and a vowel, making a syllable. For example, family would be written using the signs for the three syllables 'fa'-'mi'-'ly'. Logograms are signs that stand for a whole word. The most widely used logogram today is Chinese writing. We should not forget that Linear B was developed to suit the needs of accountants' ledgers for keeping track of tax collection and the wealth of the king. The second, social, reason why Linear B was never used to preserve the epic poems, was that the knowledge of writing was jealously guarded. A class of privileged bureaucrats or scribes who spent most of their lives mastering the intricacies of writing – giving them the power of knowledge and the associated status – wanted to maintain their privileged position. The individual writing styles of no more than 50–70 scribes have been identified on the tablets found around the Mediterranean, suggesting that at any given time there were only that many literate people in the entire Mycenaean Empire, covering the Peloponnesian peninsula, most of mainland Greece, Crete, the Cycladic Islands and the Mediterranean coastline of today's Turkey.

Here is a good example of a Linear B tablet and its interpretation by Stavroula (Stephie) Nikoloudis, Honorary Fellow of Classics and Archaeology, at the School of Historical and Philosophical Studies, University of Melbourne:

"This Linear B tablet is from Mycenae (it is formally known as Tablet MY V 659). It comprises a list of women, each of whom is allocated a bed or some kind of bedding (e.g., rugs used for a bed). There is no verb at all in this text, so we don't know for certain if we are dealing with a past or future action. On the basis of texts that do contain verbs, we know that the Linear B corpus as whole contains both sorts of records.

Linear B writing tablet

These women may have been seasonal workers who visited the palace at Mycenae to carry out specialised work for a limited period of time (e.g., in the sphere of textile production) or they may have been more permanent, dependent personnel of the palace. In either case, according to most scholars, this tablet indicates that they were provided with a bed or some kind of bedding for their personal use by the palatial administrators.

Here is a transliteration of the tablet to make it easier to follow. (The word-dividers visible in the tablets are shown in transliterations as commas.)

1. wo-di-je-ja , de-mi-ni-ja 1

2. ma-no , a-re-ka-sa-da-ra-qe 2

3. ri-su-ra , qo-ta-qe 2

4. e-ri-tu-pi-na , te-o-do-ra-qe 2

5. o-to-wo-wi-je tu-ka-te-qe 2

6. a-ne-a2 , tu-ka-te-qe 2

7. pi-ro-wo-na ki-ra-qe 2

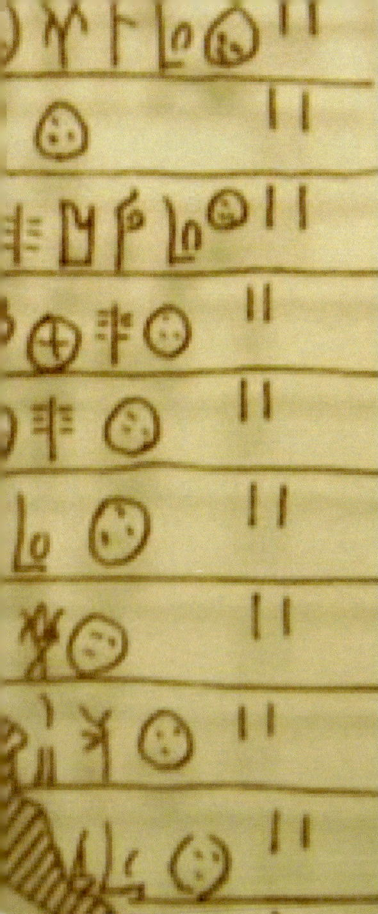

.1 wo-di-je-ja , de-mi-ni-ja 1
.2 ma-no , a-re-ka-sa-da-ra-qe 2
.3 ri-su-ra , qo-ta-qe 2
.4 e-ri-tu-pi-na , te-o-do-ra-qe 2
.5 o-to-wo-wi-je tu-ka-te-qe 2
.6 a-ne-a2 , tu-ka-te-qe 2
.7 pi-ro-wo-na ki-ra-qe 2
.8 ?]-ka-ro ke-ti-de-qe 2
.9]-ri-mo-qe 2
.10]ma-ta-qe 2

8. ?]-ka-ro ke-ti-de-qe 2

9.]-ri-mo-qe 2

10.]ma-ta-qe 2 etc.

Line 1:

The second word in the first line of the tablet is de-mi-ni-ja, taken to be a neuter plural of the Greek word 'demnion' = 'bedding', known from Homer (cf. Iliad 24.644), where it also occurs in the plural 'demnia' and seems to refer to the under-bedding laid on the ground to create a place to sleep.

There, the possibility is noted that de-mi-ni-ja (in line 1) might in fact be another woman's name, and not the word 'bedding'. This would mean that the first woman recorded on the tablet (namely Wo-di-je-ja) was in charge of the group of women workers listed below her (whose particular duties were not specified by the tablet-writer). Mycenaean palaces kept track of their workers by compiling lists of personnel, often for the purpose of distributing food rations to them. The other words on the tablet are, for the most part, women's names.

The other words on the tablet are, for the most part, women's names. Where there is only a single woman recorded in a line, the number of (implied) beds or bedding material is also 1 (number at the end of the line) - e.g, lines 1 and 11.

In most cases, though, each line features two names. The recurring "-qe" at the end of the second name in these cases is an enclitic particle (this Mycenaean Greek form becomes 'te' in later Greek): it links the two names. For example:

Line 2:

ma-no , a-re-ka-sa-da-ra-qe 2

= Mano Alexandra(-and) 2

= Mano and Alexandra 2

Most of the names are unusual compared with later Greek names, but alongside familiar 'Alexandra' from line 2, there is also 'Theodora' (the second name in line 4). The other term worth mentioning is 'tu-ka-te' (lines 5 and 6) which is the Greek word 'thugater' [my apologies for the lack of a Greek font!] meaning 'daughter'. This demonstrates that some women's daughters worked alongside their mothers.

Whichever interpretation is preferred (there are valid arguments for each), MY V 659 is, at is core, a list of female workers."

The epic poems described the heroic endeavours of the Mycenaeans and in the process provided detailed description of their ethics, characters, physical features, their joys and sorrows, the weapons and fighting styles used, how they lived and what sort of families and social structures they had. The people of the Mycenaean Empire were unified by common aims, set by their chieftains or later by their kings, using a common language, Greek, and by worshipping common gods, the 12 Gods of Olympus. They were: Zeus, the father of the Gods; Hera the goddess of marriage and the family; Poseidon, the god of sea; Athena, the goddess of wisdom; Artemis, the goddess of hunting; Apollo, the god of light and music; Hermes, the messenger of the gods; Demeter, the goddess of agriculture; Ares, the god of war; Hephaestus, the god of fire; Aphrodite, the goddess of love; and Hestia, the goddess of health.

As is very frequently the case with history, it is not well understood how and why the Mycenaean Empire collapsed in around 1100 BC. This collapse was followed by what scholars call the Dark Ages and the complete disappearance of the Mycenaean world.

The majestic palaces and fortresses were abandoned, the technical knowledge vanished and the social and administrative structure of the Mycenaean era appeared to have been all but forgotten. However, this was also the time when the genetic makeup of Ancient Greece was enriched by mass migration across the Mediterranean. The ascendance of the uncivilised, tribal, but also Greek-speaking Dorians from the northern parts of mainland Greece initiated the movement of vast amounts of people. When the social and technological fabric of a society disappears, people hibernate, concentrating on survival. They become more inward-looking and placid. Although the physical nourishment of the people of the Dark Ages may have been limited, their intellectual nurturing was rich as they listened on and on to the stories of the epic poems that later became the source material for *The Iliad* and *The Odyssey*. With the short supply of material possessions, the storytellers of the epic poems, describing the heroic and wealthy past, brought some brightness to the hard lives of people of the Dark Ages, and became the unsung heroes of the times. It is interesting to think that in spite of the existence of Linear B, Mycenaean society remained basically an oral society. The reason we today still have *The Iliad* and *The Odyssey* is because the bards of the Mycenaean world were illiterate. Telling the stories again and again, they preserved the legends of that world in spite of its total structural, physical and social collapse. Oral culture can survive until the death of the last person who is familiar with the story passes away! So, in a bizarre way, oral culture is the *pièce de resistance* of human knowledge.

Misleadingly, some anthropologists interpreted oral culture as superior to cultures that are deeply rooted in literacy. This twisted logic is of course incorrect. In spite of recognising that sometimes an oral society can be advantageous, or even be the only way to preserve the accumulated knowledge of a particular human group, generally cultures that acquire writing early in their development greatly benefit from it. After all, we are all familiar with the childhood game of Chinese whispers, where a word passed from one person to the next can morph into something completely different. Basically, a written text is the best way of maintaining continuity and understanding and establishing clear rules. Nevertheless, sometimes I do wonder, in the Internet age, when we do not have to remember anything anymore, when everything can be "Googled" and our smart phones can remind us about everything and anything, how much of our digitally stored knowledge would survive a complete meltdown of technology? Of course, there are still some libraries, giving shelter to thousands of books. However, the history of mankind does not give too much hope for the survival of libraries either.

It appears that in spite of the collapse of the Mycenaean Empire, maritime skills were more or less preserved, and trading and migration were either maintained or renewed around the 9th century BC. Through these trading routes, the Phoenician consonantal alphabet arrived in Greece in around 900 BC. This alphabet used symbols to represent individual phonemes (i.e. individual speech sounds like /b/ or /k/), rather than to represent syllables or whole words. The addition of further symbols to represent vowels, thus adapting the alphabet to better fit the needs of the Greek language, completed one of the most important, accessible writing systems of the ancient world – the Greek alphabet.

Homer

The newly acquired writing system was used to set down the world's first literary work, demonstrating a new confidence. I am fully aware of the debate regarding whether *The Iliad* and *The Odyssey* were the creations of a single individual, Homer, or several bards. For me, it is not who, but what they created that is important.

"Around 850 BC a magical event or rather a series of events took place and fortunately for us there was born among them (the Greeks), just at the right time, a genius capable of taking full advantage of the new invention and putting into writing the lays that had been chanted by the court minstrels in the Ionian world ever since the days of the Trojan War. But this genius, who is more likely to have been Homer than a series of editors, did much more than put into writing the traditional lays. He had the architectonic mind that could incorporate many separate poems in a single lengthy whole and plan the whole with a purpose. Furthermore, he could view physical and human nature alike with a detached eye; and with a robust piety he combined a strong sense of humour. He was sensitive to beauty both of the eye and of the ear, he commanded an unfailing flow of imagery, and had the great poet's power of conveying through the particular image a universal thought. And he built up and adapted to the written word a metre that still stands unrivalled as a medium for epic verse." (Hoare 1991).

The poems have been made readily accessible to the contemporary English-speaking world by the brilliant, truly modern, beautifully descriptive and most of all enjoyable translation by Robert Fagles (1990 and 1996).

The Iliad recounts the events of a few days during the Trojan War, between the Greeks and the Trojans. The cause of the war was the abduction of Helen, the daughter of Zeus and Leda and the wife of Menelaus, Kind of Sparta, by Paris, one of the sons of Priam, the King of Troy. To avenge the abduction and rescue Helen, the Greeks sailed to Troy and laid siege to the city. Prof Michael Hanly, of Washington State University, summarises the action in this way:

"A confederacy of Greek peoples is besieging the town of Troy. The siege is in its tenth year. A quarrel breaks out between Agamemnon overlord of the confederacy, and Achilles, its most effective fighter, in the field. Agamemnon takes from Achilles a prize of honour, a concubine, earlier awarded to him, and by this Achilles' honour is gravely affronted. He responds by withdrawing his services – he is a volunteer – and he prays that defeat in the field may humiliate Agamemnon and enhance his own value (honour as his prowess comes to be appreciated as indispensable.

His prayer is granted. Battle begins. The first day's fighting (rich episodes which have little coherence but considerable introductory value in relation to what follows) is inconclusive. But when after a day's interval the fighting is resumed the Trojans led by Hector (son of their king, Priam) get the upper hand. At nightfall they decide to bivouac on the battlefield with high hopes of a decisive victory the next day.

Agamemnon is now thoroughly alarmed, and admits his error. At the suggestion of Nestor, his senior adviser and a person of great age and experience, he sends honourable envoys, some of Achilles' closest friends, to appeal to him to come to the rescue, and to offer him restitution of the prize taken from him and abundant gifts in compensation for the insult done him. But Achilles, obsessed with his grievance, is obstinate. He rejects Agamemnon's amends and his friends' appeal.

The battle is resumed. The Trojans' victorious progress continues. One after another most of the principal champions of the Greeks are wounded and disabled. The Trojans storm the wall of the Greek camp, and carry the fighting into the camp itself. The Greeks make a brief recovery and drive them out; but soon the tide turns again and the Trojans fight their way into the camp for the second time and press forward to destroy the invaders' ships. Meanwhile Achilles' squire and friend Patroclus has been urged by Nestor to try himself to persuade Achilles to relent. Reproaching Achilles for his inhumanity he pleads urgently with him. Achilles is prisoner of his own earlier refusal, but he allows Patroclus to borrow his armour and lead their men out to save the ships, warning him to turn back once this has been accomplished. Patroclus saves the ships and routs the Trojans. But he forgets the instruction given him. He pursues his success too far and is killed by Hector beneath the wall of Troy. After a fierce struggle his friends bear his body back to the Greek camp.

When Achilles hears of Patroclus' death he is plunged into a frenzy of grief, remorse and rage. His anger against Agamemnon is suddenly and completely forgotten, replaced now by a far fiercer anger against the man who has killed his friend. Reconciled with Agamemnon and armed in new and splendid armor (gift of a god) to replace that lost with Patroclus he rides out in fury to find Hector and kill him. He and we know that by this he will hasten his own death too, for it is fated that his own death shall follow soon on Hector's.

Meanwhile Hector, made over-confident by his late success and unwilling to relinquish the hope of final victory that has come so very near to fulfillment, has brusquely rejected the advice of a friend that the Trojans should retire into their city and not attempt to offer battle in the new situation created by Achilles', who enraged by his friend's death returned to the field. In consequence his people are routed by Achilles with fearful slaughter. The survivors escape into the city. Hector, remorseful and ashamed, stands alone outside the wall to face Achilles, watched from above by his father and mother and fellow-citizens with agonized apprehension They fight and Hector falls. Achilles drags his body behind his chariot round the walls of Troy and back to the Greek camp.

Achilles gives Patroclus a splendid funeral. But his hatred and anger against Hector remain unappeased. He lets his body lie unburied and subjects it to persistent insults. Even the gods are indignant and disgusted.

But Priam, Hector's father, is inspired to go alone into Achilles' presence and begs to be allowed to ransom his son's body. He puts Achilles in mind of his own father, Peleus, an old man like himself, comfortless far away. Achilles' anger melts suddenly, turned to sympathy. He accepts the ransom and gives Priam what he asks, treating him with kinds and courtesy. Priam takes the body of Hector back to Troy, where his people honour his memory and give him a funeral worthy of his merits."

One of the most beautiful modern Australian literary pieces, David Malouf's *Ransom,* describes Priam's journey to recover the body of his son Hector (Malouf 2009).

But in spite of the unimaginable loss on both sides the war continues for years, and it is only through the cunning of Odysseus (Ulysses), the warlord of Ithaca, who devises a trick to win the unwinnable siege of Troy, that the Greeks are victorious. The Greeks produce an enormous wooden horse and pretend it is a gift. Once taken inside the mighty walls of Troy the soldiers hidden within open the gates of the city and finally the Greeks take Troy after 10 years of siege. The wooden horse story is mentioned in Homer's *Odyssey* but Virgil's Latin epic, *The Aeneid*, gives the best known description.

> "By destiny compell'd, and in despair
> The Greeks grew weary of the tedious war,
> And by Minerva's aid a fabric rear'd,
> Which like a steed of monstrous height appear'd:
> The sides were plank'd with pine; they feign'd it made
> For their return, and this the vow they paid.
> Thus they pretend, but in the hollow side
> Selected numbers of their soldiers hide:
> With inward arms the dire machine they load,
> And iron bowels stuff the dark abode.
>
> Laocoon, follow'd by a num'rous crowd,
> Ran from the fort, and cried, from far, aloud:
> 'O wretched countrymen! What fury reigns?
> What more than madness has possess'd your brains?
> Think you the Grecians from your coasts are gone?
> And are Ulysses' arts no better known?
> This hollow fabric either must inclose,
> Within its blind recess, our secret foes;
> Or 'tis an engine rais'd above the town,
> T'o'erlook the walls, and then to batter down
> Somewhat is sure design'd, by fraud or force:
> Trust not their presents, nor admit the horse.'"

The second epic poem of Homer, *The Odyssey,* describes the long, tortuous return of the victorious hero Odysseus from Troy to his beloved homeland,

Ithaca. The trip turned out to be the ultimate nightmare of all sailors. Compared to this, winning the war was child's play. Prof. Michael Hanly again:

"Long years have passed since Troy was taken and the victors of the siege set out for home. But Odysseus, the cunning inventor of the Trojan horse, ship wrecked after many adventures on his homeward way, has remained ever since marooned on a distant island, cherished prisoner of the sea-nymph Calypso. She loves him dearly and has offered him the gift of immortality. But he longs to return to his wife and his home.

At Odysseus' home in Ithaca, meanwhile, most people have given him up for lost. In consequence rival suitors are pestering his wife to remarry, partly because of her own attractions and partly with an eye to advancing a claim to Odysseus' royal prerogatives. Abusing the customary entitlement of visitors to hospitality they are making themselves free of Odysseus' house and eating and drinking daily at his expense. Odysseus' son Telemachus, a boy till now, has been powerless to prevent them. When the story of *The Odyssey* begins he is just emerging into manhood. His mother Penelope, as we presently learn, longs and still hopes for Odysseus' return, and the thought of marriage to any other man is repulsive to her; but her hope is fading, the pressure on her is increasing and her resources for resisting it are nearing exhaustion.

Two developments now take place, roughly simultaneously with one another. Telemachus suddenly decides to assert himself as a man and head of the household. And Calypso consents at last to let Odysseus go.

Telemachus warns the suitors (of course without effect) to leave the house, making them responsible for the consequences if they do not. Then he sets out by ship for the mainland in quest of some definite news of his father, alive or dead. From Nestor at Pylos and Menelaus at Sparta he hears the stories of what befell the other Greek chieftains after the fall of Troy, and a report that his father is alive but captive on an island far away. The suitors in Telemachus' absence plan to ambush and kill him on his way back to Ithaca.

Meanwhile on Calypso's island far away the nymph has at last been persuaded to let Odysseus go. With her help he makes a raft, and sets out in it across the sea. After some days of uneventful sailing a violent storm arises. The raft is wrecked, and Odysseus escapes with difficulty by swimming, to come ashore at last in the land of the Phaeacians, where King Alcinous receives him kindly and promises to have him carried safely home to Ithaca. In Alcinous' palace he tells his hosts (at length) the story of all his past adventures since leaving Troy (the encounters with giants and witches and sundry marvels that make up the best known part of the whole poem). That done, the Phaeacians with magical speed convey him, sleeping, home to Ithaca and land him in a remote part of the island.

Disguised and dressed as a tattered castaway, Odysseus now finds shelter (unrecognized) in the hut of his own head swineherd, from whom he learns how things stand with his family and in his home. Presently Telemachus, returned from his travels after escaping the suitors' ambush, comes to visit the swineherd. While the swineherd is temporarily absent Odysseus sheds his disguise and reveals himself to his son. Together they plan their next move. Odysseus resumes his disguise.

41

Next morning, he proceeds to his own house in the Ithacan town and enters it in the character of a beggar seeking alms. He observes and himself suffers from, the arrogant and brutal behaviour of the suitors. He waits for his chance. He dare not yet reveal himself even to his wife, with whom as mistress of the house he is invited to a private conversation. More than once he is in danger of premature recognition. The tension rises. Penelope not recognizing her husband in the tattered stranger, and seeing that her son is now grown up and able to take his place as his father's heir, decides (or appears to decide) that she must at last surrender to the suitors' importunity. She proposes a test to settle who shall have her hand and take her to his home. The test is, to string Odysseus' bow and perform with it a certain feat of archery. The bow is brought. The suitors try in turn to string it, without success. Penelope leaves the hall. The bow comes presently, despite protests from the suitors, into the hands of Odysseus himself. The dénouement follows swiftly. The suitors, taken unawares, are killed by Odysseus, helped by his son and two loyal servants to whom after cautious sounding he has already revealed himself. He sheds his disguise and resumes his natural appearance. Penelope, afraid at first to believe that her wish has at last come true, now sees him as she remembers him, and the recollection of a shared secret seals their reunion. They tell one another, as they lie in bed together, what has happened to each during their long separation; and Odysseus tells Penelope of further trials prophesied for him, though with final homecoming and a quiet end at the last the poet's tact thus tempers his happy ending with a touch of bitter in the sweet. On the next day peace is made between Odysseus and the families of the men on whom he took his vengeance."

This happy conclusion was reached after years of testing challenges when our hero was blown around the Mediterranean by unruly winds. Many Mediterranean islands eagerly claim some sort of connection to the legend. Jerba is thought to be the Land of the Lotus Eaters. After tasting the lotus fruit, the sailors and warriors found it very difficult to leave. Homer was obviously aware of man's addictive tendencies. Bonifacio on Corsica claims to be the Land of the Laestrygones, who hurled so many rocks at Odysseus' ship that the huge gap they created today serves as the harbour of the town. Beautiful Ponza could have been the island of Aeaea, where the gorgeous Circe turned Odysseus' men into pigs and captivated Odysseus. Charybdis and Scylla inhabited the Strait of Messina. I can attest that the whirlpools remain a scary feature of the strait. Malta was where Calypso seduced Odysseus to make him her immortal husband, but after seven years of captivity our hero escaped. On his raft finally he reached the island of the Phaeacians, Corfu. No one seems to claim the Land of the Cyclops, where the primordial giants lived. This is a shame, as the story is an excellent example of human ingenuity. The Cyclops, Polyphemus, had been eating Odysseus' men one by one, and the situation was dire. Asking for Odysseus' name, the hero replied that he was called "Nobody". Then, he formulated a cunning plan and blinded the single eye of the Cyclops. The monster called for help, but when asked, "Who did this to you?" He replied, "Nobody." We can imagine the rest, including the happy escape of Odysseus and his men.

Land of the
Laestrygones

Circe

Sirens

Land of the
Phaeacians

Pillars of Heracles

Troy

Island of
the Winds

Land of the
Cyclopes?

Charybdis Scylla

Ithaca
(Paliki)

Land of
the Sun

Island of
Calypso

Land of the
Lotus Eaters

200miles

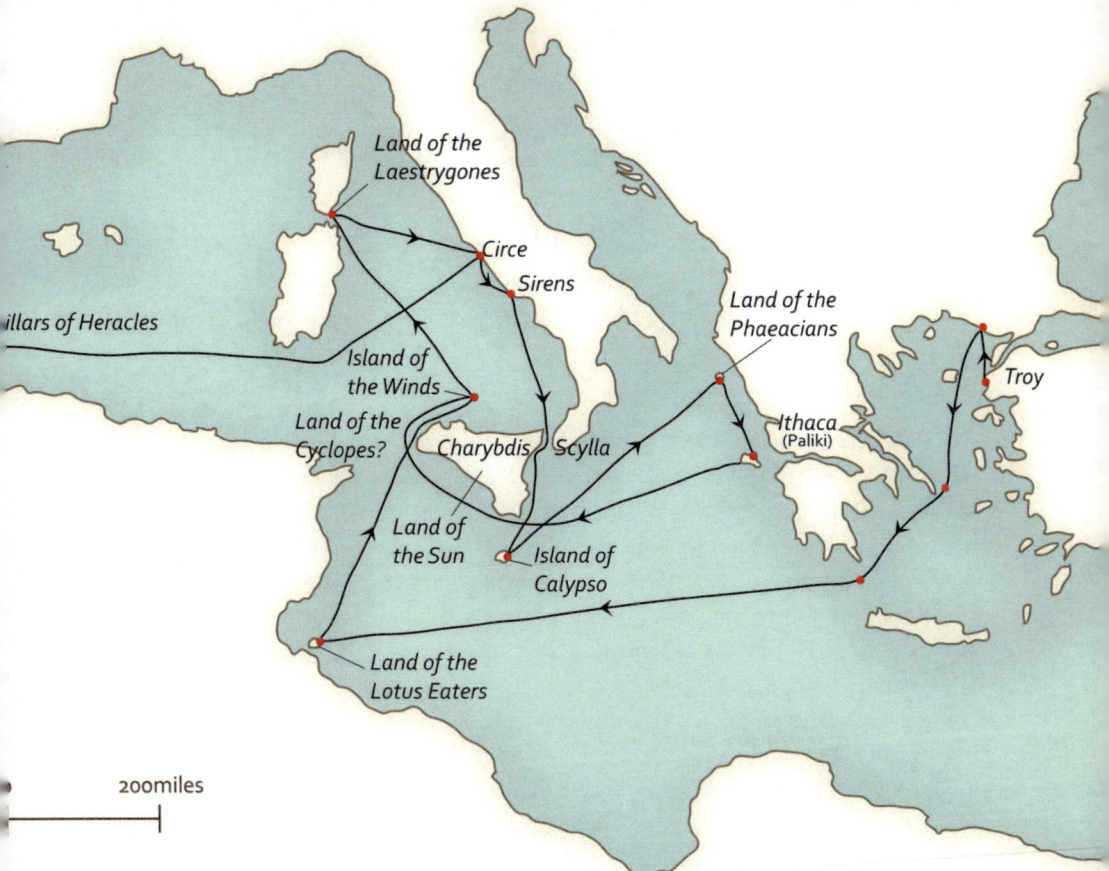

The wanderings of Odysseus

43

THE LAND OF
ST SPIRIDON

July, 2006

Corfu

I come from an era when schooling was about learning facts, when learning about other cultures was not about tasting their food or taking clumsy steps imitating folk dances, but really about studying their history, reading their literature and being able to point to their geographical location. My birthplace, Hungary, has never been a world power, so its education system lacks the arrogance of nations with more glorious histories. At school, in addition to maths, science, humanities, arts and the intricate details of the Hungarian language, we had the privilege of becoming acquainted with the enormous riches of world literature with a European focus. At the time of my graduation, an average Hungarian high school graduate, assisted by a mountain of compulsory readings every year, had a reasonable knowledge of English, American, German, Russian, French, Spanish and Italian history and literature, and an understanding of their roots in the Ancient Greek and Roman texts. Of course, the passing years have eroded my knowledge and I was more than ready for a refresher course – this time, in English. So I decided to spend the next couple of years exploring Ancient Greek history and literature. First, I was rather doubtful as to whether the ancient texts written in hexameter would be accessible for me in English. But luckily my first choice was the ancient best-seller, *The Odyssey*, in the translation of Robert Fagles (1996). Fagles is a magician in communicating the ideas of the ancient texts in contemporary words. So, I carried on reading all sorts of random pieces that took my interest. I was actually quite shaken by the immense beauty of the literary pieces, the depth and the complexity of the thoughts, the ridiculously precise understanding of the human condition and, most of all, the wisdom of the Ancient Greeks that remained relevant after almost 3,000 years.

After a year of absence, we were reunited with our beloved boat, *Fenix*, in the town of Levkas. Following 10 days of boat maintenance and improvement, expertly done by Steve and his friend, we waved goodbye to the friendly folks of Levkas, and in the early afternoon sailed into the choppy, wind-blown Ionian Sea, heading north. The fresh westerly breeze quickly carried us to a gorgeous anchorage hidden along the coast. After cooking up a storm in *Fenix*'s comfortable galley, we enjoyed a starlit dinner under the Mediterranean sky.

I quite like cooking on a boat. I pride myself as being a reasonably good cook, and love entertaining by creating complicated meals like bouillabaisse. Perhaps, because I am a scientist by trade, I always follow recipe books. Many of my friends frequently ridicule me by hinting at my lack of imagination, but I know they are wrong.

There is a lot of chemistry that happens during the process of cooking, and changing the order of administering the spices or just adding an extra minute when pan-frying meat can destroy the balance of flavours one intends to create. Of course, this disciplined way of cooking has to be abandoned once we hit the water. Although on *Fenix*, I have a spice collection that would shame most chefs, the nature of the game fundamentally changes. It is no longer about following recipes, but about using limited or unfamiliar ingredients to recreate familiar flavours from home or new ones just experienced in one of the shore tavernas. Other times, it is all about inventing new dishes that still pass the taste test even on the second day. Hunting for the right ingredients in the marvellous Mediterranean markets is always an adventure. Thus, shopping and cooking have become an integral and exciting part of our cruising life. Food consumed in the cockpit – in fact, on anything that floats – tastes markedly different and so much more flavoursome from anything prepared on land in even a three-star Michelin restaurant.

Cockpit meal

Our anchorage the night after leaving Levkas was narrow, and there was just enough space for a single boat to swing around. We were a little anxious, fearing an anchor drag, but the morning sun found us with a firmly buried anchor and in a great mood. We swam to the shore, and after a long brunch, headed to the island of Corcyra/Corfu/ Kerkira (whichever name you prefer), timing our arrival for the late afternoon. Visitors past and present praise the island as a lush green paradise that casts a soothing spell over all who visit it. To do justice to this beautifully crafted part of our planet, I turn to the words of *Prospero's Cell* (Durrell 1975).

> "Somewhere between Calabria and Corfu the blue really begins. All the way across Italy you find yourself moving through a 'landscape severely domesticated' – each valley laid out after the architect's pattern, brilliantly lighted, human. But once you strike out from the flat and desolate Calabrian mainland towards the sea, you are aware of a change in the heart of things: aware of the horizon beginning to stain at the rim of the world: aware of islands coming out of the darkness to meet you.
>
> Corcyra is all Venetian blue and gold – and utterly spoilt by the sun. Its richness cloys and enervates. The southern valleys are painted out boldly in heavy brush-strokes of yellow, red and while the Judas trees punctuate the roads with their dusty purple explosions. Everywhere you go you can lie down on grass; and even the bare northern reaches of the island are rich in olives and mineral springs.
>
> The architecture of the town is Venetian; the houses above the old port are built up elegantly into slim tiers with narrow alleys and colonnades running between them; red, yellow pink umber – a jumble of pastel shades which the moonlight transforms into a dazzling white city built for a wedding cake."

Indeed, even in the 21st century, arriving by sea and anchoring under the old fort where one can hear only the humming of the town is a magical experience.

Corfu has been inhabited for around 30,000 years, and it was an already an important centre during the Minoan and Mycenaean periods from 3000 to 1100 BC. However, today only circumstantial evidence exists to support the existence of significant habitation during that period. For example, the palace of Knossos on Crete (around 1800 BC) was built from a fir tree unique to Cephalonia, one of Corfu's neighbouring islands, suggesting a brisk trade between the islands of the Ionian Sea and faraway Crete. The long history and importance of the island is supported by the beautifully detailed description of its geography and people by Homer in *The Odyssey*.

Odysseus arrived at the island of Corfu after wandering the seas for almost ten years. The heroes of Troy had by then all returned to their homelands, but Poseidon punished the arrogant Odysseus and prevented him from reuniting with his family. After nearly ten years of wandering, the kind-hearted Athena was more than ready to help him to return to his home in Ithaca.

Unfortunately, Poseidon discovered the plot and shipwrecked the hero, who miraculously survived and landed on the island of the Phaeacians, Corfu. After a good night's sleep on the shore, he met the beautiful Nausicaa, the daughter of Alcinous, the king of the Phaeacians. Nausicaa led Odysseus to the palace, where he stood with bemusement.

> "A radiance strong as the moon or rising sun came flooding
> Through the high-roofed halls of generous King Alcinous.
> Walls plated in bronze, crowned with a circling frieze
> Lazed as blue as lapis, ran to left and right
> From outer gates to the deepest court recess,
> And solid golden doors enclosed the palace.
> Up from the bronze threshold silver doorposts rose
> with silver lintel above, and golden handles too.
> And dogs of gold and silver were stationed either side,
> forged by the god of fire with all his cunning craft
> to keep watch on generous King Alcinous' palace,
> his immortal guard-dogs, ageless, all their days.
> Inside to left and right, in a long unbroken row
> from farthest outer gate to the inmost chamber,
> thrones stood backed against the wall, each draped
> with a finely spun brocade, women's handsome work.

Here the Phaeacian lords would sit enthroned,
dining; drinking—the feast flowed on forever.
And young boys, molded of gold, set on pedestals
standing firm, were lifting torches high in their hands
to flare through the nights and light the feasters down the hall.
And Alcinous has some fifty serving-women in his house:
some, turning the handmill, grind the apple-yellow grain,
some weave at their webs or sit and spin their yarn,
fingers flickering quick as aspen leaves in the wind
and the densely woven woollens dripping oil droplets.
Just as Phaeacian men excel the world at sailing,
driving their swift ships on the open seas,
so the women excel at all the arts of weaving.
That is Athena's gift to them beyond all others
A genius for lovely work, and a fine mind too.

Outside the courtyard, fronting the high gates,
a magnificent orchard stretches four acres deep
with a strong fence running round it side-to-side.
Here luxuriant trees are always in their prime,
pomegranates and pears, and apples glowing red,
succulent figs and olives swelling sleek and dark.
And the yield of all these trees will never flag or die,
neither in winter nor in summer, a harvest all year round
for the West Wind always breathing through will bring
some fruits to the bud and others warm to ripeness
pear mellowing ripe on pear, apple on apple,
cluster of grapes on cluster, fig crowding fig.
And here is a teeming vineyard planted for the kings,
beyond it an open level bank where the vintage grapes
lie baking to raisins in the sun while pickers gather others;
some they trample down in vats, and here in the front rows
bunches of unripe grapes have hardly shed their blooms
while others under the sunlight slowly darken purple.
And there by the last rows are beds of greens,
bordered and plotted, greens of every kind,
glistening fresh, year in, year out. And last,
There are two springs, one rippling in channels
over the whole orchard—the other, flanking it,
rushes under the palace gates
To bubble up in front of the lofty roofs
where the city people come and draw their water.

Such were the gifts, the glories showered down by the gods
On King Alcinous' realm.
And there Odysseus stood,
Gazing at all this bounty, a man who'd borne so much..."

Sadly, no archaeological evidence has yet been found to confirm the existence of the rich Phaeacian kingdom described by the bard. Earthquakes are probably why there are few remains left from that period, but some stunning carved fragments show that the island was continuously inhabited from 1500 BC. In 734 BC, the innovative Corinthians established an important colony in Kerkira, just next to the modern town of Corfu. Kerkira prospered, and in 664 BC, it staged a successful revolt against Corinth. Historians partially blame this revolt for forcing Corinth into an alliance with Sparta and subsequently precipitating the Peloponnesian Wars between Athens and Sparta, which raged from 443–404 BC.

The most stunning piece of proof of the prosperity and power of Corfu during this period is the Gorgon pediment (585 BC). The pediment was part of the Temple of Artemis (590–580 BC), and remains the oldest Greek pediment in existence. As you visit the small but sweet archaeological museum and wander absent-mindedly through the rooms exhibiting the usual Greek vases, little perfectly shaped statues and ancient knick-knacks, nothing prepares you for the dramatic appearance of the Gorgon (17 m wide and more than 3 m tall). The work depicts the Gorgon and her children, who were born from her blood after Perseus cut off her head for fear of being turned into stone. We see the winged Gorgon surrounded by snakes, her two children Pegasus and Chrysaor, and two lion-panthers, while on the sides we can see scenes from the Battles of the Titans. The anger and fright was carefully carved into the Gorgon's face and you can just imagine this frieze decorating the entrance of a magnificent palace. According to archaeologists, the pediment had vivid colours.

Corfu, the city-state became a Roman protectorate around the turn of the millennium. Over the centuries, almost all major European nations have occupied and ruled Corfu at one time or another. After the collapse of the Roman Empire, it became part of the Byzantine Empire. The Byzantine period was followed by the invasions of the Normans, the Venetians, the Angevins, the Russians, the Turks, the French and the British. In 1864 Corfu became part of the recently independent Greece, but it was only after World War II that it became a fully integrated part of modern Greece. In spite of its turbulent history, Corfu remained fundamentally Greek over the millennia. This is from *The Greek Islands* (Durrell 1975):

> "A glance at the synoptic history of the place will do. Nothing to decrease the sense of being out of one's depth, submerged by too much data. But as time goes on, as Sunny Greek mornings succeed each other, you will find everything sinking to the bottom of your mind's harbour, there to take up shapes and dispositions, which are purely Greek and have no frame or reference to history anywhere else."

The lushness of Corfu is even more striking as it contrasts with the barren mountains of neighbouring Albania, clearly visible just across the narrow channel that separates the island from the mainland of Europe.

The patron saint of the island is St Spiridon. There are delightful small churches all over the town devoted to Greek-Catholic and Catholic dominations. One such a church has two doors cut on both sides of the narrow aisles, inviting a steady flow of tourists into the church all the time, even during religious services. I suppose this is a way to provide a chance for all visitors to sample the spectacular Greek-Catholic service. Perhaps it is hoped that on the spur of the moment they will be inspired to become more like the locals, and become followers of St Spiridon. The islanders have a close relationship with their patron saint, and the emergence of the cult of St Spiridon is one of the most remarkable stories I've ever heard (Durrell 1975):

> "The island is really the Saint: and the Saint is the island. Nearly all male children are named after him."

> In the chapel of the church of his name, he lies, looking trifle misanthropic but determined, as befits one who has seen most sides of life on Earth, and who is on equal terms with heaven. The sarcophagus is deeply lined and comfortable; he lies in hibernating stillness in his richly wrought casket. Who is Spiridon? His life is an amusing study in myth.

> He was born and lived in the mountains of Cyprus. When his wife died, he buried his unhappiness between the four walls of a monastery, becoming immediately remarkable for his fineness of spirit and fidelity to God ... A long life, many good works, and not a few miracles contributed to his subsequent popularity, so that when he died, this humble bishop of Trymithion (he was over ninety years old) had become the revered almost as a saint. He was buried: but the restless virtue in him could not waste in the Earth – and now exhalations of sweetness from his coffin began to trouble the orthodox. A spray of red roses broke from his tomb – today still to be seen in Cyprus. These combined omens persuaded the religious to dig his body up – and no sooner was this done than Spiridon justified his resurrection by a miracle, entering, so to speak, into posthumous life and career from the refuge of God himself. He had hardly a chance to settle down when Cyprus fell to the Saracens, his relics were removed to Constantinople; and when Constantinople itself was threatened by the locust hordes of the Moslem world, he was once more forced to change his country of operations.

> At this time, the Saint was in private ownership. A Greek, recorded as having been both priest and wealthy citizen, and whose name survives as Kalocheiritis, preserved him equally against the unbelieving Moslems and incipient decomposition. This Greek appears to have had some traffic in Saints since at the same time, he possessed the embalmed body of another saint – a lady of virtue – Saint Theodora Augusta.

> Kalocheiritis packed his two saints (very much as a peddler packs his apparatus in two shapeless sacks). He slung them, one on each side of his mule, and telling the curious that they contained animal fodder, crossed one fine spring morning into the enchanted landscapes of Greece and Parmythia in Epirus gave them refuge until 1456 when they were brought across the blue waters of the gull to Corcyra and laid in the chapel of Michael Archangel.

The three sons of Kalocheiritis, for example, inherited nothing beyond the two embalmed figures of their father. The two eldest were given half share each in Spiridon, while he youngest was forced by law to accept Theodora entire. He was obviously not content with this arrangement since he very soon relinquished the lady to the community. Spiridon, however, was a source of revenue as well as awe. By 1489, his two half shares were united in the possession of Philip the grandson – who made an attempt to carry off the relic to Venice, obviously to increase his turn over. This suggestion threw the island into a ferment, and he was forced to allow the tears and entreaties of the Corcyans to prevail. Spiridon stayed but it was not till 1598 that he got his own church."

More recently, in search of the warmth and glow of the southern European summer, millions of tourists have followed the invaders' footsteps. After such a history of occuption, one could well imagine, or even justify, signs of resentment among the islanders. However, the people of Corfu remain pleasant, polite and very helpful, and have withstood the onslaught of package tours. The services are generally good and the food is magnificent! Try Aigli, overlooking the great Corso that was built during the French occupation. Their vegetable mix entrée is exquisite.

After arriving at Corfu, the first thing one is confronted with is the sometimes loud, argumentative style of conversation. All Greeks speak and gesticulate with great enthusiasm! If you are from a country where formal and aloof behaviour is taught, appreciated or sometimes even enforced, the first confrontation with the Greek temperament is a little frightening. Greek men, unless physically doing something, spend their time in cafés, endlessly sitting and talking about important things like business and politics with strong gesticulation. While Australian men drink beer with their mates, Greek men, young and old, drink an endless amount of coffee. In Corfu, even today, most business deals are concluded in cafés!

The coffee is served in all shapes and sizes, cold or hot. Their absolute favourite is frappé a cold drink made from instant coffee that is blended with ice and mysteriously turned frothy like a good draft beer. I developed the theory that the caffeine load might be the cause of their temperament, and that a disruption of the coffee supply would turn them into a nation of reserved Victorian Englishmen.

Gesticulating and using harsh voices is a feature of communication in Corfu, and a way of talking that takes some getting used to. But don't get intimidated if and when the opportunity arises: join with your new acquaintances' discussions, which can cover everything from politics, movies, your country of origin, weather, wines, olives, women, business, tourists and family life. It seems the place and its people have not changed much since the time the Durrells were on the island (Durrell 1959):

The family was going to get into a taxi in front of the hotel.

"The taxi-drivers, perceiving our innocent appearance, scrambled from inside their cars and flocked round us like vultures, each trying to out-shout his compatriots. Their voices grew louder and louder, their eyes flashed, they clutched each other's arms and ground their teeth at one another, and then they laid hold of us as though they would tear us apart. After treated to the mildest of mild altercations not used to the Greek temperament it looked as though they were in danger of their lives.

'Can't you do something, Larry?' Mother squeaked disentangling herself with difficulty from the grasp of a huge driver.

'Tell them you'll report them to the British Consul,' suggested Larry, raising his voice above the noise.

'Don't be silly, dear,' said Mother breathlessly. 'Just explain that we don't understand.'

'Hoy!' roared a voice, 'whys donts yous have someone who can talks your own language?' Turning we saw an ancient Dodge parked by the kerb, and behind the wheel sat a short, barrel-bodied individual with ham-like hands and a great, leathery, scowling face surmounted by a jauntily-tilted peaked cap. He opened the door of the car, surged out on to the pavement, and waddled across to us. Then he stopped, scowling even more ferociously, and surveyed the group of silent cabdrivers.

'Thems been worrying yous ?' he asked Mother.

'No, no,' said Mother untruthfully; 'it was just that we had difficulty in understanding them.'

'Yous wants someones who can talks your own language,' repeated the new arrival; 'thems bastards . . . of mothers. Yous will excuses the words.... Would swindles their own mothers. Excuses me a minute and I'll fix thems.'

He turned on the drivers a blast of Greek that almost swept them off their feet. Aggrieved, gesticulating, angry, they were herded back to their cars by this extraordinary man."

Argumentative or not, the most distinctive sign of hospitality in Corfu is the friendliness of the taxi drivers. After experiencing the famous rudeness of Athenian taxi drivers, the weary tourists approaches the taxi with great care, hiding their mountains of luggage. In Athens, a ride is frequently refused if the client's luggage is too plentiful, too big, too dirty, too oddly shaped or too unpleasant-looking. In contrast, in Corfu every additional piece is a challenge that gives the driver a chance to demonstrate his excellent packing skills and is welcomed with a broad smile. Taking a taxi in Corfu is more than a fleeting anomalous relationship with a nameless driver sitting behind the wheel as a natural extension of the marvel of the 20th century. No, not in Corfu! Taking your seat, you become the natural protégé of the driver who treats you with respect, but also like an infant. Many people consider anyone who cannot speak their own native language as infants at best, and a little retarded at worst. So, the taxi drivers of Corfu look after you as they have done for at least a half a century. This is from *My Family and Other Animals* (Durrell 1959):

"'Wheres yous wants to gos ?' he asked, almost truculently.

'Can you take us to look for a villa?' asked Larry.

Sure. I'll takes yous anywheres. Just yous says.'

'We are looking,' said Mother firmly, 'for a villa with a bathroom. Do you know of one?'

The man brooded like a great, sun-tanned gargoyle, his black eyebrows twisted into a knot of thoughtfulness.

'Bathrooms?' he said. 'Yous wants a bathrooms?'

'None of the ones we have seen so far had them,' said Mother.

'Oh, I knows a villa with a bathrooms,' said the man. 'I was wondering if its was goings to be bigs enough for yous.'

'Will you take us to look at it, please?' asked Mother.

'Sure, I'll takes yous. Gets into the car.'

'Donts you worrys yourselfs about anythings, Mrs Durrells,' he had scowled; 'leaves everythings to me.'

So he would take us shopping, and after an hour's sweating and roaring he would get the price of an article reduced by perhaps two drachmas. This was approximately a penny; it was not the cash, but the principle of the thing, he explained. The fact that he was Greek and adored bargaining was, of course, another reason. It was Spiro who, on discovering that our money had not yet arrived from England, subsidized us and took it upon himself to go and speak severely to the bank manager about his lack of organization. That it was not the poor manager's fault did not deter him in the least. It was Spiro who paid our hotel bill, who organized a cart to carry our luggage to the villa, and who drove us out there himself, his car piled high with groceries that he had purchased for us.

That he knew everyone on the island, and that they all knew him, we soon discovered was no idle boast. Wherever his car stopped, half a dozen voices would shout out his name, and hands would beckon him to sit at the little tables under the trees and drink coffee. Policemen, peasants, priests waved and smiled as he passed; fishermen, grocers, and cafe-owners greeted him like a brother. 'Ah, Spiro!' they would say, and smile at him affectionately as though he was a naughty but lovable child. They respected his honesty, his belligerence, and above all, they adored his typically Greek scorn and fearlessness when dealing with any form of Governmental red tape."

Even today, 50 years on, this unique friendliness of the taxi drivers remains one of the most pleasant features of the island. We had a personal experience when we hired a taxi to find an obscure gas-fitting shop in the outskirts of the city. Stephen, the driver, with telling blue eyes a reminder of the British occupation, spent approximately half a day with us assisting in all our shopping needs and was only satisfied with himself after overseeing the loading of our groceries and other essentials into our dinghy.

In Corfu, the sea is part of people's lives. In the past, the ever-present sea abolished the need for bathrooms for centuries, so when Madame Durrell was looking for a villa with a bathroom on Corfu in the 1950s, it caused considerable difficulties.

"'They seem a helpful crowd,' Larry went on. 'The manager himself shifted my bed nearer the window.'

'He wasn't very helpful when I asked for paper,' said Leslie.

'Paper?' asked Mother. 'What did you want paper for?'

'For the lavatory… there wasn't any in there,' explained Leslie.

'Shhh! Not at the table,' whispered Mother.

'You obviously don't look,' said Margo in a clear and penetrating voice; 'they've got a little box full by the pan.'

'Margo, dear,' exclaimed Mother, horrified. 'What's the matter? Didn't you see the little box?'

Larry gave a snort of laughter.

'Owing to the somewhat eccentric plumbing system of the town,' he explained to Margo kindly, 'that little box is provided for the… er… debris as it were, when you have finished communing with nature.'

Margo's face turned scarlet with a mixture of embarrassment and disgust.

'You mean… you mean… that was… My God! I might have caught some foul disease,' she wailed, and, bursting into tears, fled from the dining-room.

'The next morning, we started … 'Didn't you notice?' she asked. 'None of them had a bathroom.'

Mr Beeler stared at Mother with bulging eyes.

'But Madame,' he wailed in genuine anguish, 'you want a bathroom? Have you not got the sea?'

Of course, in today's EU-trained Greece, there are bathrooms in most houses and in all hotels and motels – although it appears that the quality of the plumbing, in spite of acquiring all the technical miracles of the 21st century, has not improved during the 60 years since the Durrells spent those memorable five years on the island. Thus, they still keep buckets for collecting used toilet paper, even in six-star hotels equipped with all luxuries known to mankind.

Greek Sirens

The sea that surrounds the island of Corfu remains part of the daily life of its inhabitants. Regardless of their everyday occupation, the men fish and the women, young or old, gracefully immerse themselves every morning in the sparkling sea, emerging like 21st-century Aphrodites. Today's Greek women, all shapes and sizes, regardless of their age, continue to adore the sea and swimming is part of their daily routine. The young arrive with springy steps, jump from rocks or run into the sea. Young people all over the world enjoy water thus; it's not something specific to Greece. But on the Ionian Islands, even older women remain devotees of the sun and water, as they have been for thousands of years. There is a delightful description of the swimming habits of Greek women in the 1950s in *Mermaid Singing* (Clift 1956):

> "Even though Kalymnians are the most aquatic of all islanders, little boys and girls of five and six and seven have separate areas of play in the sea. The boundaries are fluid, and they cross and recross and jumble together while they are still small, but as they grow older this segregation becomes distinct and rigid. Nubile girls and women not only swim in concealed coves and beaches away from the eyes of men but wear (except for the rich or educated who have learned foreign customs) an enveloping garment that is rather like a square-necked nightgown. Actually it is very graceful and pretty. It is usually made another colour, so a group of women going into the sea achieve a formal, fluid grace of line and colour that you will never find on Western beaches. But if the purpose of the garment is modesty it defeats itself, for the moment it is wet it becomes transparent and clings provocatively to breast and belly and thighs.

> 'You admire them going into the water, my sweet,' says George, blissfully stuffing himself with black figs under the twisted tree where we have paused to rest above the little pebbled cove. 'Just tell me when they are coming out.'

> Obviously, too, in this trammelling garment the women's aquatic exercises are restricted. They never manage anything more strenuous than the breast-stroke, the side-stroke or a form of gentle dog-paddle. One day I was lured by an overweening pride into demonstrating the Australian crawl. The women, after their first stunned and gratifying surprise, averted their eyes. My performance, I realised, was to them something as grotesque as a trapeze act or a performing seal."

Clift might have been proud of her ability to master the Australian crawl (overarm swimming style), but in real terms her Australian sisters were not much ahead of the Greek women in the 1950s. Symbolically, by the 1950s, Australian women "crawled" towards equal rights, but – as shocking as it might be today – they were not only banned from having a bank accounts but also, in Australia's top academic institute (CSIRO), female researchers had to quit after marrying.

Nowadays, people even in the most remote Greek islands shun the ridiculous outfits described in Clift's book. The elderly women arrive slowly, walking or dragging themselves out of expensive new cars driven by their children or grandchildren to the shore. The sun has just risen above the horizon, the sea is blue and, cheerfully talking to each other, they take off their old-fashioned clothes that cover their proud but somewhat shapeless bodies. The dresses are a simple variety of the shirt-dress. They are usually made of black or dark blue cotton, sometimes with small flowers breaking the monotony of the single colour, straight cut, leaving plenty of space for the hips and bosoms. At the front of the dress there is a line of buttons for easy changing, beginning at their sharp chins and pointing to their legs, which resemble Corinthian columns. I have never seen these dresses anywhere in the world other than Central Europe, worn by village women. Having removed their dresses, the women in their modest swimming costumes slowly immerse themselves in the soothing sea, all the while continuing to chat about the latest exciting stories in their families. The ritual is finished by lying down on the small walls separating the sea from the bustling town and letting themselves leisurely dry in the life-giving sun. Then they quickly dress and drag themselves back towards their home. I observed this ritual all over Corfu and other Greek islands.

Enjoy swimming!

Corfu is a delightful place to visit. There is an excellent anchorage under the old fort with good access to the town. The French-built Spinada is wonderful: a little, neglected park that provides young and old with lots of opportunities to play and talk in the evening. From 7 pm until the early hours, the park is busy: children riding their bikes while adults merrily chat. In 2006, the town was free of beggars and of peddlers selling unwanted holiday bric-à-brac and, more importantly, it was safe and orderly. This was surprising, as it is only a stone's throw from Albania, which at the time of our visit was considered to be a kingdom of thieves and was responsible for the export of prostitutes, beggars and thieves all over Europe. In 2007, George Bush, the American president, was accused of removing his wristwatch while visiting the country. It was liberating not to be worried about thieves and safety when one ventured away from the brightly lit main tourist tracks. In Corfu, people wander about freely. The best example of the excellent safety record of the town was that even small children were allowed to ride their bikes and little rented electric cars into the darkness of the park. Corfu is one of the most exciting holiday destinations in Europe. It offers something for everyone: the sports enthusiast, families, the history geek and for the average person just wanting to have a good time.

ATLANTIS

August, 2006

Crete

I would have preferred to arrive at Crete on *Fenix*, but I had to leave her in Athens to fulfill my obligation as an organiser and founder of a breakaway conference, in Cambridge. We, modern scientists are the followers of the Greek mindset. Thus we continue our independent investigations into the world regardless of what other people might think. As my colleague Barry Marshall stated:

> "Science is not democracy or religion. The truth cannot be voted in or out or believed in. The scientific hypothesis is rigorously tested by independent investigators who provide the ultimate answers to our enquiries." – Barry Marshall, 2005 Noble Laureate for Medicine, National Press Club Address 2006.

In this spirit, a group of scientists organised the conference. The aim was to examine the development of eye disease not from the viewpoint of genetics, fashionable at the time, but from the perspective of cell biology, which focuses on cellular function. So Steve and our son Gavin sailed *Fenix* from Athens to Crete on a route that has been plied by an endless number of vessels over the millennia. As for me, I had to negotiate the challenges of peak European summer air traffic from Athens to Cambridge and back to Crete.

Olympic Airlines, in pursuit of the largest profit possible, overbooked the plane by 30 passengers. As this became obvious, everyone started to shout: customers, clerks and supervisors. No one knew what to do, so no one was doing anything useful. After a while, things settled down and the clerks made an attempt to put the excess passengers on planes. An administrative nightmare ensued as tickets had to be refunded, new ones paid for, lunch coupons distributed…

> "Many people think that the biggest difference between females and males is the ability to multitask." – Kathy Lette, *How to Kill my Husband* (2007).

Perhaps all Greeks are descendants of the mysterious female warrior tribe, the Amazons, because the Greeks are the ultimate champions of multitasking. At any time any self-respecting employee performs a minimum of two, but preferably three, vastly different tasks at the same time. The very best can even handle four!

In this spirit, the clerk reached for my papers while simultaneously answering the phone and also responding to the enquiries of a colleague. After studying my papers, he came to the conclusion that he needed some forms – at Olympic Airlines no employee ever has the necessary papers in his desk – so my man left his phone dangling and wandered into the next-door office to retrieve the relevant forms.

Apparently, he was some sort of oracle, as his colleagues were anxiously waiting for his wise comments on a variety of matters: as soon as he entered the room, the forms were forgotten and they immediately started to discuss all sorts of unrelated issues, which delayed his return to his desk, where in the meantime a long queue had formed from his more-or-less patiently waiting customers. When he returned without the forms, instead of sorting out my problem – "Too hard!" – he started to deal with new customers, hoping for something easier to handle. This attitude created a never-ending pile of papers on his desk, all representing unfinished matters. My plane was not scheduled to leave for another five hours, so I was not particularly fussed, but passengers who were trying to catch earlier flights and not to miss their connections were really frustrated.

I think the origins of this multitasking are closely connected to the habit of Mediterranean people combining work and family. I had observed that the family business means "family always present in the business": the children happily pottering around their parents or chasing each other between the legs of the customers; the owners eating their daily meals and attending to their own private needs while also serving their customers. All these habits inevitably lead to a mastery of multitasking. Although, the now defunct Olympic Airlines, with the best intentions, could not be called a traditional family business, old habits die hard and multitasking, with all its inefficiencies, continues to be a prevalent and idiosyncratic feature of Greek business.

Warning! If you're a tourist, you may risk your sanity by attempting to navigate Greek bureaucracy. Use postal, banking and real estate services at your own risk! The general environment tends to be totally disorganised, chaotic and laid back. As Seascape owner Diane Edwards put it, "People operate on GMT: Greek Maybe Time".

Arriving from Athens to charming Cambridge was wonderful. It was the end of August and there were only a few particularly eager students around. The town was quiet but at the same time busy enough to make me feel that I had entered the cathedral of scholarly life. Walking in the beautiful tranquil gardens of the colleges, I could almost hear all those "big brains" working behind the centuries' old walls. The influence of Oxbridge (the universities of Oxford and Cambridge) on human knowledge is comparable only to that of Athens.

The first recorded date connected with Cambridge University was 1209. After a disagreement with the local council, some students from Oxford moved to Cambridge and the first college was founded in 1284. During the reign of Henry VIII, several new colleges were built, splendid gatehouses were erected and the most beautiful church in England, King's College Chapel, was completed. More importantly, Henry VIII removed the university colleges from the religious bodies, thus re-establishing the foundations of independent academic thinking. In late Victorian times, further colleges were founded, including the first women's colleges (although degrees were not awarded to women until 1948). The university gradually developed into a centre of scientific research. Several discoveries that changed our world forever were made by famous scientists at Cambridge University. To mention just a few:

- William Harvey   - discovered the circulation of the blood in 1628

- Isaac Newton   - described universal gravitation in 1687

- Charles Darwin   - described the mechanism of evolution in 1859

- Ernest Rutherford   - split the atom in 1903

- Francis Crick and James Watson - discovered the structure of DNA in 1953

- Stephen Hawking   - published *A Brief History of Time* in 1988

It is interesting to consider that the very existence of the university can be directly connected to Greeks living in Athens 2,500 years earlier. In one way or another the Greeks defined scholarly work and developed the idea of independent scientific investigation. They devised the investigative techniques that have been used since their inception to advance, expand and improve our knowledge and understanding. Just to mention a few:

- Homer (850BC? 1200 BC?)   - literature

- Socrates (470–399 BC)   - philosophy

- Hippocrates (460–370 BC)   - medicine

- Hippodamus (498–408 BC)   - architecture

- Pythagoras (580–500? BC)   - geometry

- Herodotus (484–425 BC)   - history

- Strabo (63 BC–24 AD)   - geography

While I was savouring the fruits of the Ancient Greeks' labours, Steve and Gavin sailed the boat from Athens to Crete. The history of Crete goes back to 6000 BC and this long, uninterrupted human presence produced some of the best-known and most thrilling mythological characters. We were excited to visit this island, which lies halfway between the continents of Africa and Europe, and were expecting all those characters to come alive and greet us. The reality was not much less exciting.

The trip from Athens to Iraklion was characterised by huge seas and big winds hitting 35 knots again and again. Gavin is anything but an avid sailor. He quickly declared that if the waves entered the cockpit he would go down below to sleep and forget about the huge seas. Until then, he and Steve shared the three-hour watches, looking out for boats under the dark sky. Careful watch on this very busy waterway, where traffic was from every direction day and night, was essential: our small sailing boat was hidden by the huge waves. It is well known to every sailor that large cargo or cruise ships can run into a small boat without anyone other than the people on the smaller vessel noticing. A small boat might have the right-of-way, but if a collision happens it could disappear without a trace. It might take weeks for the relatives to raise the alarm – far too late to do anything! Around 3 am Steve woke up to a restrained, then hysterical, laugh. He quickly emerged fearing that Gavin had freaked out. He found our son happily sitting in the cockpit, looking at something in his hand that was

Sailing towards Crete

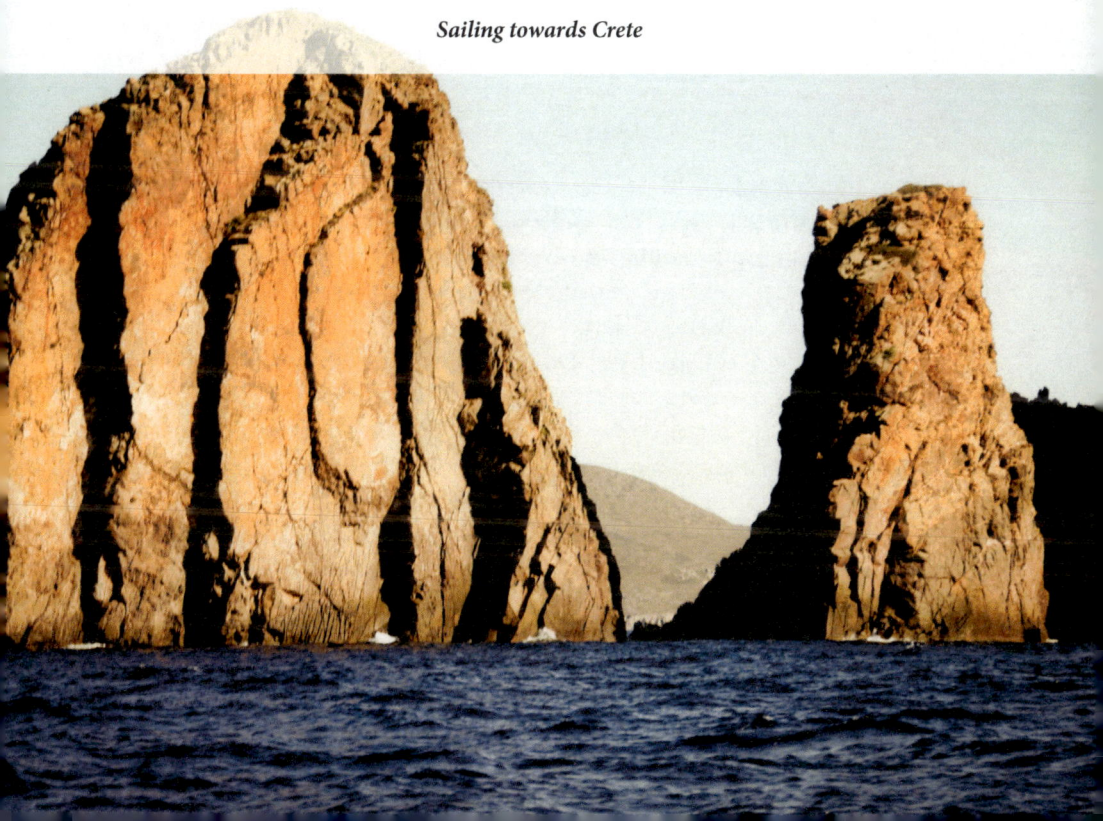

glowing in the darkness. He was watching his favourite *Seinfeld* on his iPod and enjoying every minute of it. Gavin happily continued his watch, facing the rough seas on his own and having fun all the way to Crete.

After being thrown around for 30 hours, Steve and Gavin arrived exhausted at Iraklion and sailed into the commercial harbour. The northern coast of Crete is continually battered by huge waves and lacks harbours or marinas that can accommodate relatively small yachts. Tying up in a commercial harbour, where the quay is designed for much bigger vessels, is a real challenge. Having carefully lined *Fenix* up, they realised that the bollards were at least a metre above their heads. With some acrobatic manoeuvring, they somehow managed to tie her up. Soon they found themselves taking care of the bizarre administrative requirements of the Greek authorities, which included the purchase of a cruising permit, a transit log and paying all sorts of other fees. All of these payments resulted in a nice collection of stamps from a variety of offices: Health, Harbour Master, Port Police, and Coast Guard. It was as if they had arrived not from Athens, but from Sulawesi. However, they soon realised that the authorities were correct after all: in Crete, there is the feeling of being in a very foreign land, rich in historical references.

Perhaps these administrative measures were nothing but reminders of the tumultuous history between Athens and Crete. During the Bronze Age (2700–1450 BC), Athens was not the strong power it later became; the Minoans ruled the Mediterranean world. According to legend, King Minos of Crete forced Athens to pay tribute for the loss of his son who died while trying to kill the bull of Marathon. The tribute consisted of seven youths and seven girls, who were fed to the half-man, half-bull monster, the Minotaur, the offspring of Minos' wife Pasiphae and a bull.

The Minotaur was held in the middle of an intricate maze called the Labyrinth, which was designed and constructed by Daedalus. Fearing the secret of the Labyrinth would be revealed, King Minos kept Daedalus in a tower as a virtual prisoner. Unfortunately, for Minos, he misjudged Daedalus' genius. Daedalus constructed large wings from feathers held together with threads and wax. Wearing these, Daedalus and his young son Icarus leapt from the tower and, legend has it, became the first men to fly. However, even then, youngsters did not listen to their elders: in spite of Daedalus' warning, Icarus flew too close to the blazing sun. The wax holding the feathers together softened, and one by one, the feathers fell into the sea. Icarus duly followed. His father wept, blaming himself. Eventually, however, Daedalus arrived safely in Sicily, where he built the magnificent Temple of Apollo.

No one could escape from the Labyrinth, however. It held the Minotaur, which was fed on young Athenians, sacrificed in order to stay a terrible plague. But then came Theseus, a later Athenian hero, who distinguished himself in early youth. First he killed a number of monsters, then restored his father Aegeus to the throne of Athens. Theseus offered himself as one of the sacrifices to the Minotaur and sailed to Crete. He was a dashing fellow and Ariadne, the daughter of King Minos, fell in love with him at first sight. The love-struck Ariadne gave Theseus a roll of wool, which he unravelled at the entrance of the Labyrinth to help him to trace his footsteps back. Theseus killed the Minotaur, retraced his steps through the maze and ran away with Ariadne, whom he later abandoned on Naxos. On his return to Athens, he forgot to hoist the prearranged signal of white sails to indicate that he was alive. When his father saw the ship's black sails, he threw himself into the sea in despair.

Theseus took the Athenian throne and married the Amazon queen Antiope, and they had a son, Hippolytus. Later Theseus married Phaedra, who Theseus loved but who was disliked by Hippolytus. From here, we know how the story continues: it was immortalised by Euripides in his play, *Hippolytus*.

Today, very few remember the original tale of Ariadne's Thread. The term is used to describe a problem-solving method where the truth is found by tracing steps, point by point, through an exhaustive application of logic to all available routes. It can be used to solve the problems of a physical maze, a logic puzzle or an ethical dilemma.

The history of Crete reaches back into the dark, cold Neolithic period. Over the millennia, the people of the island remained attached to their religious beliefs and continued to worship the Goddess of Fertility. Perhaps this is how her story started.

"I was born a long, long time ago. My mother was a good mother, but she was used to losing one child after another. At the time of my arrival she was still breastfeeding a small underdeveloped girl and there was a boy running around her in the muddy cave. I delayed my arrival in the hope of being welcomed by my parents. It was as if I knew all the horrors of hunger that were waiting for me once I left the nice warm environment of my mother's womb.

After an uneventful delivery, people were amazed by the birth of the strong girl with snow white skin, as white as the mountains' tops in the cold weather. Unusually, I had long black hair and a very strong body. Even during those early days of semi-conscious existence I knew my mother's milk was not only the key to my survival but to the emergence of a new world. I suckled on my mother's breast with brute force, never leaving anything for my older sister. She subsequently died from starvation, or disease – who knows? I grew quickly during the spring and summer months when food was more plentiful than during the dark, cold winter. Winter was always hard, as our grain storage ran out well before the new harvest. My parents could never collect enough food to last through the cold season. They tried hunting and gathering with varying success. One day, my mother was chasing a wild boar towards my father and his brothers. They attacked the beast with their spears and primitive chipped stone tools, but sadly they only managed to injure it. The enraged animal rushed into the undergrowth of the forest where it came across my little brother, looking for berries. He was simply eaten by the beast. My parents and other tribe members arrived just in time to witness the final moments of the gory scene.

During this disaster, I was comfortably sleeping in my cot in the cave. Since my parents had lost all their other children, as if to compensate for their loss, the tribe treated me as their favourite. Being liked by everyone meant that I was well-nourished compared to my peers. There was always a bit of grain or a scrap of meat for me, so I became stronger and stronger and grew into a tall young woman with muscular legs and arms, an ample bosom and wide hips. By this time, my father had died and I lived alone in our cave with my mother.

One spring the strongest young man in the village came to talk to my mother. His father was the best hunter in the tribe and they were known to tame wild animals. So his family was blessed with plenty of meat: far more than I could imagine. The parents of this young man were kind to me as far as I can remember. Perhaps they recognised my true nature.

I became the wife of this man, and without much ceremony he moved into our cave with a large animal in tow. The animal was white and made silly noises like meh, meh. He said it was a goat. We never had an animal live with us before, but I followed his instructions and kept it inside for the night, milked it and let it out in the morning to graze. One morning when I went to let the goat out, I found that she had given birth to two kids. She was a dutiful doe but the new additions kept me very busy, and to be honest it was only the promise of all that meat that prevented me from shooing them off. I did not understand then how lucky we were to have three domesticated goats. My mother knew the best places to find berries and our little primitive plot of land provided some much-needed grain. The three of us working together managed to provide enough food to last through most of the winter months. That following spring our son was born. I recalled my own thirst for my mother's milk and I kept the child on my breast day and night to provide him with a continuous flow of life. My son grew pink, fat, inquisitive and good-natured on the inexhaustible life I gave him, as did all my five children. Our dwelling was well located: it faced south and the early spring sun always shone into our cave. I still recall the warmth it delivered into our half-frozen bodies after the long, cold winter winds. We built a small fence in front of the cave that provided shelter from the wind and kept wild animals away. In the cave we had a well-protected sleeping place that was dry and reasonably warm during winter and nice and cool during summer. My children grew strong in the protective environment of our dwelling, away from the curious eyes of the rest of the tribe. I was unique among the tribe as all my children were born alive and survived beyond their early years.

My mother was very strict and kept our dwelling clean, removing all the things we could not use anymore. Not that there was much rubbish left after we finished feeding ourselves. I followed this custom, throwing the stuff collected day by day from our cave onto a swampy field behind the cave: the charcoal pieces, the droppings of our sickly goat, the white clean bones. Sometimes our grain rotted, so instead of nourishing us it also ended up on the field. Incidentally, we also used the same place to relieve ourselves.

One spring, I was astonished to notice that this field had become very green – greener than anything I had ever seen – and that year by autumn we had twice as much grain as the years before. The area was infested with snakes so very few people went there. Fortunately the snakes were harmless. I knew as they bit me couple of times when I startled them, I bled a little, sucked the wound and continued my work. However, the tribespeople believed what they believed and thought the snakes were poisonous. So, the snakes in my field and around our dwelling scared the living daylights out of most people. In many ways, they were a blessing in disguise because it took a long time for the tribe to discover the excess grain we stuffed into ourselves year after year without sharing it around.

Of course, after seeing my children nice and pink from the good grain harvest, from the milk of the goats and from the occasional hunting of prey, people became interested in my success. I think I was the only woman in our tribe, potentially in the whole world, who successfully raised all her children to adulthood.

People started to ask questions and they began to invite me to their homes to give my blessing on the birth of a child or to bless sowing seeds in spring time. It took me while to work out why my field was greener. Rightly I guessed that it was associated with using it as a rubbish tip. Not that we had too much rubbish: we used everything until it had disintegrated into pieces, every bone was chewed by several of us until it was broken down into snow-white pieces. Most of the rubbish on that tip was nothing more than human and animal faeces. By this time, my daughters' husbands moved into our home, as was custom, and my married sons moved into their in-laws' home. Two of my sons were strong and adventurous, and walked and hunted all over our island. One day, they came across something on the shore that they had never seen before – a floating object that enabled people to walk and sit on water. It carried strange-looking people that turned up on the horizon from nowhere. I was told that they stepped onto those contraptions – later I learned they were called ships – and the wind blew them away.

I continued to carry out my duties as the Goddess of Fertility. Yes, that's what they called me. Goddess? Goddesses are supposed to be beautiful with full breasts and fertile wombs. By this time my heyday was long over. I was pale and skinny, and only my long black hair was a reminder of my better days. But my field was as green as ever! So I advised people and blessed their crops for a small fee, a share of their grain or a cup of milk. They prospered, and more and more of them came to seek my advice about all sorts of family disputes. I always considered what was best for the children and gave my advice accordingly and never ever advised them to fight.

People! Although, they could clearly see that they benefited from the blessings I gave them in person, they thought that they could avoid needing to give that small donation by manufacturing ridiculous statuettes of me at the peak of my fertility. These statuettes featured a big-breasted woman with snakes in her hands. They thought that my power was something to do with the snakes and they did not realise for a long time that it was the manure on the fields that had done the trick! They put these statuettes where I used to stand and – fools that they were – expected the same result. Well, more often than not they were bitterly disappointed and starved! So they came back to me and this small community kept me alive with their donations, even after my daughters and their husbands had passed away.

One beautiful sunny morning, I heard hurried steps and to my astonishment I found my two long-lost sons standing in front of me. They were dressed in strange but colourful clothes and carried a big sack with them. The sack was huge and made from fine material never seen on our island before. The sack was filled with all sorts of objects unknown to any of us.

My sons and the people they came with on those huge ships brought prosperity to my people from a faraway land. We had always been quick learners, and all of us rapidly acquired the skills of making bronze, jewellery and pottery and the art of animal husbandry.

My people were used to hardships and they were grateful for the knowledge brought by my sons and their companions. For me it was becoming harder and harder to move around, so it was time to make use of the beautiful statuettes some talented people made for the spring fertility festivals. These beautiful statuettes were created with the refined techniques of the faraway land and were decorated with jewellery. Because of my blessings my tribe became more and more numerous and stronger, and under the leadership of my sons our land became a prosperous place. I was happy when I closed my eyes as a very old woman. I knew that our descendants would fill this land with lots of joyful people."

The legend of the fertility goddess endured even after Egyptian influence brought fast development to the region. The distance of the island from other lands allowed the people of Minoan Crete to develop their own unique culture. The rapid technical development, which affected pottery, metalwork, jewellery production and stone carvings, also led to social development. More and more people lived closer together in towns, and the first labyrinthine palaces were constructed. By 1700 BC, the golden age of Minoan Crete had arrived. During this period there were at least three large centres on Crete: Phaistos, Malia and Zakros, with palaces and large populations. The best known, next to present day Iraklion, is Knossos. English archaeologist Arthur Evans excavated the palace in 1900. He was astonished and delighted with his significant find

Minoan Garden of Eden

Minoan fertility goddess

of wonderful architecture and art from a civilisation comparable only to that of Egypt. In a bold move, he rebuilt parts of the palace, trying to recreate a complete picture of Minoan life and art. His recreated archaeological wonder made Knossos one of the prime tourist destinations on Earth. Although today many would say that this rebuilt Knossos represents Evans' interpretation of the Minoan civilisation, I think making it accessible for many meant he made an enormous contribution to human culture.

The Palace of Knossos was the largest and grandest palace of Crete covering 22,000 m^2. There was peace in Minoan Crete. As far as we can tell, the towns and palaces did not have defences. Knossos consisted of a maze of rooms of all sizes, large halls, storerooms, workshops, staircases and corridors. Perhaps there is a less interesting explanation for the labyrinth-like structure of the palaces than the mythological story of Daedalus.

The maze-like arrangement of the palace was probably due to the Minoan builders' lack of understanding of how to build arches or curved structures. The wedge-shaped elements that make up an arch and keep one another in place transform the vertical pressure of the structure above into lateral pressure.

The labyrinth-like structure of the Palace of Knossos

In Minoan palaces, the weight of the roof was borne by the columns directly as vertical pressure, so it was necessary for the columns to be wide and heavy. This also limited the distance between the walls to narrow corridors.

Nevertheless, the Palace of Knossos is a magnificent sight. In the eastern wing, there were four levels of royal apartments, and in the western wing, there were sacred places, shrines and the throne room. Unbelievably, the alabaster throne was found intact. In a nice reference to peace and order, a copy of the throne serves as the seat for the President of the International Court of Justice in The Hague.

Although Minoans continued to worship the Goddess of Fertility, by this time, the King acted as the High Priest and was considered to embody their deity. This might have something to do with Egyptian influence.

Minoans were hooked on bulls, and these appear everywhere in their art. A small, refined sculpture of a bull's head with crystal eyes, elegant gilded horns and white pearl muzzle from circa 1600 BC was found in the Palace. The wall paintings or frescoes produced by the Minoans are simply fabulous. One of the

The Minoan bull leapers

most famous, "Bull-leaping", depicts an acrobat leaping across a bull's back with two assistants at either end. One holds the horns of the animal and the other is ready to catch the flying acrobat. As fabulous as the depiction is, the most interesting thing about the painting is its border. Recently it was proposed that the intricate border, which looks like a modern barcode, represents a kind of calendar with magic nine-year cycles.

The Queen's apartment in Knossos is decorated with a fabulous fresco of vivid blue dolphins playing in the Mediterranean Sea. The openings, windows and the door frames are decorated with artful border designs symbolising the waves of the sea. Perhaps all this high-quality, interior design was due to the refined taste of Minoan women, who adorned themselves with astoundingly beautiful and colourful jewellery, found scattered all over their palaces.

Minoan writing – so-called Linear A – was similar to hieroglyphic characters and was arranged in a spiral. Despite huge efforts by academics, it has not yet been deciphered. The Minoans were a peace-loving people and their economy was based on agriculture, manufacturing industries, shipping and trade. They traded effortlessly across the Mediterranean, particularly with the Cyclades, Egypt, the rest of the Greek world, and the East. Unfortunately, the destruction of the great palace centres by a series of earthquakes and tidal waves caused by the eruption of the volcano on Santorini in 1630 BC deny us more details about their lives. After the destruction of the palace centres, the Mycenaeans established themselves on the island. The Palace of Knossos was rebuilt to some extent and became the centre of Mycenaean power. The culture of the island now became imbued with a new, more martial spirit. Shortly after 1400 BC, the Palace of Knossos was destroyed for the last time and the colourful world of Minoan Crete was replaced by the harsh Megalomes of Mycene. I could not help thinking that had Minoan Crete not been destroyed, the Western world/culture would have developed in a completely different way.

After the final collapse of the Mycenaean empire around 1000 BC, Crete and the rest of Greece descended into a Dark Age. Most of the achievements of the Minoans and Mycenaeans were forgotten. While the rest of Greece soon recovered with a vengeance, creating one of the greatest cultures in the history of mankind with an unprecedented influence on today's world, the Dark Age continued for the Cretans. They remained poor, and sometimes backwards, but proud of their Greek-Cretan origin. Crete emerged as the centre of the Greek independence movement against the Turks in the 19th century. The free spirit and temperament of the Cretans was celebrated in the book of Nikos Kazantzakis, *Zorba the Greek* (Kazantzakis 2000). In the character of Zorba, Kazantzakis masterfully summarised his philosophical views, which are engraved onto his headstone: "I hope for nothing. I fear nothing. I am free".

On my return to Crete, I read the book again and I was surprised that this best-seller of the 1970s was not that interesting anymore, and how dated its mixture of leftist, Buddhist and nationalistic ideas had become. I was particularly surprised by the male chauvinist views of Zorba that I hadn't noticed during the excitement of reading the book the first time. Nevertheless, it still remains a good read of a bygone era and it gives us a good description of Crete and the Cretan mindset through the most irresponsible, exhilarating, havoc-making adventures of Zorba. The adventures start with the hesitant attempt to establish a coal mine which turns out to be only an excuse to live life to the full:

"Towards the end of the afternoon we berthed by the sandy shore and saw finely sifted white sand, oleanders still in flower, fig and carob trees, and, further to the right, a low grey hill without a tree, resembling the face of a woman resting. And beneath her chin, along her neck, brown veins of lignite.

An autumnal wind was blowing, frayed clouds were passing slowly over the Earth and softening its contours with shadow. Other clouds were rising menacingly in the sky. The sun appeared and disappeared, and the Earth's surface was brightened and darkened like a living and perturbed face.

I stopped for a moment on the sand and looked. A sacred solitude lay before me, deadly and yet fascinating, like the desert. The Buddhist song rose out of the very soil and found its, way to the depths of my being. 'When shall I at last retire into solitude, alone, without companions, without joy and without sorrow, with only the sacred certainty that all is a dream? When, in my rags – without desires – shall retire contented into the mountains? When, seeing that my body is merely sickness and crime, age and death, shall I – feeless and blissful – retire into the forest? When? When oh when?'

"That man has not been to school, I thought, and his brains I have not been perverted. He has had all manner of experiences; his mind is open and his heart has grown bigger, without his losing one ounce of his primitive boldness. All the problems which we find so complicated or insoluble he cuts through as if with a sword, like Alexander the Great cutting the Gordian knot. It is difficult for him to miss his aim, because his two feet are held firmly planted on the ground by the weight of his whole body. African savages worship the serpent because its whole body touches the ground and must, therefore, know all the Earth's secrets. It knows them with its belly, with its tail, with its head. It is always in contact or mingled with the Mother. The same is true of Zorba. We educated people are just empty-headed birds of the air."

Zorba craned his neck, looked at me with joy and fear.

'Speak plainly, boss!' he cried. 'Didn't we come here for the coal?'

'The coal was a pretext, just to stop the locals being too inquisitive, so that they took us for sober contractors and didn't greet us by slinging tomatoes at us. Do you understand, Zorba?'

'Then I'll dance, boss. Sit further away, so that I don't barge into you.'

He made a leap, rushed out of the hut, cast off his shoes, his coat, his vest, rolled his trousers up to his knees, and started dancing. His face was still black with coal. The whites of his eyes gleamed.

He threw himself into the dance, clapping his hands, leaping and pirouetting in the air, falling on to his knees, leaping again with his legs tucked up – it was as if he were made of rubber. He suddenly made tremendous bounds into the air, as if he wished to conquer the laws of nature and flyaway. One felt that in this old body of his there was a soul struggling to carry away this flesh and cast itself like a meteor into the darkness. It shook the body which fell back to Earth, since it could not stay very long in the air; it shook it again pitilessly, this time a little higher, but the poor body fell again, breathless."

An example of his shocking thinking on women:

"'Yesterday there was a fete on in a village near Candia devil take me if I know what saint it was in aid of! Lola – ah! true enough, I'd forgotten to introduce her to you; her name's Lola – she says to me:

"Grandad!" She calls me granddad once more, but now it's a pet-name, boss.
"Grandad," she says, "I'd like to go to the fete!"
"Go on, then, Grandma," I say to her.
"But I want to go with you."
"I'm not going. l don't like saints. You go by yourself."
"All right, I shan't go either."
I stared at her.
"You won't? Why not? Don't you want to?"
"If you come with me, I do. If not, I don't."
"Why not? You're a free person, aren't you?"
"No, I'm not."
"You don't want to be free?"
"No, I don't."
I thought I must be hearing voices. I really did.
"You don't want to be free?" I cried.
"No, I don't! I don't! I don't!"

Boss, I'm writing this in Lola's room, on Lola's paper; for God's sake, listen carefully. I think only people who want to be free are human beings. Women don't want to be free. Well, is woman a human being?'"

After my arrival we visited Knossos, and drove a rented car on the inland roads of the island. The plains and valleys of inland Crete are reminiscent of an enormous Garden of Eden. Perhaps a more realistic description is an enormous market garden. Every inch was planted with either olive or fruit trees, grapes or vegetables. Even at the end of summer, everything was lush and green. The vines of the famous Cretan wineries run up high into the mountains. The mountainsides were busy with people harvesting the fruits of their labour. It was a wonderful, unforgettable sight.

Unfortunately, our temporary marina was untenable in the large swell entering from the north. Foolishly, we had used our sea-anchor rope to secure the boat to a bollard and a lamp-post. After the continuous movement back and forth destroyed it, we decided to leave Heraklion. We sailed to the eastern most side of the island to Ayios Nikolaos. We anchored in the beautiful sheltered waters of the Spinalongas Lagoon for a couple of days and enjoyed the warmth of the late summer. Then we reluctantly moved to the local marina, to pack up the boat for the season. As we settled into the marina, a storm, called the Livas, that had been brewing for a couple of days finally arrived. It came all the way from Africa to cover our pride and joy with red African sand.

———◆◆●◆◆———

Santorini/Thera

July, 2007

Thera had been the subject of my dreams for years. But it is hard to reach with a sailing boat, as it is out of the way and lacks a safe harbour. Thus, after years of ruminating over the best way to get ourselves onto this mythical island at last we decided to use the fast ferry from Mykonos to Santorini. It seemed less troublesome than sailing on the angry sea, which continued to be torn, by the Meltemi (another of the quickly developing Mediterranean storms), the strong, dry north wind of the Aegean Sea. We expected a leisurely ride without the usual challenges of sailing *Fenix*. How silly we were! At the ferry terminal, we were confronted by hundreds of people. The rowdy crowd was waiting. They were sitting on benches, on the floor, on their suitcases. Some were determined enough to push back and forth through the crowd to get water or ice cream, to find lost friends and family members, to access the cashier to buy tickets, or just to visit the toilet. In an attempt to create something resembling an order, people were herded into a space separated by columns, and I mean truly separated! Between the columns, a waist-high brick wall had been erected to prevent crossing from one lane to another. We faced the two long, winding lines; there was no way to tell which one was for Santorini. It was hellishly hot despite a near storm-force wind blowing. The chaos was further enhanced by the noise of the arriving and departing ships running their engines at full throttle to keep them at the quay in the strong wind. When a ship pulled up, the shouting really reached a crescendo as people moved suddenly in unpredictable directions, trying to make their way to the ship's gangplank. Miraculously, some people presented the correct ticket to the gatekeepers.

Somehow we also managed to work out which ship was ours and presented our ticket at the right place. As we entered into the huge underbelly of the ship, it unexpectedly became quiet, and simply by climbing a couple of flights of stairs, we ascended from Hell to Heaven. We found ourselves in a huge futuristic space with airplane-style seats, air-conditioning, soothing music and a bar serving excellent coffee. We were pleased to see that it was an Australian-made catamaran. The Fast Cat was not bothered by the rather large waves as it almost flew over the surface of the water. We thoroughly enjoyed our ride to Santorini and were pleased with ourselves for making the right decision.

The island we were heading to is known by several names: Thera, Thira and Santorini. I liked the name Santorini as it somehow sounded mysterious. Arriving at Santorini was a unique experience. As we approached the island, the Fast Cat, travelling at 35–40 knots, suddenly dropped its speed and glided into a inky blue coloured lake, the Caldera, surrounded by strange-looking mountains aiming to touch the sky. God must have had something more important to do when creating this landscape, as it would appear that halfway through he abruptly dropped the unfinished land into the sea straight from the sky. This hastily finished business created a somewhat alien scene. We later learnt that this strange landscape was created not by a forgetful God but by frequent volcanic activity and recurrent earthquakes.

We took a taxi from the harbour to the capital, Fira, climbing the 300-400 m, almost vertical volcanic rock along a winding road that went up and up. The top was nothing like the moon-like landscape of the harbour. There was a wide green plain where the volcanic soil nourished blond wheat, large fruit and vegetable gardens and huge wineries. The trees, nourished by the sun and rocked by the gentle wind, were laden with colourful fruits.

The town of Fira clings to the volcanic rock, with narrow, winding streets that are just capable of accommodating the ever-increasing numbers of pedestrians. No traffic is allowed in the western part of the town, so everyone walks. Our taxi dropped us a couple of hundred metres from our hotel, and although it was somewhat demanding, we enjoyed the walk across the pebble-paved white steps among the white houses and hotels sparkling in the afternoon sun. Our gorgeous little hotel perched on the edge of the land

View of Fira, Santorini

overlooking the Caldera. We were towards the end of our trip, so we decided to make it memorable by "living it up" in luxury, hence the tastefully decorated suite with a steep set of steps leading to the bedroom on the mezzanine, a huge bathroom and a glorious pink and purple mosaic-decorated spa with a view. The living room opened onto a small balcony where one could sip champagne while watching the red Aegean sun slowly dip into the blue sea. It was exactly what the doctor ordered for a weary traveller like me!

Today, the island cleverly exploits its wonderful geography and unique past. In modern Santorini, the name of the game is whether your property faces west and whether or not it overlooks the Caldera. Those who were born lucky inherited dwellings on the west side of the town that they developed into small hotels, for today's tourists pay crazy amounts of money to stay in a room with a view. Those who did not fancy becoming hoteliers opened restaurants or cafés, serving mediocre food. The quality of the food or service, however, is irrelevant. No one ever cares about anything but the unique red sunset created by the perpetual Mediterranean mist. Inspired by this exceptional landscape and its glorious history reaching back 4,000 years, the town's architects also tried to incorporate memorable touches into their designs. They did not have to go far for inspiration, as a large number of artefacts, wall paintings, statues and unusual and beautifully formed vases were found in the ancient town of Akrotiri, only 50 km from Fira.

A happy couple in the Santorini sunset

Steve was absolutely overwhelmed by the beauty of the place. He went for a walk only to turn back and drag me out to witness the birth of the first-ever "gold street". As the sun set, the town's main street glowed joyfully, its golden rays glittering and turning every shop window into an oversized jewellery box. Many of the shops were real Aladdin's caves, filled with watches and a wide selection of rather tasteless but expensive jewellery.

Right beneath the town was the old harbour. It could be reached by cable car or – for the more adventurous – there were plenty of donkeys. Donkeys traditionally carried goods from the old harbour to the towns of the plain, and nowadays, with the same patience, carry tourists up and down the 500 or so steps. Unfortunately, Santorini's donkey drivers did not pick up the droppings of their animals, so donkeys, asses, mules, their drivers and tourists alike walked the steep steps in a permanent stench.

The island of Santorini has a tumultuous geological and mythical history. What we know for sure is that in 1630 BC a destructive eruption of the ancient volcano and the subsequent collapse of the magma created the magnificent Caldera. The edges of the ancient volcano endured the eruptions and formed the small islands of Santorini, Nea Kameni and Thirasia. Greek geographer Strabo was the first to describe the emergence of these new islands in 197 BC. It is this violent geological history that has shaped the dramatic shores of Santorini and the lake-like Caldera, creating an unbelievable view.

Nea Kameni, the daughter of the ancient volcano, is a black, lifeless volcanic rock. We visited the island on a small, overcrowded tourist boat that departed from the old harbour. We climbed to the top of the volcano in just 45 minutes. The air was filled with rancid sulphuric gas, hissing from cracks like angry witches. At the top, we looked at the black volcanic rock formations with bewilderment and left quickly so as not to challenge our luck. Who knows, the volcano may not be dormant after all!

At sea level, encouraged by the promise of good health forever, we braved the red/yellow/green volcanic spring water and had a swim. It was somewhat disgusting to swim in a yellowish sludge that smelled like my son's socks after a day of training. The experience was not enhanced by the large numbers of volcanic stones (pumice) which were floating around us, giving an impression of swimming in a sewerage plant. Chasing eternal youth, I covered my face with the questionable-looking yellowish mud. After couple of minutes, the mud dried and cracks started to appear on my eternal youth, so I decided to wash it off. I looked optimistically at Steve, hoping for praise or something like, "You look great!" – but he remained silent.

The island, or rather different varieties of the land mass we today call Santorini, has been inhabited from the Neolithic age (5000 BC). It became a highly developed society at the site of Akrotiri (2000–1500 BC). Between 1600 and 1500 BC, the volcanic activity on the islands increased, and after several warnings from Mother Nature, the citizens abandoned the islands before the most destructive eruption took place. Athough Akrotiri survived the eruption, its inhabitants never returned. The volcanic activity continued and slowly the abandoned city was covered with volcanic ash. Slumbering undisturbed underneath this grey ash for centuries, its beauty was preserved, creating a gold mine for today's archaeologists. Their investigations recovered beautiful objects, particularly wall paintings, small statues and pottery, all exhibited in a splendid archaeological museum. I found the pottery particularly imaginative. The jugs, shaped like birds with long necks and spouts, were decorated with colourful drawings of plants and animals from both land and sea. The wall paintings were also unique in their colourful depiction of everyday life. There were also lots of movements: monkeys jumping around, boys boxing, or a fisherman walking with his catch. In their use of colours they were very similar to the wall paintings we saw in Knossos. The facial features and the body shapes of their subjects were also similar to those found in Knossos. Archaeological diggings in Akrotiri revealed multi-storey, exquisitely decorated buildings, complete with bathrooms and running water, all signs of a complex society!

After the site was abandoned, the island remained uninhabited for centuries, but Herodotus informs us that in 1200 BC Dorian settlers, led by King Theras, arrived from Sparta. So it is not surprising that, during the Peloponnesian Wars, Santorini (Thera) was allied with the Spartans. However, later the victory of Athens forced it into the Delian League. Santorini's modern history is not too exciting. Until the 1970s, when tourism rediscovered the island, it remained impoverished and large numbers of its inhabitants migrated to greener pastures.

There is a beautiful tale connecting Santorini to the legendary island society of Atlantis. Atlantis, a continent inhabited by peaceful people who ran a highly developed society, sank to the bottom of the sea at its zenith. The mystery surrounding the destruction of this legendary continent has preoccupied historians, scientists and artists for hundreds of generations. The first reference to Atlantis is found in Plato's dialogues, *Timaeus* and *Critias*. Plato said that the continent was in the Atlantic Ocean near the Straits of Gibraltar until its destruction 10,000 years earlier. The description goes like this:

"First of all, they bridged over the zones of sea which surrounded the ancient metropolis, making a road to and from the royal palace. And at the very beginning, they built the palace

Mountains

Chequer Pattern of Canals

Capital City

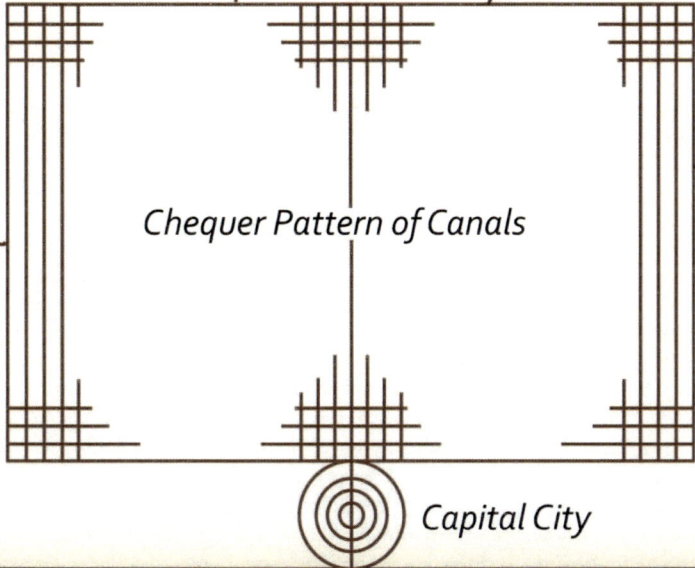

The Map of Atlantis after Plato

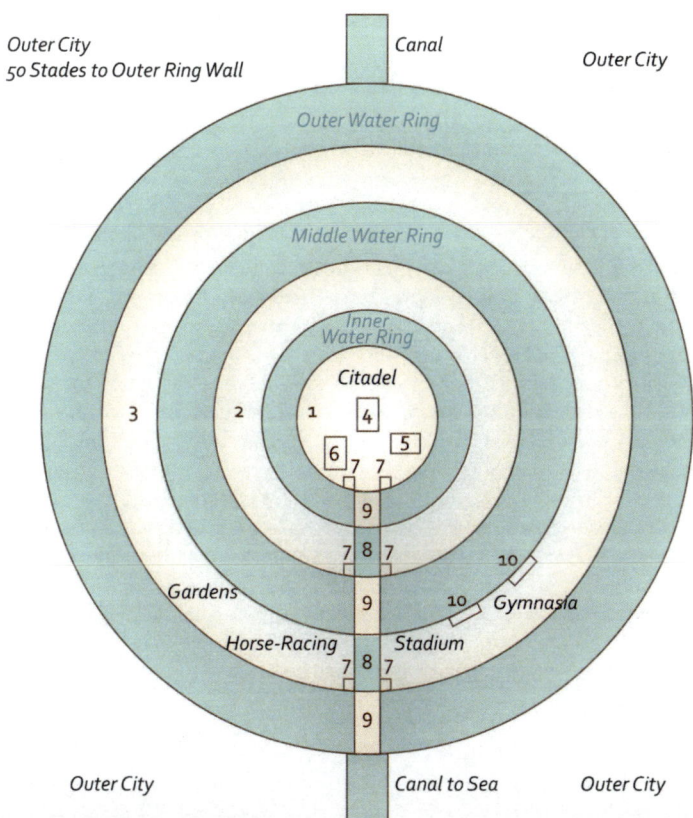

Outer City
50 Stades to Outer Ring Wall

Canal

Outer City

Outer Water Ring

Middle Water Ring

Inner Water Ring

Citadel

3   2   1   4   5   6   7 7

9

7 8 7

10

Gardens

9   10   Gymnasia

Horse-Racing   Stadium

7 8 7

9

Outer City

Canal to Sea

Outer City

in the habitation of the god and of their ancestors, which they continued to ornament in successive generations, every king surpassing the one who went before him to the utmost of his power, until they made the building a marvel to behold for size and for beauty. And beginning from the sea they bored a canal of three hundred feet in width and one hundred feet in depth and fifty stadia in length, which they carried through to the outermost zone, making a passage from the sea up to this, which became a harbour, and leaving an opening sufficient to enable the largest vessels to find ingress. Moreover, they divided at the bridges the zones of land which parted the zones of sea, leaving room for a single trireme to pass out of one zone into another, and they covered over the channels so as to leave a way underneath for the ships; for the banks were raised considerably above the water...

Now the largest of the zones into which a passage was cut from the sea was three stadia in breadth, and the zone of land which came next of equal breadth; but the next two zones, the one of water, the other of land, were two stadia, and the one which surrounded the central island was a stadium only in width. The island in which the palace was situated had a diameter of five stadia. All this including the zones and the bridge, which was the sixth part of a stadium in width, they surrounded by a stone wall on every side, placing towers and gates on the bridges where the sea passed in. The stone which was used in the work they quarried from underneath the centre island, and from underneath the zones, on the outer as well as the inner side. One kind was white, another black, and a third red, and as they quarried, they at the same time hollowed out double docks, having roofs formed out of the native rock. Some of their buildings were simple, but in others they put together different stones, varying the colour to please the eye, and to be a natural source of delight. The entire circuit of the wall, which went round the outermost zone, they covered with a coating of brass, and the circuit of the next wall they coated with tin, and the third, which encompassed the citadel, flashed with the red light of orichalcum.

The palaces in the interior of the citadel were constructed on this wise: in the centre was a holy temple dedicated to Cleito and Poseidon, which remained inaccessible, and was surrounded by an enclosure of gold; this was the spot where the family of the ten princes first saw the light, and thither the people annually brought the fruits of the Earth in their season from all the ten portions, to be an offering to each of the ten. Here was Poseidon's own temple which was a stadium in length, and half a stadium in width, and of a proportionate height, having a strange barbaric appearance. All the outside of the temple, with the exception of the pinnacles, they covered with silver, and the pinnacles with gold. In the interior of the temple the roof was of ivory, curiously wrought everywhere with gold and silver and orichalcum; and all the other parts, the walls and pillars and floor, they coated with orichalcum. In the temple they placed statues of gold: there was the god himself standing in a chariot – the charioteer of six winged horses – and of such a size that he touched the roof of the building with his head; around him there were a hundred Nereids riding on dolphins, for such was thought to be the number of them by the men of those days. There were also in the interior of the temple other images which had been dedicated by private persons. And around the temple on the outside were placed statues of gold of all the descendants of the ten kings and of their wives, and there were many other great offerings of kings and of private persons, coming both from the city itself and from the foreign cities over which they held sway. There was an altar too, which in size and workmanship corresponded to this magnificence, and the palaces, in like manner, answered to the greatness of the kingdom and the glory of the temple.

In the next place, they had fountains, one of cold and another of hot water, in gracious plenty flowing; and they were wonderfully adapted for use by reason of the pleasantness and excellence of their waters. They constructed buildings about them and planted suitable trees, also they made cisterns, some open to the heavens, others roofed over, to be used in winter as warm baths; there were the kings' baths, and the baths of private persons, which were kept apart; and there were separate baths for women, and for horses and cattle, and to each of them they gave as much adornment as was suitable.

Of the water which ran off they carried some to the grove of Poseidon, where were growing all manner of trees of wonderful height and beauty, owing to the excellence of the soil, while the remainder was conveyed by aqueducts along the bridges to the outer circles; and there were many temples built and dedicated to many gods; also gardens and places of exercise, some for men, and others for horses in both of the two islands formed by the zones; and in the centre of the larger of the two there was set apart a race-course of a stadium in width, and in length allowed to extend all round the island, for horses to race in. Also there were guardhouses at intervals for the guards, the more trusted of whom were appointed to keep watch in the lesser zone, which was nearer the Acropolis while the most trusted of all had houses given them within the citadel, near the persons of the kings. The docks were full of triremes and naval stores, and all things were quite ready for use. Enough of the plan of the royal palace.

Leaving the palace and passing out across the three you came to a wall which began at the sea and went all round: this was everywhere distant fifty stadia from the largest zone or harbour, and enclosed the whole, the ends meeting at the mouth of the channel which led to the sea. The entire area was densely crowded with habitations; and the canal and the largest of the harbours were full of vessels and merchants coming from all parts, who, from their numbers, kept up a multitudinous sound of human voices, and din and clatter of all sorts night and day.

I have described the city and the environs of the ancient palace nearly in the words of Solon, and now I must endeavour to represent the nature and arrangement of the rest of the land. The whole country was said by him to be very lofty and precipitous on the side of the sea, but the country immediately about and surrounding the city was a level plain, itself surrounded by mountains which descended towards the sea; it was smooth and even, and of an oblong shape, extending in one direction three thousand stadia, but across the centre inland it was two thousand stadia. This part of the island looked towards the south, and was sheltered from the north.

The surrounding mountains were celebrated for their number and size and beauty, far beyond any which still exist, having in them also many wealthy villages of country folk, and rivers, and lakes, and meadows supplying food enough for every animal, wild or tame, and much wood of various sorts, abundant for each and every kind of work.

I will now describe the plain, as it was fashioned by nature and by the labours of many generations of kings through long ages. It was for the most part rectangular and oblong, and where falling out of the straight line followed the circular ditch. The depth, and width, and length of this ditch were incredible, and gave the impression that a work of such extent, in addition to so many others, could never have been artificial. Nevertheless I must say what I was told. It was excavated to the depth of a hundred, feet, and its breadth was a stadium everywhere; it was carried round the whole of the plain, and was ten thousand stadia in length. It received the streams which came down from the mountains, and winding round the plain and meeting at the city, was there let off into the sea.

Further inland, likewise, straight canals of a hundred feet in width were cut from it through the plain, and again let off into the ditch leading to the sea: these canals were at intervals of a hundred stadia, and by them they brought down the wood from the mountains to the city, and conveyed the fruits of the Earth in ships, cutting transverse passages from one canal into another, and to the city. Twice in the year, they gathered the fruits of the Earth: in winter having the benefit of the rains of heaven, and in summer the water which the land supplied by introducing streams from the canals."

Plato preserved enough detail about Atlantis that its identification now seems very likely, and rather less mysterious than many of us would like. It is likely that Atlantis was the land of Minoan culture, namely the islands of Ancient Crete and Santorini. Although the excavations from Akrotiri on Santorini indicate the highest level of civilisation at the time and suggest that they met with a catastrophic end, scholars think that Atlantis was not Santorini but the Minoan palaces on Crete. Crete was the larger island that housed the royal city, while Santorini, the smaller island, was the metropolis. Although volcanic activity on Santorini did not directly cause the disappearance of the Minoan civilisation on Crete, it destroyed Akrotiri and the subsequent tsunami and earthquakes resulted in the permanent decline of the peaceful Minoan world. If this hypothesis is correct, Plato never realised that the land of Atlantis was already so familiar to him. Nevertheless, the archaeological proof is by no means conclusive and it remains open to interpretation whether the mystical perfect city of Atlantis really existed or whether Plato, wishing to instruct his compatriots on the consequences of disrespect for the gods, fabricated the myth of this continent by drawing on the destruction of the real island of Santorini.

Santorini deserves all the hype it receives from the tourist promoters, as it is a magnificent place to visit. Whether or not it is the legendary island of Atlantis, its exciting history and breathtaking scenery charmed us forever.

THE HOME OF
GOOD MEDICINE

June, 2007

Cos

After the usual boat maintenance that always awaits us at the beginning
of the season, we enjoyed a spectacular, picturesque sail from Crete
to Cos. Cos is a beautiful town with a history that stretches back to
the Bronze Age. Architecturally, the town comprises numerous ancient ruins
that happily embrace the remnants of the Ottoman era, the grandiose houses
of the Italian occupation, the less imaginative dwellings of the local people,
and the ugly modern buildings of the present tourist trade. Inhabitants and
visitors experience a flawless flow of history when walking around the town.
Everything is real! Every stone is genuine! The attitude of the Koians (the
people of Cos) to their long history is very similar to that of the inhabitants of
the modern city of Rome.

The Koians are proud, easy-going and move through the world with the
confidence of people who have the firm knowledge that this blessed island
is theirs forever. History for them is not a boring, irrelevant subject they are
forced to learn at school. On the contrary, they take great interest in their
own history, which helps them to treat the thousands of tourists that wash
up on their shores with courtesy. Courtesy, politeness and respect towards
tourists (who brought wealth to modern Greece) are not often accorded high
importance in the Greek mind, but unlike their mainland counterparts, the
majority of Koians have a philosophical approach. In the shops, restaurants
and cafés, or for a couple of euros around the ruins, they were ready to tell us
their meandering stories where facts and mythology were pleasantly mixed.

To move the summer crowds around, all sorts of transport options
are available for hire. There are bikes, mountain bikes, tricycles, mopeds,
motorbikes with two, three or four wheels, cars, buses, four-wheel drives,
and other strange-looking motorised contraptions. We hired bikes and cycled
around the town for chores, pleasure and exercise and to be able to get around
quickly. The afternoon sea breeze helped to ease the midday heat and the
surrounding hills covered by cypresses protected the town from reaching
unbearable temperatures, even right in the heat of summer.

The town, with its medieval castle, is stunning as it sizzles in the Aegean sun!
Inspired by the picturesque site, I developed the most pleasant morning routine.

The day started with a cappuccino at the Italian café. Then, fuelled by caffeine and the heat of the morning sun, I ran every day from the marina along the sea in the shade of plane trees covering the promenade to the Knight's Castle. I strolled across the busy passenger harbour and walked through the old port. According to ancient writers, the port could offer refuge to 100 galleys from the ever-threatening Meltemi. It is still a busy port where local excursion boats jockey for spots with Turkish gulets and visiting yachts. Considering its strategic importance, it is not surprising that in medieval times, on the southern side of the port, a huge castle was built to protect this ideal harbour. After turning away from the port, I found myself in a medieval street. It used to be a waterway connecting the port with the sea and is simply the most delightful path in the whole of the Mediterranean! Running in the shade of the castle wall was a totally enjoyable experience. Then, I usually passed under the ancient stone bridge that since antiquity has linked the small island to the mainland.

Of course, the bridge has been modified over the centuries but fundamentally it has not changed since medieval times. Even today, the bridge is the only way to access the castle from the famous square where tired visitors rest under the 500-year-old tree that is thought to be a descendant of the plane tree under which Hippocrates, the father of medicine, taught his pupils. A sudden turn to the right and I found myself back at the sparkling blue Mediterranean Sea.

Castle museum in Cos

The sight of the sea filled my heart with immeasurable pleasure and gave me strength for my run back to the marina.

Cos is one of the few places where remnants of the past continue to fulfill a function, even if it is not their original one. One of the busiest commercial streets of the town runs alongside the ancient agora, or market. The ruins of the agora are surrounded by the town's cathedral, modern houses, hotels, office buildings, tiny shops and miniature squares.

The agora, the Knight's Castle and the Turkish baths are all organic parts of the town's everyday life. They are not lifeless piles of stones with a couple of randomly toppled columns hinting at the passing of better times. In Cos, walking through the narrow winding streets, we came across buildings that were built from stones of the distant past. Some buildings bear the coat of arms of the Knights of St John of God, an Ottoman fountain decorates the garden of one of the busiest cafés, and a Greek column is used as a base for a counter. Life goes on, and the inhabitants of places with a long history have always made use of the remains of the past in the best way they can.

However, we couldn't help but observe a disturbingly nonchalant approach towards these ancient pieces. We were shocked to see Roman murals left unprotected in the Asclepeion of Cos. Used to the shoddy workmanship of the modern building industry, I was gobsmacked to find frescos that even after 2,000 years were sporting glowing red and brown colours. Regardless of their condition, they were left at the mercy of the elements and were battered by the sun and rain. The clay water-pipes were overgrown with weeds and neglect was obvious all around the ruins.

Sometimes, this nonchalant attitude rewards those who are ready to venture outside of the better-known tourist destinations. Perhaps due to a lack of resources, a lack of attention or a combination of both, with a little luck, it is still possible to find sites that seem to be remote and untouched, in spite of the fact the Greek islands are among the busiest tourist destinations in the world.

Our discovery of an abandoned 3,000-year-old quarry on the Cycladian island of Naxos felt like a real time-travel experience. As we walked out of the village of Appolonas we found strange unfinished statues, columns, and carved building stones lying half-buried and covered with high grass on the nearby hills. The scale of the abandoned operation was astonishing. We are all familiar with the huge columns of the Acropolis, the theatres with acoustics and capacity that put modern structures to shame, but one hardly ever thinks about the engineering and artistic marvels that were necessary to create those everlasting beauties.

Halfway between the quarry and the smallish village port, there is a 10–12m high half-carved statue of Apollo lying abandoned. It was left there because the statue cracked while being moved from the quarry to the harbour. The quarrying, carving, moving and transporting by sea of this enormous statue must have been a logistical nightmare. We spent hours discussing how we could apply our supposedly superior knowledge of science and engineering to perform these tasks using the tools available to the ancient craftsman. I clearly remember the discussion and our bewilderment when we realised that even today it might take years to develop the necessary infrastructure to achieve the production and delivery of these enormous statues to Athens or other corners of the Hellenic empire.

Of course, the controversial subject of where and how historical objects should be explored preserved, collected and exhibited or – God forbid! – used is the subject of heated debate between purists, more pragmatic archaeologists, historians and tour operators. There is no easy answer to this question and, as much as we enjoyed seeing the integration of historical objects into the everyday lives of the Greeks, we were saddened by their casual approach to the management of their heritage. I guess one has to re-evaluate the meaning of archaeology in a country where every square centimetre is covered by remains of the past.

Cos is famous for its mosaics and sculptures. The mosaics were made from marble, colourful stone, glass and terracotta pieces that were cut to small rectangular or irregular shapes, or pounded into powder. According to the locals, mosaics were invented in Cos! Unfortunately, most of them were transported to Rhodes during the Italian occupation. The Italians, even today, feel very much at home in the Mediterranean basin. Their ancestors, the Romans, dominated what used to be Ancient Greece for hundreds of years. Later the Venetian and Genoese galleys roamed the waterways of the Mediterranean, and more recently Benito Mussolini tried to rekindle long-lost glory.

Modern Italian forces occupied the Greek islands for approximately 25 years around the time of WWI. In a controversial project in Rhodes, the castle of the Grand Master of the Knights of St John (later the Knights of Malta) was renovated. With famous Italian confidence, the project was conducted without any consultation with the locals. Thus, as a sad outcome, the renovated castle most probably buried the foundations of the Colossus of Rhodes forever. With total disregard for local sensitivities, the most beautiful mosaics from Cos were moved to Rhodes to decorate the renovated Castle. Those remaining in Cos can be seen in the small archaeological museum or in the Casa Romana.

Fortunately, the most beautiful mosaic ever created, in my opinion, remained in Cos. Perhaps it stayed because of its incompleteness, size and mundane subject. The small (50–40 cm) mosaic depicts a variety of fish swimming in the depths of the sea. They are lively, with water flittering in their gills. Their green, silver and orange colours sparkle in the water and change colours as you move around. The unique lifelike features were created with the use of extremely small, 3x3 mm carefully cut colourful pieces of stones. As with hand-made carpets, where more knots per square inch result in more delightful details and colours, the use of tiny pieces of stone offered the unknown artist an unprecedented artistic freedom to create this unique beauty. I loved the fish swimming in their green pool!

Fish depicted in a Koian mosaic

Asclepeion

One of the most famous mosaics remaining in Cos is the mosaic floor depicting the arrival of Asclepius on Cos. A Koian on foot and Hippocrates welcome him. In the middle of the mosaic, we also see the Koian symbol of medicine, a snake entwined around a staff, which has become the universally recognised symbol of medicine all over the world. The story of how a small island destroyed regularly by earthquakes ended up giving the world the symbol of medicine is fascinating.

The Asclepeion of Cos, named after Asclepius the Healer, is the reason that Cos has been rebuilt again and again on this earthquake-prone terrain over the millennia. Asclepius was born in Tikke, in Thessaly. According to *The Iliad*, he was the father of the two skilled healers who took part in the Trojan War.

His healings must have been very successful, as Asclepius acquired divine status and his cult spread very rapidly from the 5th century BC. Over the next 500 years, around 500 Asclepeia or healing complexes were developed across the Greek world, with the Asclepeion of Cos providing the blueprint for them.

The Koians welcome Asclepius, in a mosaic from Cos

The Asclepeia functioned as sanctuaries of Asclepius, Athena and Apollo. They were usually placed in areas with a mild climate on tree-covered hills with a good breeze and abundant hot and cold springs. Even from the earliest days, these places of worship also served as therapy centres. The therapy was a mixture of rituals and healing practices and was administered by a large group of specially trained priests, assistants and therapists. The therapy itself had a fundamentally mystic character, and ultimately divine intervention was expected to deliver relief or cure.

Had it not been for Hippocrates (460–370 BC), the greatest of the Ancient Asclepians (physicians), the Asclepians would have continued their well-rehearsed activities for millennia to come.

Hippocrates studied at the Asclepeion of Cos and read the papyri Heraclitus dedicated to the Asclepeion of Ephesus. He was also well travelled: he visited Macedonia, Thrace, Scythia, the islands of the Aegean, Smyrna, Athens, Egypt, Libya, the Peloponnese and Thessaly. In addition to the secret of healing, he was also educated in philosophy and rhetoric. Equipped with all this education, he came up with the idea of systematically classifying and methodically treating disease.

The Hippocratic system of diagnosis was based on careful clinical observation, logic, and rigorous analysis. To the best of our knowledge, he was the first person to treat sickness in anything resembling a methodical manner. Diseases were no longer considered a curse of the gods, but were interpreted rationally: the art of healing was liberated from demons, magic and superstitions. He also had enormous sympathy for human suffering and placed the patient at the centre of his attention. He stated simply: "The place of the physician is at the pillow of his patient."

Hippocrates was a generous teacher and a prolific writer and we are lucky that 57 of his works have survived.

• **General:** *The Oath, The Law, Ancient Medicine*

• **The Doctor:** *Art, Fitness, Instructions, Aphorisms*

• **Anatomy and physiology:** 8 books: *Dietary, Food, Healthy Diet*

• **Pathology:** 6 books

• **Prognostics:** 3 books

• **Works, particularly nosology:** 6 books

- **Therapy:** *Diet Acid, Liquids*

- **Surgery:** 8 books

- **Ophthalmology:** *Sight*

- **Obstetrics and gynaecology:** 7 books

- **Paediatrics:** *Teething*

- **Various works:** including 24 letters of Hippocrates

John Fabre's book, *The Hippocratic Doctor: Ancient Lessons for the Modern World* (Fabre 1997), makes the writings of Hippocrates accessible to the *contemporary* world. In Chapter I of *On Fractures*, and in *On the Law*, respectively, Hippocrates writes (Fabre's translation):

> "In fact the treatment of a fractured arm is not difficult, and is almost any practitioner's job, but I have to write a good deal about it because I know practitioners who have got credit for wisdom by putting arms in positions which ought rather to have given them a name for ignorance. And many other parts of this art are judged thus: for they praise what seems outlandish before they know whether it is good, rather than the customary which they already know to be good; the bizarre rather than the obvious."

> "Medicine is the most distinguished of all the arts, but through the ignorance of those who practise it, and of those who casually judge such practitioners, it is now of all the arts by far the least esteemed. The chief reason for this error seems to me to be this: medicine is the only art which our states have made subject to no penalty save that of dishonour, and dishonour does not wound those who are compacted of it. Such men in fact are very like the supernumeraries in tragedies. Just as these have the appearance, dress and mask of an actor without being actors, so too with physicians; many are physicians by repute, very few are such in reality."

To clean up the mess about who could and should act as a physician, Hippocrates wrote his code of ethics for doctors , the so-called *Hippocratic Oath*:

> "I swear by the physician Apollo and by Asklepios and
> by Hygeia and by Panacea and by all the gods and
> goddesses, who shall be my witnesses, that I shall fulfil
> this my oath and contract with all my power and judgement.
>
> I will look upon him who shall have taught me this Art
> even as one of my parents. I will share my substance
> with him, and I will supply his necessities, if he be in
> need. I will regard his offspring even as my own
> brethren, and I will teach them this Art, if they would
> learn it, without fee or covenant.

I will impart this Art by precept, by lecture
And by every mode of teaching, not only to my
Own sons but to the sons of him who has taught
Me, and to disciples bound by covenant and
Oath, according to the Law of Medicine.

The regimen I adopt shall be for the benefit
of my patients according to my ability and judgement,
and not for their hurt or for any wrong.

I will give no deadly drug to any, though it be
asked of me, nor will I counsel such, and
especially I will not aid a woman to procure abortion.

I will keep my life and my Art pure and clean.

I will not engage in surgery upon those who suffer from
stones, but will leave this task to those who are experienced.

Whatever house I enter, there will I go for
the benefit of the sick, refraining from all wrongdoing
or corruption, and especially from any act of seduction,
of male or female, of bond or free.

Whatsoever things I see or hear concerning
the life of men, in my attendance on the sick or
even apart there from, which ought not to be
noised abroad, I will keep silence thereon,
counting such things to be as sacred secrets.

As long as I will keep this my oath, and as
long as I will not violate it, may I be successful
in my life and Art, and may I always have a
good name among men; but if I infringe this
oath and become an oath-breaker. May my fate
be contrary."

From his writings it becomes clear that the Hippocratic instructions were not limited to methodical diagnosis and treatment but encouraged a healthy lifestyle, exercise, good food, and clean air and water. The methodical healing practices based on memory, diagnosis and therapy were combined with the features of a modern-day wellness centre. In addition to undergoing treatments, the patients were encouraged to take long walks, eat a healthy diet, and enjoy massages and baths. Entertainment was also provided in the form of theatrical performances while the priests continued to perform religious ceremonies and sacrifices to ask the gods to help the patient's recovery. In Cos, the religion-based therapy of the earlier Asclepians (faith, dreams) was married with the rigorous Hippocratic medical method. This new approach had a decisive influence on the therapeutic success of the Asclepeion of Cos and drew thousands of people. Their money delivered prosperity to the Koians and ensured that the island was rebuilt after every earthquake. The tales of the success of the Asclepians survived thousands of years of history, so even today when the serpent-entwined Rod of Asclepius is spotted, the sick sigh with relief, trusting that one of the followers of the Father of Medicine will take care of them.

During the Peloponnesian War (431–404 BC), between Athens and Sparta, Athens was struck by a terrible epidemic of cholera. Pericles summoned Hippocrates to Athens. He came and saved the city. The grateful Athenians admitted him to the Eleusinian Mysteries, awarded him a gold wreath, and he and his descendants were entitled to dine free of charge in the chief magistrates' quarters.

It is interesting to note that the Ancient Greeks not only clearly understood that the beginning of human life was in the form of a pile of cells in the woman's womb, but were also proficient in disrupting the development of these cells by performing abortions, a service administered by women. However, they also held a strong opinion on the subject and, as far as physicians were concerned, the performance of abortion was banned, well before the emergence of Christian belief.

The Asclepeion is an amazing site. It is more like a medical precinct than a hospital, with at least 24 hospital rooms easily identifiable among the ruins. It is blessed by a cypress forest, gentle sea breeze, fantastic view, and hot and cold springs.

The complex that moved the art of healing from faith-based treatments to an independent scientific field continues to function in a new role. Tens of thousands of doctors visit the complex, and every summer the re-enactment of the Hippocratic Oath is held at the Asclepeion. Several international societies celebrate the legacy of Asclepius, such as The Hippocratic Society or the biannual Greek Conference, where doctors, lawyers, scientists and ethicists gather to discuss the latest developments in medical sciences and their impact on society. With the fast development of stem cell research, gene therapy and xenotransplantation, they have had a lot to talk about recently!

Layout of the Asclepeion of Cos after a local map

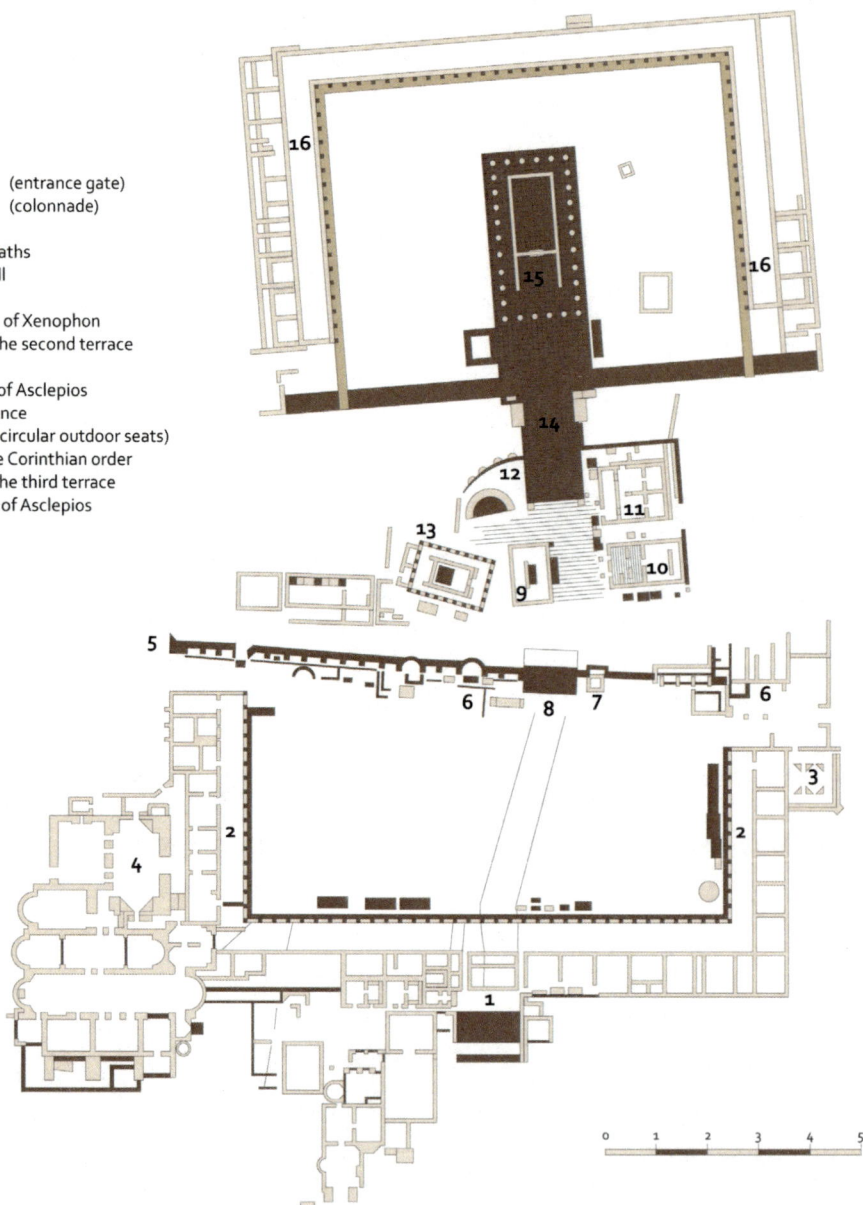

1. Propylon (entrance gate)
2. Stoa (colonnade)
3. Toilettes
4. The female baths
5. Retaining wall
6. Springs
7. Small temple of Xenophon
8. Staircase to the second terrace
9. Altar
10. Ionic temple of Asclepios
11. Priests residence
12. Exedra (semi circular outdoor seats)
13. Temple of the Corinthian order
14. Staircase to the third terrace
15. Doric temple of Asclepios
16. Stoa

Cos-Asclepeion

Human Rights

Another unique feature of Cos was that it provided immunity for political refugees. From 242 BC the Asclepeion of Cos was proclaimed to provide immunity for the whole of Greece. Of course, throughout history warring powers have provided refuge to their enemies' enemies. As the saying goes, "Your enemies' enemy is your friend." What made the Cos immunity different is that it provided refuge for all Greeks in need, without any discrimination. Following in the footsteps of Cos in the Hellenic period, it became common practice to declare certain Greek temples and cities sacred and inviolable. *Asylia* was the practice of declaring religious precincts places of asylum, meaning they were immune to violence and civil authority. There is plenty of evidence for this, mainly in the form of inscriptions and coins. Of course, nothing is ever perfect and the well-intentioned laws were frequently broken, but the Romans and other powers in the region largely accepted the right of the Asclepeion of Cos to function as a sanctuary. A famous setback happened in 102 BC: Cleopatra (not the beautiful one, but the wife of Ptolemy Evergetes) left her grandson on Cos with most of her fortune at the Asclepeion. However, Mirthiades seized Cos and failed to respect its immunity, taking off with the son, and the treasures of Cleopatra.

As I had seen before, another great idea of the enlightened 20th century is deeply rooted in Ancient Greece. After the disaster of the Holocaust, and after 2,000 years of absence, the ancient idea of asylum was officially renewed by the United Nations in 1948 in the UN Charter for Refugees! Unfortunately, the well-intentioned Charter is widely misused and Australia and other developed countries are forced to deal with hundreds of thousands of economic refugees trying to exploit the system. It is a shame, as those who are really in need of protection frequently miss out.

Sailors

As Steve pointed out, the best thing in sailing is that you meet people whose views might be fundamentally different from yours, people who move outside of your social circle whom you otherwise would never have met. But contrary to all expectations you are swept together with one common interest: boats. No, not yachts – boats. Small, big, ugly, beautiful, weird, shiny, neglected, cheap or expensive, they have one thing in common: they are all adored by their owners. All in all, boats are like a mother's womb, carrying their human cargo safely around in the sea of troubles. Sailors therefore have a unique relationship with the rest of mankind and there remains a strong camaraderie and community feeling among them.

Unlike car owners, sailors continue to maintain enormous brand loyalty. Boats are much more than vehicles for getting from A to B. The boat you own is much less a reflection of your financial status than it is a manifestation of your personality. The boat is your home, friend, reliable cocoon where you can hide from the problems of the world, your safety valve and source of pride. Regardless of the sometimes not-so-pleasing outcome, your boat is a silent and tolerant recipient of your thriving creativity. A boat can also help people to get to know themselves, to get closer to their hidden inner self, the free natural man. They bring out the best and the worst in us! Boats can help us to test our self-reliance and our ability to cope with the challenges of nature, outside of the reach of the Western nanny-states. Sailing on the seemingly endless waters of the world's oceans gives us the impression of a borderless world. At the end of the day, if we do not like something, we can move our boat a couple of metres or a few thousand miles away. This impression unfortunately only lasts until one experiences the first arrival into a new country. The process of check-in incorporates a more than healthy portion of kowtowing to customs, health and passport control offices, drug agents, harbour masters, and an endless number of other public servants – whatever the country's bureaucracy can muster. Some places have simply declared new arrivals incapable of following the intricate rules and have thus created a new industry. Special agents, for a good price, gather all the necessary stamps and hand back the passports to the hapless sailors, who tentatively regain the impression of a borderless world once more.

We met two couples in Cos. Both of them, just like us, were proud owners of Swedish boats. Udo and Lissi had owned a Najad for 25 years, but the boat was in immaculate condition – I thought it was brand new! We spent a peaceful afternoon sipping sparkling mineral water and discussing their meticulous maintenance schedule. We also got the address of the best marina in the whole Mediterranean: Marti Marina in Turkey, which, unknown to Udo and Lissi, later became the source of endless arguments between Steve and I. While we admired Udo and Lissi's commitment to their boat, I didn't think it would suit me as a way of life. I do not have any ambition to own the best-looking Hallberg-Rassy in the world, a point on which my husband and I respectfully disagree.

On the other end of the scale, Alfredo and Paula, owners of a five-year-old Hallberg-Rassy, were casual about their boat. The laid-back Alfredo had sold his father's business in 2002 and bought a basic 45-foot model. The boat's cockpit lacked any protection from the elements. He was not bothered by the merciless Mediterranean sun or by the salty sea sprays, but with his tiny wife cheerfully ploughed the Mediterranean waters every summer.

We first spotted them at the Italian restaurant in the marina. In my urgent need for some food other than Greek salad or souvlaki or the ever-present stuffed tomatoes and peppers, consumed endlessly with great enthusiasm by Steve, after some nagging, we abandoned our favourite Greek restaurants and went for a real Italian pizza. Indeed, it was a real pizza prepared and delivered to our table from a wood-fired oven by one of the restaurant's all-Italian staff. Next to us sat an Italian couple who were apparently well known to the staff. As with Italians everywhere, they were loud, confident, enviably well dressed and behaved as if they owned the place. But the star of the show was the cook, who said "hello" to all the customers and stopped for a chat with the couple. They were obviously very satisfied with the meal and praised his art. He accepted the praises with the generosity of a sovereign, sat down and would probably have spent the rest of the afternoon talking to them had fate not intervened in the form of an ignorant non-Italian couple – us. After lunch, they consumed a white frothy substance with such delight that we could not resist in asking them what it was. It was a simple lemon sorbet. We also ordered one.

Italians are welcoming and generous, so it did not take long for us to became part of the gang and join the conversation about boats, visits to different islands and so on. We continued our afternoon by sipping espresso in our cockpit, and later they invited us to join them for dinner with a Greek friend. We met around 9 pm, and while we waited for their Greek friend, we ended up in the Italian restaurant again, in search of an aperitif. Soon the specialty of the house was on its way. The cocktails were served in long glasses, and they looked stunning: chopped strawberries, gin and tonic with lots of ice. This was the Italian version of a humble gin and tonic. What a delicious treat it was!

In Greece, 9 pm means anything but, so it was around 9.45 pm when the friend arrived. She suggested going to a special Greek restaurant, Maistrali, that served nothing but mezze (like tapas). We were taken to a gorgeous garden restaurant hiding under the shade of hundred-year-old trees. The restaurant was tastefully decorated and we received around 10 small dishes of exquisite flavours: pepper stuffed with feta and herbs; tiny, oven-roasted pork fillets; tiny squid; grilled veal liver; and aubergines prepared several ways – baked with lemon and garlic in olive oil, stuffed with mince, with fresh grape tomatoes, mashed and flavoured with herbs – every way incredibly delicious!'

The meal was complemented by good white and red house wines from Crete and finished with a semolina cake topped with vanilla-bean ice cream and flavoured with mastica.

> "Mastic gum is a resinous sweet extract from the Pistacia lentiscus tree, indigenous to the Mediterranean islands. The mastic tree thrives especially well in the southern part of the island of Chios, due to the mild climate and characteristics of the soil. Mastic trees found elsewhere, even in other parts of Chios, do not produce mastic gum. The plant itself is known for its lemony balsam-like smell, which can permeate the air of the 'Mastichochoria', the villages on Chios that produce mastic gum. Interestingly, the Ancient Egyptians used mastic gum, imported from Chios, in the incense they burned as a tonic for exhaustion and to restore mental clarity." (Wikipedia 2012).

Steve picked up the bill (€63 for six people!) to the delight and praise of all. He was very popular that night! We parted as friends and Alberto made us promise to get in touch should we return to Italy and visit Sardinia. After all, Paula was from Sardinia and her numerous relatives would be happy to look after us if we were to visit that mysterious island.

After these happy encounters, following the rules of sailors' friendships, we waved goodbye and all went our separate ways. "Boaties" are people who like their freedom and only rarely commit to dates. "See you next year!" – which miraculously happens from time to time – is the closest thing you'll get to a full commitment. Interestingly, this casual attitude does not prevent people from forming long friendships that last for decades. Like the ever-changing sea, people are forever popping up and disappearing from our lives, leaving their marks and their memories behind forever. We were sad to leave the delightful city of Cos but after three visits it was time to move on.

THE ISLANDS OF THE
SPONGE DIVERS

July, 2007

Kalimnos

We started in the late morning for the short sail to Kalimnos. To our pleasure, another Hallberg-Rassy was making the same journey and we engaged in a friendly race. We arrived at Kalimnos, tired and excited, and haphazardly, tied the boat up to the town quay. Without too much delay, we joined the citizens of the town and retired for our siesta. We had finally arrived at this faraway island where Australian journalist and author Charmian Clift spent a couple of years in the 1950s with her family and wrote the fascinating book *Mermaid Singing* (Clift 1956) about the life of the villagers. I was looking forward to seeing the island with my own eyes and to meeting the islanders myself. Kalimnos is widely acknowledged as the sponge-diving capital of the Mediterranean. Technology has transformed diving from an excessively hazardous to a merely dangerous activity, yet until the late 20th century it remained one of the most perilous professions on the poor island of Kalimnos.

"We know many of them now the crippled men: from old Emmanuele Manglis, the doyen of divers, who was paralysed late in life – and in a dive any boy in his first lesson could have made – to eighteen-year-old Panorimides Katapoulis, who was paralysed a few weeks after our arrival, on the last dive of the last day of his first cruise.

Panorimides comes from a family of divers (his father was drowned diving off Cyprus three years ago), which means a large family, although the family of Panorimides, with eight brothers and three sisters, is larger than most. Now, until the other boys become old enough, only one brother Themoli, will be able to go away diving.

From the balcony of our yellow house, we saw Panorimides taking his first walk since he left hospital. He came all the way down the broad street that separates the coffee-houses from the harbour with his brother Themoli on one side of him and another lad in a seaman's cap on the other. The curved stick dangled over his arm, because he couldn't quite get the hang of it yet. Instead he grasped his brother's arm, and when they came below our balcony we could see Themoli's arm shaking with the pressure of that angry white-knuckled hand and the dumb ferocity in the eyes of Panorimides as he tried to force the useless trailing leg to move.

The other thing you notice about the crippled men is that they cannot keep away from the sea. In the upper reaches of the town where the majority of them live because it is the poorer quarter, the houses are small and bright and cosy and you can grasp your neighbour's hand across the windows. There are no streets, only the loose mountain boulders and scoured fissures of clay and cracked mountain soil to walk on, with a rough step or two hacked out from the rocks in the really precipitous places. But down they come, heaving and stumbling and clutching at walls and doors and boulders for support, making their painful progress to the sea. During the day you find them at the coffee tables on the waterfront, always on the waterfront, selling fish or the soft herb-wrapped cheeses of Kalymnos, or oranges or cigarettes or peanuts. At night they limp among the harbour tavernas, and occasionally they put down their trays and drink a beaker or two of retzina with the men who still wear black cans and have two sound legs tucked under the table. The men who drink and gamble all winter long and sometimes spill a furtive libation on the floor before they raise their glasses … a libation to what, I wonder?"

Although diving is one of the oldest human activities, the physiology of diving was poorly understood until the late 19th century.

According to Aristotle (384–322 BC), the Ancient Greeks attempted to supply air to underwater sponge divers by lowering cauldrons to the seabed. The diver would then insert his head into the cauldron to take a gulp of air. The methods by which air could be supplied to divers improved over the centuries as ingenious men built diving bells, breathing bags, diving barrels and diving hoses attached to a pressure pump.

Yet it soon became apparent that inadequate access to an air supply was not the only obstacle faced by divers. The deeper a human dives, the greater the pressure exerted upon him becomes, and a man approximately 10 m underwater will be subject to twice the pressure he would experience on the surface.

The effects of pressure on the human body were first scientifically observed during the frenetic tunnelling and bridge-building projects of 19th-century America. One such project was the Brooklyn Bridge, which spans the East River on pillars dug deep into the riverbed. To dig the deep underwater foundations, workers toiled in sealed airtight chambers called caissons. Pressure inside the caissons had to equal or be somewhat higher than that experienced at the bottom of the river to keep water out of the chamber and provide workers with an adequate air supply. The air was pumped into the caissons from the surface.

While the caissons may have ensured that workers had air to breathe, they also caused many to become afflicted with the debilitating "caisson disease", also known as "the bends". Afflicted workers experienced symptoms including itchy skin, a red rash, severe headaches, blurred vision and such severe joint pain that it would make them scream. Even less fortunate workers would experience a loss of feeling in their legs, paralysis and, in the most severe cases, a loss of consciousness and death. Slowly, people came to understand that "caisson disease" resulted not from breathing under pressure but from leaving the high-pressure environment.

The air we breathe is 78% nitrogen and only 21% oxygen. An inert gas, nitrogen does not play a physiological role, but under increased pressure, excess nitrogen passes from the bloodstream and is absorbed into surrounding tissue. This process remains harmless until the pressure quickly decreases, such as when a diver swims to the surface for fresh air or a worker exits a caisson at the end of his shift. This rapid decrease in pressure releases nitrogen bubbles from the tissue, causing tissue damage. When these bubbles enter the central nervous system, irreversible nerve damage occurs, causing pain, paralysis and even death. Under atmospheric pressure or when ascending at a safe speed, however, the slow release of nitrogen does not form bubbles and is cleared by normal respiration without causing damage. The trick was therefore to provide divers and caisson workers with plenty of air, ensuring both a slow descent and ascent.

Tragically, and like so many of those who laboured for him, the man who was the Brooklyn Bridge's designer, engineer and project manager was also struck down by "caisson disease". Becoming paralysed halfway through construction of one of the technological wonders of the 19th century, his devoted wife became a "go-between" for her husband and his workers. Tirelessly she communicated his detailed instructions, imaginative engineering solutions, advice and encouragement, and at times his disappointment, in their progress. Miraculously, they completed construction of the bridge, now one of the main arteries channelling ever-increasing traffic between Manhattan and Brooklyn. Today, the Brooklyn Bridge stands as a monument to human ingenuity, imagination and determination.

Unfortunately, even in the 1950s, when the knowledge and expensive diving equipment to counter the bends were readily available in more prosperous parts of the world, they remained beyond the reach of the impoverished inhabitants of Kalimnos.

Traditionally, the sponge divers of Kalimnos left on their boat around April, only returning to their homes in the autumn:

> "The sponge boats leave in April or early May. Between sixty and a hundred of them sail out to Alexandria and Derna and Crete and Benghazi and Tripoli. For a few weeks before

their departure, when the banks advance the yearly loans to the captains, the town has a misleading air of prosperity. The boats must be equipped and stocked with food for seven months. Money is in circulation millions, even billions of drachmae! Children appear in cheap new dresses, new sandals. This is the time for weddings, for christenings, for parties. In the tavernas and coffee-houses business booms. The gambling tables have the air and atmosphere of a little Monte Carlo. Men walk the streets with springier step, as if it were really their money and not the banks'.

All summer long, while the boats are away, the town lies in a torpor of heat and idleness. Everyone who can goes to the other side of the island, to little houses at Brosta or Merthies. If one has no house he erects a makeshift tent of striped rugs strung on bamboo poles. For the hot months Kalymnians live close to the sea on the fish they catch and the figs and prickly pear and grapes that grow around them and the sweet water from the wells. There is a charming unwritten law that any person, man, woman or child may satisfy his hunger by taking what fruit he can eat from anybody's property, so long as he eats it there by the tree or the vine. He is only guilty of theft if he carries the fruit away in a basket or stuffed into his pocket to eat later."

Diving into the sea stark naked, carrying only a heavy, chiselled stone, the divers propelled themselves into the depths of the sea. Once they reached the bottom, they walked along the seabed searching for sponges. After cutting the sponge from its tuft, they returned to the surface as quickly as possible, gasping for air. Within a year, the tufts regrew, delivering a new supply so people could return and repeat the harvest. After the sponge was cleaned on the boat and dried, its rubbery skin was beaten with a mallet and removed. The now relatively skinless sponge was washed several times to remove any remaining skin tissue. Finally, it was dried, trimmed and perhaps bleached to make it more desirable for the beauty parlours of Paris, London and New York.

The sponge divers of Kalimnos, young and old, risked their lives on a daily basis to carve out a miserable living and dreamed constantly of migrating to America or Australia. Many of those who departed the shores of Kalimnos with access to capital and modern equipment went on to establish thriving sponge diving and fishing industries in their adopted countries, including such renowned locations as Tarpon Springs, USA and Fremantle, Australia.

"'Well, I've got my papers,' said the freckle-faced twenty year-old who had joined us at the café table. 'They'll send a telegram when I have to go up to Piraeus. In five weeks or so I'll be off to Australia.'

'You're really happy about it?' George asked.

'Well,' he said matter-of-factly, 'I'm glad it was settled before I signed up for another season's diving. There are better ways of making a living. This diving, it's not a good life.'

The crippled diver Dionyssos was limping down through the tables garishly hung with little sandals and children's clothes and tablecloths and women's pullovers on wooden hangers, crying the merits of a new shop opened in the narrow street beside Agios Christos.

The freckled boy turned his head away and drained the little cup of coffee in a gulp, and in doing so he brushed my cigarette case off the table. I bent to retrieve it, and under the concealing table I saw that his legs were moving reassuringly, one against the other."

Today, Kalimnos is a thriving town where no one limps anymore. Thanks to the return of hundreds of migrants like the young, freckled man described with such emotion by Clift, Kalimnos boasts prosperous-looking houses, well-run cafés and restaurants enticing tourists and locals alike. Most people work in the tourism and fishing industries and the harbour is constantly busy. While the beaches are not the best you will ever gaze upon, once you have convinced yourself to jump from the rocks, the sea is crystal clear and balmy. Surrounded by large mountains, the town gasps for air in the seemingly endless glow of the summer heat. The trees from these mountains were first felled centuries ago to construct the fast galleys of the ancient seamen, the war machines of the Turks, and later, the sponge divers' fishing boats. Now the barren, pale grey rocks act like giant mirrors, reflecting the midday heat onto the houses and punishing the townsfolk with excessive summer temperatures for their careless handling of the natural resources.

Throughout Greece, we observed that with their increasing prosperity, the original migrants and their descendants, born in faraway places like New York or Melbourne, were returning to their homeland or that of their parents. Fluent in several languages, they possessed excellent business skills and understood the needs of their customers. Generally, these "returnees" became the driving force behind the tourism industry. In Kalimnos we met several café owners who, after 20 years in London or Melbourne, had returned to their place of birth. When asked why, they replied, "Life might be harder in Kalimnos, but we simply love this island".

The women and men of Kalimnos are kind, with clear, proud brown eyes, straight backs and big bones. The women are the strong, stocky type, with wide hips and ample bosoms. Kalimnian girls develop very early and, according to one local barman, there is a saying, "The girls in Kalimnos develop tits before their teeth". Kalimnian women bear more of a resemblance to their ancient sister the Willendorf Venus (22000 BC) than the relatively recent Venus of Milos (400 BC). They are nothing like present-day anorexic goddesses.

The sponges of Kalimnos

Kalimnians are well dressed and, as in all Mediterranean countries, after the temperature has dropped slightly around sunset, they come out in their droves to parade around in the summer night. In Kalimnos the siesta lasts until 6 pm, unusual even for a Mediterranean country. At about this time, the first dogs and cats emerge, followed by young children, and by 6.30 pm one can see the first shopkeepers walking slowly towards their shop. The town unhurriedly comes to life from its daily Cinderella sleep, a state imposed on it by the heat. By 9 pm most townsfolk have returned to the streets, jostling for the best seats in the cafés. Having successfully acquired a table, they merrily greet each other and passers-by, taking short breaks from sipping their seemingly bottomless frappés. The children play happily in large groups, industrious men and women discuss the latest business deals, while their more relaxed peers chat idly, the guys ogle the girls and the girls giggle, as they would anywhere in the world, except that by now the town clock has already struck midnight.

Kalimnos and its mountains stripped of trees

The Flying
Dutchman

From Kalimnos we sailed to the southern corner of the island of Simi, where a small natural bay, Panormitis, provided shelter from a raging force 7 Meltemi. We knew the bay was small, as the Global Positioning System (GPS) showed an opening only a few metres wide, connecting a miniscule lake-like area with the open sea. The GPS is a modern-day marvel that, using satellites, can give the position of your boat anytime, anywhere on the planet within a couple of metres. The existence of the GPS has simply made traditional navigation irrelevant, until someone decides to shut down the satellites and leaves most of the ships and pleasure crafts plying the waters of the Earth in a dire state.

Nothing prepared us, however, for the hair-raising experience of entering the bay via a channel of about seven or eight metres in width in the midst of a furious Meltemi. Once inside, we were shocked to see the bay practically filled with boats also taking refuge from the raging wind. More shocks awaited us as this windy night drew on. Desperate to find a place to anchor and with the sun setting fast, we wandered in a somewhat aimless but determined manner searching for space in order to swing around in the swirling wind. Leaving the bay through that narrow channel was something we were neither ready nor willing to contemplate. In the tiny bay the water was frothy. White horses were energetically racing with the wind to the shore only to be turned back in the form of large waves. It was impossible to predict the wind direction. I felt like a ping-pong ball sitting in a washing machine. The majority of boats were tenaciously hanging onto their anchors with their fluke driven deep into the sand. Some were not so lucky and dragged their anchor, helplessly bumping into their neighbours.

The contrast between land and sea was startling. Along the shore, just metres from the anchored boats, was a large monastery. Its majestic buildings and fully lit clock tower alluded to a civilised past – contemplating the world, searching for God, researching the accumulated knowledge of mankind in the large library, sipping tea, chanting religious hymns – and yet, only metres away from this civilised calmness, nature was truly raging.

Finally, we found a spot, turned into the wind and started to lower our anchor. It did not hold. This was not that surprising, as our Rake anchor had a very unpleasant feature: it was impossible to make it "bite" – i.e. to convince it to bury itself deep in the sand, instead of sliding once it hit the bottom. The anchor had an obvious aversion to sand, or, had it been a human, we would call it an allergy. This was an anchor that promised to hold *Fenix* even in hurricane-strength wind. Unfortunately for us, we hardly ever sailed in hurricane-affected regions, but almost every night we had to go through the painful procedure of struggling with our "sliding" anchor.

The failure of our anchor to hold, not once but twice, was problematic enough, without the situation being aggravated further by our broken anchor winch, or windlass. Steve had no alternative but to haul the anchor up by hand, a painstakingly slow process. Slowly, slowly, slowly, just 30 cm at a time, the 40 m deployed chain became shorter and shorter until finally the anchor was dangling in the air. Meanwhile, the storm-strength winds were blowing the boat in whatever direction they pleased. Using the full force of our 100 HP engine to counter the gigantic washing-machine effect of the waves, I tried desperately to steer *Fenix* away from the boats fortunate enough to be anchored safely. Then, it was a case of third time lucky, and as the anchor held, we were saved from leaving this one and only refuge along the coast of Simi.

By now, the impressive clock tower bells had tolled 11 pm. Lights were being turned off as most residents of this small community went to sleep; yet the not-so-small task of repairing the winch in the darkness awaited Steve. We simply could not afford to spend this stormy night with a broken winch. The raging winds continued to take their toll and two boats dragged their anchors in quick succession. They too started the "Flying Dutchman" routine, pioneered by us, in search of a safe haven for anchoring.

The *Flying Dutchman* is one of Wagner's most famous operas. Faced with daunting storms, a Dutch sea captain swears to sail for all eternity if necessary to reach his destination. However, you should be as careful in what you swear as in what you wish for: in a Faustian turn, Satan condemns the Dutchman to sail the seas forever, with his only hope for redemption the unconditional love of a woman. Once every seven years he may leave his ship in search of a woman who will redeem him from his deathless wandering if she gives him faithful, absolute love; failing this, he is condemned to roam the seas until the Day of Judgement. Guess what? He never finds her, but the music is fantastic anyway! Within the ornate confines of an opera house and using the magic of human voice and musical instruments, Wagner's masterpiece perfectly recreates a Nordic storm. Having been exposed to this stormy music at the Vienna Opera only a few weeks before our trip, I was surprised to find myself humming the now familiar tunes in the middle of this complicated night.

By midnight, every boat had managed to settle and Steve's magical engineering skills had repaired the faulty windlass. During these trips, Steve was the Managing Director and owner of a midsize tech company and I was a Professor at the Medical School of the University of Western Australia. As such, regardless of the conditions, our sailing had to take a back seat from time to time to enable our work to take priority. While he was busy working on the windlass, I kept watch over the raging seas and revised a Centre of Excellence Grant Application. It was around 2 am when I gladly emailed it to my work, for even in this isolated region of the Mediterranean, a mobile telephone network and GPRS were both available thanks to the presence of the monastery. Religious organisations are experts in using the power of communication to spread the word of God. Thus, it was not surprising that they had been quick to recognise the importance of modern communication technologies. Today, most monasteries in Europe, Asia and Latin America have Internet access and use mobile phones.

After fabricating a very simple anchor alarm, consisting of a weight, an empty plastic water bottle and around 20 m of fishing line, we turned in at around 3 am. I can still recall the feeling of complete satisfaction and the calmness of my mind and body after this long, busy day, full of challenges. The wind remained strong, hot and dry, full of dust from the surrounding mountains, and, satisfied or not, it was nonetheless an extremely uncomfortable night.

The monastery of Panormitis

The morning sun arrived early and we found ourselves in a completely changed world. As if it had been only a bad dream, the wind had disappeared. The sun was smiling on the horizon and we enjoyed our miniature Eden. The morning quickly brought with it more heat, and without too much hesitation, we jumped into the crystal-clear sea to cool down. The monastery, with its lights so mesmerising at night, looked majestic by day, surrounded by gentle hills covered with olive groves. A gorgeous windmill perched at the entrance of this little natural harbour and the uninhabited, huge, grey mountains, covered by inhospitable rocks that loomed in the distance, further emphasised the beauty of the bay. We visited the monastery but missed out on the museum as it only opened once the tourist boats arrived.

And my God, were they tourist boats! During our sailing in Greece, we have seen big boats squeezed into small harbours, but what we were about to experience was unprecedented. In Greece, anything that floats and is not bigger than the shortest diameter of an anchorage or a harbour can and will manoeuvre into these microscopic harbours to disgorge its human cargo onto the unsuspecting idyllic islands. To be fair, without tourism, these islands are hardly suitable for supporting human life. In the modern age, inhabitants of the Greek islands were until recently poor, and it is only in recent times, and thanks to the millions of admirers of both the sun and sea that they have become prosperous again.

Around 3 pm, which everyone in Greece seems to observe as the perfect time for a siesta, a monster arrived in the narrow channel leading to our peaceful anchorage. As high as the three-storey monastery buildings and almost as wide as the channel, this behemoth was slowly but surely heading towards our safely moored boat. With a strong blast from its horn, its captain tried to convince us to move, but we were not in the mood to pick up our anchor, deployed with so much difficulty. Eventually, the behemoth manoeuvred itself around us and tied up to the quay, lowering one anchor and leaving the other hopelessly dangling at the side of the boat. The crew, using a boat hook and a rope totally inadequate for the task, tried to do something with the anchor from the deck towering two stories above the waterline.

We watched their activities with great interest and Steve eventually went to help them. Approaching with the dinghy, he could see that a huge rock, a metre in diameter, had lodged itself between the shank and the fluke of the anchor, preventing its deposition into its holder. He jumped onto the anchor and tried to dislodge the rock, and as I watched my man trying to deal with something larger than himself, it reminded me of the picture of Atlas carrying the Earth on his shoulders. Unable to do too much with the rock, he recruited a crew member to assist him, so two of them were now struggling with this giant stone lodged in the anchor. After around 15 minutes of struggling they managed to convince the rock to leave its comfortable position and rolled it into the sea.

In the meantime, hundreds of tourists had walked to the monastery to join a guided tour hosted by one of the monks. Due to the anchor adventure, we again missed the tour, but we were glad that we had been able to help the crew. The bay soon became unbearably hot as the surrounding bare mountains reflected back the dry heat, and the next morning we therefore left this place of excitement to visit Simi.

The rock that refused to dislodge, Panormitis

Simi

Simi is a beautiful little place that for years has contested Kalimnos' title as home of the best sponge fishermen in the Mediterranean. With its rich architecture and brightly coloured houses, it is a pleasant tourist destination with a particularly good seafood restaurant (Manos) along the town quay. The service in general in Simi, however, is quite shabby in several places. The laundry service produced atrociously creased clothes and a local café definitely made the world's worst fruit salad, which consisted of a small pile of chopped pale apples and bananas topped with an uninviting lump of yoghurt.

We were relived when we came across Ay Marina, at the south entrance of the city, where the traditional Greek taverna, under the management of a French couple, has evolved into a stylish beach café. The food, a mixture of Greek and French cuisine, was delicious. The salads were glorious and even a simple moussaka had some French finesse. The small quay, built from local stones and surrounded by the bluest of blue water, allowed visitors arriving on speedboats from the nearby towns to tie up. There were comfortable sun loungers, big, bright sun umbrellas and excellent drinks served from the garden bar. The beach, overlooking a small chapel on an even tinier island at the

The beautiful Simi

entrance of the bay, completed this picture-postcard scene. When tired of the sun, you could retreat to the garden, play table tennis or cool off with a cocktail in colourful, soft armchairs in the gazebo. This little paradise contrasted starkly with the surrounding lifeless mountains covered with nothing but grey stones of different shapes and sizes. But, nothing is ever perfect!

The service was also rather French in nature, arrogant and patchy. Patrons were not expected to be too demanding. In most countries of the world, hospitality services are frequently provided by a mix of illegal migrants, students and housewives short of money. In contrast, the majority of French hospitality workers are true professionals and, as with all professionals, exhibit a healthy pride and a hint of arrogance all buried deep in history.

The arrogance of French waiters goes back to the French Revolution. With the demise of the aristocracy, servants were forced to work for the less-educated and less-refined revolutionaries. Surprise, surprise, the revolutionaries soon acquired a taste for the luxurious lifestyle of the hastily beheaded aristocracy, and the servants of the aristocracy soon found themselves teaching their revolutionary masters to the etiquette of a lost era. Naturally, a teacher always carries a sense of authority over his pupils. It is hardly surprising then that the servants' confidence eventually evolved into a sense of superiority over their masters. This attitude, acquired during the tumultuous years of the French Revolution, has been handed down faultlessly through generations of waiters. Even today, more than 200 years on, French waiters make great efforts to impart proper etiquette to their less-educated and less and less willing patrons. In this spirit, the impatient patrons of this restaurant were simply told to wait and adhere to the serving routine of the restaurant: "You are on holiday anyway! You don't have to run anywhere!" said the owner to the thirsty crowd.

Another time, in another French restaurant – Katherina's on Mykonos – we were reprimanded for wishing to order wine before the meal was selected: "*Quelle horreur!* An incompatible wine with your meal!" Unfortunately, in this hot climate we had become used to ordering our drinks first, usually a large bottle of sparkling mineral water and a bottle of the dry Greek wine, so we were quite persistent. To avoid a verbal confrontation, the waiter simply refused to come to our table to take our drinks order until our meals were selected. We learnt our lesson and never returned to the restaurant. If you are not overly sensitive to such behaviours, however, the gorgeous Ay Marina is well worth a visit for a refreshing swim and great food in an exquisite location.

SAINTS FOR ALL TASTES

Patmos

After spending much of the day motoring from the island of Leros, with its green anchorage surrounded by green eucalyptus trees and crimson and purple bougainvilleas, we arrived at the island of Patmos. Anchoring in the small bay opposite the town quay, we discarded our colourful sailing attire in favour of more serene apparel and headed by scooter towards the imposing monastery dominating the skyline.

The fortress-like Monastery of St John the Theologian is one of the holiest sites of the Orthodox Christian Church. After a falling out between its faithful in 1054 AD, the Christian Church was divided into Eastern and Western Christian Churches. Today, the Eastern Christian Church dominates the Middle East and Eastern Europe, while the Western Christian Churches dominate Western and Central Europe. The Eastern Christian Church is also referred to as the Orthodox Christian Church, the Greek Orthodox Church, the Orthodox Catholic Church, or more simply, the Orthodox Church.

The contemporary Orthodox Church asserts direct continuity from the earliest Christian communities founded in regions of the Eastern Mediterranean by the Apostles of Jesus. As such, it claims to have preserved the original and Apostolic Christian faith. In 320 AD, Constantine I, the first Christian Roman Emperor, transferred the imperial capital of the Roman Empire from Rome to Constantinople. Consequently, the first eight centuries of Christian history, most major intellectual, cultural, and social developments, occurred in this region. The fact that all the ecumenical councils of that period met in either Constantinople or its vicinity typifies this state of affairs. As missionaries from Constantinople converted the Slavs and other peoples of Eastern Europe to Christianity, including Bulgaria in 864 AD and Russia in 988 AD, they translated scripture and liturgical texts into the vernacular languages of the various regions. The liturgy, traditions, and practices of the church of Constantinople, so closely reflecting the Apostolic Christian faith, became adopted by all. Even today, these texts provide the basic patterns and ethos of contemporary Orthodoxy.

There are two major differences of opinion between the Orthodox and Western Christian Churches. The first, the *"filioque* clause", ultimately led to the split of the Christian Church in 1054 AD. The word *filioque* means "and son" in Latin. The Orthodox position is that the Holy Spirit proceeds from the Father and is sent on the Day of Pentecost from the Father through the Son. The Latin West states that the Holy Spirit proceeds equally from the Father and the Son (*filioque*), attesting the full divinity of both the Spirit and the Son. The *"filioque* clause" was, and remains, a contentious issue in the Christian Church. Fundamentally, the question remains unanswered: "Can a human being like Jesus become God?"

The second disagreement relates to the centre of power within the Church. In Western Christianity, the Bishop of Rome, more commonly referred to as the Pope, is considered the successor of the Apostle Peter and head of the universal church by divine appointment. The Orthodox Church, however, remains a fellowship of administratively independent, or self-governing, local churches. United in faith, sacraments and canonical discipline, each enjoys the right to elect its own head and bishops. Possessing privileges of chairmanship and initiative but without direct doctrinal or administrative authority, the ecumenical patriarch of Constantinople (Istanbul) is traditionally recognised as the "first among equals" of Orthodox bishops. Thus, the second serious disagreement is therefore based on Orthodox Christians refusing to accept the divine appointment of the Pope.

These two differing points of views were responsible for many of the incidents that ultimately escalated into an estrangement so deep between the Orthodox and Western Christian Churches that it continues even today. The authority of the Pope even in the Western Christian Church was later challenged by Luther in the 16th century and contributed to the division of Western Christian Churches into Catholic and Protestant denominations.

Perched upon a huge rounded mountain that covers most of the island, the monastery's interconnecting courtyards, chapels, stairways, arcades, galleries and roof-top terraces were an intriguing sight. Situated at sea level, the town of Patmos (the Chora) is nothing but a busy landing point for the many visitors arriving on massive ferries and cruise ships. When these large ships are in port, the small natural haven appears to burst its boundaries, creating the impression of an enormous cruise ship display on dry land.

The winding road to the monastery had an incline of 10% in places, and buses, cars and the occasional motorbike, engulfed in fumes, arrived slowly at the monastery wall. They transported people of all sorts and ages: cheerful holiday makers, school groups, young backpackers, retirees and serene pilgrims. I even spotted a couple of pious monks. Despite some protest from our 50cc scooter, we cajoled it into delivering us to our destination.

Jumping off the motorbike, we took to the large steps with gusto, only to realise we were facing more than a 100 m dash to the entrance.

Puffed out and sweltering in the afternoon sun, we climbed and climbed and eventually reached a small courtyard. Surrounded by three- and four-storey buildings partially carved out of mountain rock, at its centre was a small well that must have been providing the monks with water for centuries. On the left of the courtyard's entrance, we found ourselves looking into the dark interior of a mystical chapel. We entered and, after our eyes had adjusted to the darkness, the chapel's beautiful decoration revealed itself. As we stepped into one of several smaller alcoves, we noticed immediately that the theme of the frescoes had become darker and the ornaments richer. Soon, we were staring at human skulls, including that of St Thomas, and other pieces of bone braced in gold and silver. These valuable remains of saints from the time of Jesus had been deposited with tender love and care in small ornate glass cabinets. While I found this display of human bones disturbing, it did not bother the numerous pilgrims who tenderly kissed the glass cabinets, piously kneeled down and began to pray.

We left this world of the dead for the bright sunshine and walked into a museum exhibiting both religious ornaments and fascinating books. The glass display cabinets were filled with holy books, some more than a thousand years old. A 7th-century copy of the Book of Job caught my eye. It was in excellent condition and I was surprised by the quality of the approximately A3-sized paper, albeit now thin and yellow with the passage of time. Its colour unwittingly enhanced the clear, crisp handwriting and the pitch-black, shiny ink used by the monk who had copied these words of Job. After 1,300 years, the text was clearly legible for anyone who could read Ancient Greek. The richly decorated initials remained brightly coloured and their intricate designs delighted present-day visitors just as they had the early Christians.

Narrow corridors carved into the rock's surface led from the courtyard to the monks' living quarters and the main entrance of a fascinating old church featuring a valuable mosaic. Although we did not see any of the monks, our impression was that it was a working monastery with its cells all occupied. There was definitely a fully functional kitchen, for we saw baskets laden with colourful lettuces, aubergines, cucumbers and tomatoes. With its bells tolling, calling all visitors to leave this holy place, we bade farewell to the monastery.

Following a short ride towards the Chora, we descended into the cave where St John, having received the revelation of the Holy Trinity and having been banished to the island of Patmos in AD 95, spent his final years. Some scholars state that John the Apostle, John the Evangelist and John of Patmos were three separate individuals. Whether they were or not, St John of Patmos made a crucial contribution to Christian theology with the Book of Revelation. While different Christian denominations continue to debate the significance and correct interpretation of this work, the Book of Revelation is largely recognised as one of the last canonical works of the Christian Church.

Exiled for the sake of the word of God to the island of Patmos and under the influence of the Holy Spirit, St John's symbolic visions helped interpret and clarify things that were happening, or were going to happen, in the life of the Church.

Behind the images of the beast and the prostitute, for example, were the persecutions of Christians by political and religious opponents of the Church, particularly the Roman Empire. Always hidden behind these opponents was the ancient serpent, the dragon, the devil, Satan himself, who deceives nations and turns them against the Church. The fundamental idea of the Book of Revelation is the belief that Christ is the Lamb, sacrificed for us. I am not that familiar with religious texts but found this snippet from the *Summary of the Apocalypse* by Bishop Gerasimos of Abydos interesting.

"In chapter 1, St. John speaks about the origin of his revelation. The source of the revelation is God Himself, but it is Christ who, through an angel, reveals to St. John things which must shortly take place. Christ, the second person of the Holy Trinity, is always the mediator between God and the world. The Father through the Son in the Holy Spirit creates and saves everything. In chapters 2-3, St. John has visions on the contemporary spiritual condition of the Church in Asia. Christ exhorts the leaders of the churches to be steadfast in their faith and promises rewards for the victorious ones. These promises are mentioned throughout the whole book and especially in chapters 21-22. In chapters 4-5, St. John is in heaven in spirit and sees heavenly visions. We have similar visions in the Old Testament (cf. Is. 6:1f.; Ezek. 1:1f.; 2 Cor. 12:2-4).

He sees the throne of God in all of its glory. Around the throne are twenty-four presbyters and four living creatures who represent the Church of the Old and the New Testament and the world, and they praise God the Creator. Between them and the throne stands Christ as the Lamb sacrificed, slain, for our salvation. The picture signifies the mystery of our salvation in Christ. At the right hand of God there is a book that is sealed with seven seals. No one can open, understand, or even look upon the book. Only Christ the Victor can open it; only the mystery of Christ can shed light on the mystery of the world. The book must symbolize the eternal will of God for the destiny of the world, and what is to happen to it, as St. John sees it in the Spirit in chapters 6-20. Christ who opens the seals of the book is the center and the ruler of history and the world. He lives and continues the work of salvation to the end.

The vision in chapters 4-5 is truly magnificent. God the creator and ruler of the universe is there in the brightness of the throne. Christ, through whom all things are created and through whom the plan of salvation is realized, is there as the Lamb slain for the salvation of the world. The entire Church and the whole world, in heaven and on Earth, glorify God and the Lamb who was sacrificed for the sins of the world. God and Christ are inseparable and the Church glorifies them together (Rev. 4:9; 5:8-14). St. John has seen this vision on the "Lord's day" (Rev. 1:10), and chapters 4 and 5 have been considered as a prototype for the Divine Liturgy where the one Church of God lives the blessedness of salvation. In our worship, Earth and heaven, time and eternity become one eternal present in the presence of God.

The magnificent vision which St. John saw in chapters 4-5 will be the main consolation for him and for the struggling Church and an assurance for the final victory. God and Christ are in control of history, and truth and love will prevail, while evil will finally disappear from the world and a new life will come to the world created and saved by God in Christ."

The cave had been lovingly converted into a small church and pilgrims from across Greece braved the long uphill walk through the forest to visit this most holy place. After prayer, with their heads bowed, they would slowly approach the holy items. Sometimes overwhelmed by emotion and with tears in their eyes, they would timidly touch and kiss the stone where St John rested his head, the little nook he used as a handle to get up in his old age, and the numerous icons covering the wall of the cave. I observed that people not only pretended to kiss but actually placed their lips firmly on the stone objects, converting the dark, granite looking lifeless stones into beautiful, dark, shiny reliefs as if promoting the power of faith.

The habit of kissing religious objects and thereby unknowingly spreading infectious disease has been around forever. Practically any bacteria or virus that lives in saliva or other bodily fluid is deposited on the surface of the item kissed. Outside of the body bacteria and viruses have a limited lifespan, but if the next pious pilgrim follows fast enough, the surviving microbes will find a new home in his or her body. Influenza, herpes and glandular fever are the least dangerous diseases to be spread in this manner. Centuries ago, a lack of understanding about the significance of hygiene was instrumental in spreading the plague, a disease that wiped out almost the entire population of some countries in the 14th century.

Plague is an infectious disease that affects animals and humans. It is caused by the bacterium Yersinia pestis (Y. pestis). This bacterium is found in rodents and their fleas and occurs in many areas of the world. The first recording of a plague outbreak comes from Egypt in 450 AD.

Y. pestis is easily destroyed by sunlight and drying. Even so, when released into air, the bacterium will survive for up to one hour, although this could vary depending on conditions. Plague has several forms depending on the site where primary infection occurs. Pneumonic plague occurs when Y. pestis infects the lungs. This type of plague can spread from person to person through the air. Bubonic plague is the most common form of plague. This occurs when an infected flea bites a person or when materials contaminated with Y. pestis enter through a break in a person's skin. Septicaemic plague occurs when plague bacteria multiply in the blood. It can be a complication of pneumonic or bubonic plague or it can occur by itself. Septicemic plague does not spread from person to person.

Surrounded by death day in and day out, plague survivors became increasingly pious and participated in more and more religious ceremonies involving the kissing of both holy objects and the bishop's hand and shoes in quick succession. Following every evening prayer I guess those in the latent phase of infection spread the bacteria through their "kiss of death". The resulting devastation, which reduced the population of Europe by 50%, ultimately led to the rise of the Ottoman Turks in the East and some even claim to the emergence of the industrial revolution in the West.

It took another 400 years for the likes of Robert Koch, Louis Pasteur, Paul Erlich and many others to establish firmly the correlation between microbes and diseases. Not until the 20th century, with the introduction of improved measures of hygiene, did humans obtain the upper hand in the battle with microbes for the first time in history.

These breakthroughs, along with continuing improvements in hygiene and the invention of antibiotics, prompted unprecedented growth of the world's human population and in health and well-being. In light of these advances, it is astonishing that many of Africa's present leaders, including South Africa's President Thabo Mbeki, stubbornly denied as late as in 2007 that AIDS was caused by HIV infection.

The little church had a couple of rows of seats and I chose one in the last row next to a small window carved into the rock. The window offered an uninterrupted view of the glorious Mediterranean Sea, its trafficking boats painting long, frothy marks on the blue surface as if they were decorating a weird, astonishingly blue cake. This contrast between the calm within this little church and the hectic nature of 21st-century life beyond its doors was quite remarkable. In this small dark cave, sitting in the last row on that uncomfortable bench, I experienced unexpected tranquillity and happiness. I guess this was the closest I have come to what I think may have been a spiritual experience.

The spirituality of this little haven lasted only until its priest arrived, a middle-aged man in a long black cotton coat who wore his long hair bundled under his cap. He noisily started to prepare for Mass, angrily removing the candles placed onto the candle holders with so much care. As he shuffled in and out of the little alcove behind the altar carrying the symbols of his trade his long beard was blown by a light breeze and appeared to follow him, constantly. Unlike their Roman Catholic counterparts, Greek Orthodox priests are permitted to marry. Perhaps he had quarrelled with his wife or his noisy children had annoyed the hell out of him!

Orthodox priesthood provides a reasonable living for a pious man without sacrificing some of life's great human experiences, such as the love of a woman or of your own child. It is also thought that Orthodox priests, with their first-hand experience of domestic life, can better advise their flock. On the other hand, one could argue that all their personal problems make them biased arbitrators in many situations, for their attention is divided not only between their flock and God but is also shared with their family. He was annoyed not only by the tourists, but also by the faithful. When a pious lady who had been praying there for 15 minutes wanted to know more about St John, he gave a short abrupt response. I suppose priests are human too, but it was nonetheless disappointing that a man supposed to assist others to experience spirituality spoiled the atmosphere.

Since discarding the requirement for celibacy, the Orthodox priesthood has become a profession like any other. In contrast, the Catholic Church insists on maintaining celibacy among its priests. Although celibacy is not an infallible dogma, the inflexible Catholic response to the question of lifting the requirement for celibacy can be seen from a recording of French Catholic philosopher Etienne Gilson's private audience with Pope John XXIII in December 1960 (Gilson 1964):

"The Pope's face became gloomy, darkened by a rising inner cloud," Gilson later reported.

"Then the Pope added in a violent tone, almost a cry: 'For some of them it is martyrdom. Yes, a sort of martyrdom. It seems to me that sometimes I hear a sort of moan, as if many voices were asking the church for liberation from the burden. What can I do? Ecclesiastical celibacy is not a dogma. It is not imposed in the Scriptures. How simple it would be: we take up a pen, sign an act, and priests who so desire can marry tomorrow. But this is impossible. Celibacy is a sacrifice which the church has imposed upon herself – freely, generously and heroically.'"

The decision to maintain celibacy for its priests has landed the Catholic Church in a dire situation, for in developed countries there are simply not enough priests to lead the congregations. Some years ago, I heard the unbelievable story of a Swiss village that ended up with a priest from Nigeria.

"Desperate to find someone to lead the Sunday Mass, the Catholic hierarchy of Switzerland began to look for priests overseas. After some searching they selected a priest from, of all places, Nigeria. He relinquished the hot rainforest for the snow-covered slopes of a small Swiss village of 80 houses. It so happened that on the day of his arrival the temperature hit an all-time

low of -30°C after three consecutive days of snow. Everything – the streets, the houses, the mountains – was white. Wrapped up in their winter clothes, the translucent white faces of the sun-deprived residents expressed surprise as they set their inquisitive blue eyes firmly upon a man whose smiling face was shining like ebony. The priest looked up at the sky, then at the steep mountain sides, and questioned the wisdom of his Church. Wasn't God expecting too much from him? How could he relate to people who had never felt the warmth of the African sun? But, to both his and his congregation's surprise, his Church had prepared him well. The liturgy, traditions and practices were the same in the high mountains of Switzerland as in the lowlands of Nigeria. Slowly the small hamlet and its priest developed a certain level of mutual understanding, although this relationship did not last long and he soon returned happily to his country of origin."

I have no idea what happened to the Sunday Mass after his departure.

Remembering this little story, it struck me that religious organisations were the first to invent globalisation! While we tend to think of it as a recent phenomenon, globalisation has been widespread for millennia. By their very nature, all belief systems are keen to spread their point of view, and some even believe that their God is the true and only one! Perhaps the spread of Buddhism and Hinduism in Asia was less bloody than the forceful conversion of millions to Christianity or Islam, but whichever way the conversion was achieved, the converted millions became "consumers" of a particular belief system. By converting more and more people, the power of the group within the community increased and it slowly started to dominate social and economic life. Over time, the selfless holy men expected more than a praise for their services, and places of worship were built and decorated. It is no wonder that churches, stupas, temples, synagogues, mosques and other holy places around the world are laden with gold and precious stones. Fundamentally, I think there is no difference between the spread of Christianity, Islam or the Hare Krishna movement, and that of consumer giants such as McDonalds, Coca Cola and Ford. Different religions crave world domination just as much as multinational corporations. The desire to control, whether it be the mind or the market, has the same root: the desire to rule.

After visiting these holy places and becoming acquainted with some of the great debates within the Christian Church, we were ready to return to the pleasures of the 21st century. We quickly changed for dinner at "home" on the boat and, decked out nicely, drove our dinghy to the Chora through the enchanting natural harbour where the twinkling monastery lights on top of the mountain presided over peace and harmony.

Even by Greek standards, the night was exceptionally hot and humid. Unable to resist the sound of a humming air-conditioning unit, we entered the pleasantly cool sanctuary of an elegant shop. While I was delighted with its range of modern merchandise, so refreshingly different from the usual knick-knacks sold by souvenir shops, Steve simply enjoyed the cool air. We started to chat with the shopkeeper, who also turned out to be the owner. Originally from Amsterdam, she was one of the many Northern Europeans who willingly exchanged the dark, wet climate of their country of birth for the soothing warmth of a Mediterranean island. The locals had mixed feelings about these new settlers. The shopkeeper told us that she lived on Patmos for five months each year and to occupy a couple of hours each day she managed this shop selling fine shoes and clothes. I so loved one of the pairs of elegantly styled shoes that I ended up purchasing a pair – it may well have been the highest price ever paid for 15 minutes of air-conditioning! On her recommendation, we went to a local taverna on the first floor of a house. The advantage of going to a restaurant on the first floor is obvious: wandering tourists do not find these places easily, so the restaurant must produce quality food so that the mostly local patrons who keep the place afloat at will return. We were not disappointed. Sitting on the balcony with a gentle breeze easing the sweltering heat, we enjoyed excellent Greek mezze (with the best peppered pork in all of Greece!) and brought this interesting day to a joyful conclusion by finishing a small bottle of raki.

Samos

The next day we sailed to Samos where, after some searching, we found, hiding behind a large outcrop of rock, the brand new marina of Pithagoreio. While perfectly functional, the marina was completely lacking in charm and bore no resemblance to its halcyon days when Samos, with its own colonies, was an ancient naval power. Samos' glory was achieved and sustained by its talented engineers who constructed revolutionary ships called the Samaina, which could carry 50 oarsmen.

In the 6th century BC, Samos was home to the most spectacular engineering achievements of the age, reaching its pinnacle during the rule of Polycrates (532–522 BC). The most famous of all scientists, engineers, architects and philosophers was Pythagoras (580–500 BC). Pythagoras was all in one: a philosopher, a mathematician and a musician (Chalcis 2011). His genius, combined with deep study and asceticism, resulted in the most fundamental discoveries in mathematical theory and geometry. The Pythagorean theorem in geometry that describing a right-angled triangle ($a^2 + b^2 = c^2$) is still used in geometry, as are the Pythagorean tables in arithmetic.

Ancient Samos was a splendid city and its excellent harbour was protected by a huge wave breaker 370 m in length and 35 m deep into the sea. Climbing a nearby hill, the well-preserved ancient harbour was clearly identifiable. The harbour lies next to the international airport and offers a startling contrast between the scale, size and speed of transportation methods today and those of 2,000 years ago. The huge jumbo jets, approximately the size of the entire harbour, climb noisily into the sky with a speed unimaginable to our ancestors. On the other hand, we should not forget that people of the ancient world safely and effectively navigated and sailed the Mediterranean Sea. I can attest that this is no small achievement.

The ancient city was built on the slopes of today's hill of the Virgin Mary of Spilianis. Surrounded by 7 km of walls featuring 31 small towers, the city was connected to the harbour through a tunnel. While we were told that the tunnel remains operational today, it was unfortunately closed at the time of our visit. The green island of Samos, with its pleasant climate and sophisticated, cultured cities, remained an important meeting place for hundreds of years. Before the ill-fated Battle of Actium, Anthony and Cleopatra threw a famous party on Samos, inviting a "who's who" of the ancient world. The party lasted for months. It is just as well they enjoyed themselves, as some months later their armies were defeated and the victors forced them to commit suicide.

The northern part of Samos is beautiful. Covered with steep mountains and lush vegetation, it reminded us of Switzerland. Perhaps if the Orthodox and Catholic churches could manage to sort out their differences, a priest who originates from this island will find more common ground with the people of the Swiss mountains than did the hapless priest from Nigeria.

The second-largest town and harbour of Samos, Karlovassi, offers the only harbour on the north-western side of the island before setting out to Mykonos. The seaside is quite pleasant and provides a wide walkway for the promenading townsfolk in the evenings. In this part of the Mediterranean, where foreign tourists are few and far between, the locals still carve out their living from fishing, agriculture and some unidentifiable industrial activities. During our night-time promenade, we were pleased to see that small fishing boats came back laden with a rich catch. The fish were sold on the spot to the passing crowds. Among these ordinary people, I noticed a priest jostling for position, reminding me of a lovely little story I heard somewhere that gave some insight into the everyday life of an Orthodox priest.

"It was dawn. The alarm clock of the auctioneer noisily played the programmed digital tune. It was totally out of tune. Perhaps, it was deliberately designed to annoy the listener into action.

His urge to silence the offending clock was so strong that he jumped out of bed. There was no time for turning around between the warm bed sheets, pulling the pillow over his head or just having another lazy stretch of his tired bones under the quilt. The out-of-tune music reminded him of the fishermen who were on their way with their cargo from their night fishing. He quickly put on his cloak and hurriedly walked towards the town's only sandy beach. On the horizon, lit only by a hint of the morning sun, he could make out five fishing boats, slowly emerging from the East. They would all bring their catch to the jetty where he would auction them to the villagers, restaurateurs and shopkeepers from nearby towns and to the occasional tourists. He was wondering how he, the village priest, ended up becoming the only fish-auctioneer on these shores."

Mykonos

We departed at 9 am the next morning, and after a full day's sailing, we reached the small island of Mykonos. The tiny harbour in the town of Mykonos only provides shelter from the prevailing northerly winds for the local ferries and tourist boats. Pleasure crafts have been banned from this harbour for decades. I searched the Internet in vain for the Mykonos Marina, rumoured to have been started during our first visit in the 1990s. After a while I found a posting by a sailor who informed me that the Marina remained unfinished in 2007! I found this unbelievable, especially considering that during the last 10–15 years new marinas with first-class facilities had popped up everywhere along the Turkish coast. Silly me! Mykonos doesn't need additional tourists. It's already full!

I remember our first visit to the town on a rented boat when we made a mad dash from Athens to Rhodes in 10 days. We approached Mykonos in an unseasonably strong wind and were delighted to reach the town harbour around sunset. Feeling satisfied with ourselves, we entered and were busily searching for a suitable spot on the town quay when a whistle was fiercely blown somewhere on the shore. We were at that time still inexperienced in this special Greek way of herding the tourists, so we innocently continued our search. The whistle was blown again, now twice in a row. Searching the shore, we identified the source of the sound.

It was officialdom at its best! A fresh white uniform covering legs, arms and torso was attached to a head that was ferociously blowing the whistle. The two white-gloved hands were emphatically directing us out of the harbour. No knowledge of Greek was necessary to understand his uncompromising hand signals. When we approached him, without hesitation he shouted at us to leave the harbour immediately. We meekly asked, "Where to?" as to the best of our knowledge this was the only harbour for 50 nautical miles. But he convincingly shouted back, "Go to the marina just north of the town's harbour."

We sailed north, but even a binocular-aided search could not identify the marina. We sailed up and down the coast until we identified some sailing boats in a place that looked more like a dumping ground for old abandoned boats than a marina. However, further investigation confirmed our fears: this was the marina. The official forgot to mention that it was a marina under construction. We spent a miserable time rafted up to other boats, generally feeling very uncomfortable about the whole arrangement. But I have to admit the beauty of the town compensated for all the inconveniences.

This time, discouraged by the news from the Internet, we omitted the search for the marina and carefully skirted the island on its southern side, sailing into every small cove in search of a suitable long-term anchorage. This exercise was made more interesting by the Beaufort 5 force wind blowing from the north. We planned to spend a week in Mykonos and then, leaving the boat behind, take a fast ferry to the mythical island of Santorini. The wind was around 25 knots and the forecast was quite bleak for the following week. With the Meltemi season in full swing, we could expect strong winds for up to 10 days in a row. Mykonos was formed by erosion caused by the waves and the ceaseless wind. The combination of these created something like an isthmus on the south-western end of the island, with bays to its north and south. Approaching the southern side of the isthmus, the bay of Ormos, we noticed approximately 30–40 yachts that were braving the increasing winds. After some searching, we identified a suitable position and anchored a couple of hundred metres from the shore. To ensure that we would not drag our anchor and end up on one of the colourful sun loungers on the beach, we also deployed our second anchor. Riding out the Meltemi on two anchors gave us an additional sense of security in the roaring wind. Satisfied with ourselves, we left he boat behind a set out to discover the Mykonos town of Chora.

Windmills, Mykonos

The gay community discovered Mykonos in the 1970s, and by the 1990s, most of the old, abandoned houses had been painted sparkling white and the streets cleaned. Even then it was an absolute delight to walk its winding streets, filled with cute little shops and cafés offering mainly local products.

A street in Mykonos

The Mykonos of today is like something out of a fairytale. There is no word other than dazzling to describe 21st-century Mykonos. It is the modern-day equivalent of the once famous Delos, minus the cultural attributes. So incredibly narrow are the streets that you can sometimes reach from one side of the street to the other. The all-white two- and three-storey buildings, with their blue window- and door-frames, were spotless. The ground floors of every building had been converted into shops and provided a natural glittering edge to the streets. Each and every shop was a little gem and the individual designs adorning the beautifully decorated shops reflected their owners' personalities.

Jewellery shop, Mykonos

These lovely, innocent-looking shops sold quality luxury products from across the world for very inflated prices. Then there were the bars, back to back, enticing customers with the most exciting cocktail menus on Earth. Once darkness fell, small light-bulbs illuminated the town streets. As we walked along, I felt like I was walking on a brightly lit path of the Milky Way, stars twinkling all around me. It was a magical experience! I did not even mind the thousands of fellow human beings shuffling up and down the bright little alleyways. There was music, fabulous cocktails and restaurants representing all the regions of Europe. The average age of the visitors and the townsfolk alike seemed to be below 30, and those who appeared to be older did their best to fit into this seemingly forever-young community.

The town is a frequent port of call for American cruise ships. And who said Americans were fat? The Americans walking off these modern versions of the ill-fated Titanic were certainly not. Slim and toned with beautiful bodies, they carried an aura of confidence that only Americans can. The blonde and auburn girls wore incredibly small shorts and big smiles. Cashed up by their parents, they cheerfully carried environmentally friendly shopping bags advertising exclusive boutiques and international brands on their early evening stroll. The boys, tall and masculine, also had impeccable white smiles. They brought their famous rowdiness with them, so well described by Tom Wolfe in the book *I am Charlotte Simmons*, and walked up and down the narrow streets shouting ceaselessly to each other. The days of young people backpacking are gone!

Today's youngsters arrive on planes, cruise ships or private yachts and live in studios, apartments or hotels. I am not even sure whether a single campsite remains on Mykonos today!

On the other hand, the Greek taverna remains indestructible, continuing to provide excellent food, entertainment and ambiance. Near to our anchorage at Ormos was one of our favourite haunts, a huge establishment next to the beach that served simple Greek fare. Its speciality was mouth-watering grilled meats produced on a huge charcoal-fired grill. The place was absolutely packed from 8 pm until midnight, serving several rounds of customers. On our first visit, we arrived desperately hungry around at 10 pm and found the taverna packed to capacity. We approached the middle-aged lady apparently in charge to ask whether we could have a table for two at this late hour. She cheerfully assured us that there would be a vacancy in 15 minutes and we set off for a walk on the moonlit beach in the meantime.

We returned desperate, to find our table, and there it was, set in Greek taverna style. White paper sporting a nautical theme lay atop a checkered tablecloth, and our white plates, surrounded by glasses and cutlery, smiled at us optimistically. Within minutes, a waiter, literally running, arrived with a bottle of water, two glasses and the menus. Looking around I noticed that all the waiters were all running to serve their customers as fast as possible. We ordered our drinks straight-away and without too much hesitation: a large bottle of sparkling mineral water and a bottle of house wine, our usual order. After studying at length the fantastic grilled meat dishes on the menu, I ordered what turned out to be the best dish in the house, chicken portions, and Steve settled for his favourite mixed grill. Since the place was packed, we resigned ourselves to spending the remainder of the evening sipping our wine and water, but within 30 minutes the dishes had arrived, and my God, what dishes they were! Mine was an entire half of a chicken cut into small pieces accompanied by a huge Greek salad. I left aside the compulsory chips. I carefully cut a piece of chicken and put it into my mouth, expecting the usual "grilled chicken" flavour, but then I stopped. It was nothing like the grilled chicken you find in so many other establishments, dripping with grease and saturated with salt. It was a dish from heaven – the moist meat simply melted in my mouth, leaving behind the flavours of Mediterranean herbs and a slight hint of charcoal. It must first have been marinated in herbs such as oregano, thyme and rosemary before being grilled to absolute perfection. Even today, years later as I recount the experience, I can smell and taste this wonderful dish.

The strong winds showed no signs of abating and sooner or later we would had to decide if we were willing to leave *Fenix* unattended for a week. We decided to put it to the test by undertaking a full-day excursion to Delos. Swinging space in the bay was fairly limited and we resolved to purchase another anchor from the local chandlery. The new anchor would enable us to put out an extra stern anchor to prevent Fenix swinging if the wind direction changed. Fellow yachties advised us of a chandlery on the opposing steep hill.

Having climbed the hill on our scooter, we found it "manned" by two boys. The younger one, around 10, must have been the owner's son and spoke some rudimentary English. The older, around 14, was the shopkeeper in charge. Both were extremely helpful, attentive and smart. We held a deep admiration for Greek island parents who, even with the influence of television, computer games, violent movies and other undesirable distractions of today's world, maintain a balanced upbringing of their children. Perhaps the boys' participation in "real life" scenarios, being in charge of a business worth tens of thousands of euros and selling to real customers, made their days more interesting than playing with fake money or shooting make-believe guns on a screen.

It was only after their excellent service, as the boys carried our newly purchased 20 m chain and a 10 kg fisherman's anchor out to our scooter, that the realities of our situation became clear to them. It was obvious that even contemplating carrying these two items and two passengers on the scooter was impossible and they looked at us with bewilderment as they tried to predict our next move. What these boys had never encountered, however, was the innovative use of the scooter as implemented on the Indian subcontinent in the 1970s.

While living in India, we discovered that the humble scooter, the symbol of middle-class prosperity, could carry much more than it was designed for. At a minimum, two adults and two children could enjoy a relatively comfortable journey on a scooter. One child would usually stand in front of the driver while the other would squeeze between the parents. The lady of the house would always sit modestly sideways, the edges of her colourful sari floating behind the scooter like a kite. Without fail, a variety of bags would also be distributed around the bike, whether on handle-bars, hooks, or carefully carried in the lady's arms. Still, I suspect the eventual decline of fertility in India was directly related to the existence of the humble scooter, for even the best-intentioned, most accomplished engineer could not fit more than a family of four and a tiny baby on this extraordinary transport device.

Inspired by the remarkable achievements of the Indians, a mere anchor and chain was simply not going to become an obstacle to our trip to Delos. We soon loaded the chain into the holding space under the seat and the captain began attaching the anchor to the handle bar in front of the seat. Upon noticing that tying the anchor to the handle bar would limit the scooter's manoeuvrability to a single direction – straight ahead – his recalcitrant first mate (myself), brought up on the ever-questioning Homeric poetry, voiced her objection. Captain Steve looked at me with disbelief and said: "I can't believe that after so many years you continue to distrust my engineering ability!" Then, upon looking at the anchor again, he quietly muttered, "Actually, you are right!"

After centuries of denial that the female brain can process the same complex thoughts as a male intellect, at last, in the 20th century, females started to gain some recognition for their cerebral abilities. Three-dimensional seeing, however, continues to be considered a trait exclusive to the male half of the human species, so I quietly acknowledged this small success for my gender.

We were soon on our way with our chain, anchor and some other small purchases. The beauty of boating is that the simplest of everyday activities become extremely complicated when you live on a boat. A boat anchored a couple of hundred metres off shore challenges your stamina, resourcefulness and self-reliance again and again. After arriving at the shore, we packed our purchases into the dinghy and motored back to *Fenix*. Contorting like two circus acrobats, we transferred the anchor and the chain a metre above the violently moving dinghy onto the deck. We began to assemble the gear that was supposed to keep *Fenix* in place even during a hurricane. The anchor, now attached to the chain, which was in turn affixed to a long rope, was packed carefully back into the dinghy so it would run out smoothly. As Steve started motoring slowly away from the yacht I released first the rope and then the chain. When we reached the limits of both the rope and chain Steve dropped the anchor into the water. We drove back to *Fenix* and tightened the rope. Easy – and it only took three hours! Without further delay, we transformed ourselves into tourists to visit Delos, one of the most remarkable ancient towns in the Cyclades.

Delos

We were late, very late, but nonetheless managed to arrive in Mykonos five minutes before the tourist ferry departed. As vehicles were not permitted in the centre of Mykonos, we left the scooter at the windmills and ran through the winding alley towards the assumed direction of the harbour. In the distance, we could hear the ferry motors running at full throttle. With a heroic effort, we made the 100 m dash to the ramp, jumping aboard the ferry as the sailors pulled up the gangplank, and waved good bye to the windmills facing the harbour.

As soon as we left the harbour, we felt the full force of the northerly wind. The huge waves reached the windows and it looked as if we were travelling on a kind of U-boat, a class of submersible that almost won WWII for Germany, instead of on a ship. It was a bumpy ride and the crew soon started distributing paper bags for the seasick passengers. In spite of the wind, the sky remained crystal clear and the sea incredibly blue, bluer than one could imagine and the bluest that I had ever seen.

After a 30-minute roller coaster ride, we pulled into the strait between Delos and Rinia. Suddenly, the raging seas calmed. Given that seafaring people from the Bronze Age had frequented both islands, we were obviously not the first to notice this favourable change. The outline of the small harbour on Delos soon became visible and we could clearly see that the ruins covering most of the island resembled a modern city ravaged by a savage war.

Delos, located in the very centre of the Aegean Sea, was according to mythology the birthplace of Apollo and Artemis and therefore, since around 900 BC, the most significant pan-Hellenic holy place. There is archaeological proof that the island was inhabited before the Bronze Age and several ruins of Mycenaean civilisation have been found. It actually strikes the present-day visitor, surely wondering how this little, less than 3.5 square-mile stony island, be called Asteria – the Star – could have been such a holy and rich place 2,500 years ago. Nevertheless, this flat, round rock, midway between Athens and Crete, as well as equidistant from continental Greece and the Ionian colonies of the past, in spite of its bare, rocky and poor landscape, inspired some of the most famous verses of Ancient Greek poetry. Moreover, many cities and lands were devoted and supposed to belong to Apollo, but he was said to mainly delight in Delos, where the Ionians gathered together in song and dance in his honour.

In the Homeric Hymn to Apollo (probably one of the two earliest hymns, possibly composed around the 8th century BC), the birth of Apollo takes place in Delos as Leto (pregnant by Zeus, has been rejected by every other place; no land wants to hoast this tremendous event. Thus she begs the island of Delos to allow her to deliver the baby Apollo on its land (Atheneion):

> "Delos, if you would be willing to be the abode of my son Phoebus Apollo and make him a rich temple; for no other will touch you, as you will find: and I think you will never be rich in oxen and sheep, nor bear vintage nor yet produce plants abundantly. But if you have the temple of far-shooting Apollo, all men will bring you hecatombs and gather here, and incessant savour of rich sacrifice will always arise, and you will feed those who dwell in you from the hand of strangers; for truly your own soil is not rich."

And the island responds:

> "Leto, daughter most renowned of mighty Coeus, right gladly would I welcome the birth of the Archer Prince, for verily of me there goes an evil report among men, and thus would I wax mightiest of renown. But at this Word, Leto, I tremble, nor will I hide it from thee, for the saying is that Apollo will be mighty of mood, and mightily will lord it over mortals and immortals far and wide over the Earth, the grain-giver.

> Therefore, I deeply dread in heart and soul lest, when first he looks upon the sunlight, he disdain my island, for rocky of soil am I, and spurn me with his feet and drive me down in the gulfs of the salt sea. Then should a great sea-wave wash mightily above my head forever but he will fare to another land, which so pleases him, to fashion him a temple and groves of trees. But in me would many-footed sea-beasts and black seals make their chambers securely, no men dwelling by me. Nay, still, if thou hast the heart, Goddess, to swear a great oath that here first he will build a beautiful temple, to be the shrine oracular of men – thereafter among all men let him raise him shrines, since his renown shall be the widest."

Leto's delivery was somewhat delayed by the jealousy of Hera; however, eventually Eilithyia, the goddess of childbirth, came and the goddess was able to bring forth her son. He immediately broke open his swaddling-bands and claimed his skills: the bow, the lyre and the endowment of divination.

Delos' history dates back to the Mycenaean period, but it really gained prominence with the establishment of the Delian League by the Greek city-states after the Persian Wars. Xerxes, the King of Persia, first attacked the Greek colonies along the eastern coast of the Mediterranean before attempting to occupy Athens, the most developed city-state of its time. The Persians suffered a decisive defeat at Salamis in 480 BC in a sea battle. Under the leadership of Athens, the Delian League (477–404 BC) was formed in an effort to keep the Persian threat away from the Greek states. The treasures of these city-states were hoarded at Delos, creating a most impressive city on this barren island. The Temple of Apollo housed the treasury of the members of the Delian

League and was exclusively managed and guarded by Athenian personnel. The Delian League subsequently evolved into Athenian hegemony. The treasures of all member states were transferred to Athens, and not without some debate – after all, this was a democracy – were used to pay for the construction of the Acropolis. As Plutarch tells us in his work *Lives*:

> "The enemies of Pericles were crying out how that the commonwealth of Athens had lost its reputation and was ill-spoken of abroad for removing the common treasure of the Greeks from the isle of Delos into their own custody; and how that their fairest excuse for so doing, namely, that they took it away for fear the barbarians should seize it, and on purpose to secure it in a safe place, this Pericles had made unavailable, and how that 'Greece cannot but resent it as an insufferable affront, and consider herself to be tyrannized over openly, when she sees the treasure, which was contributed by her upon a necessity for the war, wantonly lavished out by us upon our city, to gild her all over, and to adorn and set her forth, as it were some vain woman, hung round with precious stones and figures and temples, which cost a world of money.'

> Pericles, on the other hand, informed the people, that they were in no way obliged to give any account of those moneys to their allies, so long as they maintained their defense, and kept off the barbarians from attacking them."

Arrival to Delos

Perhaps it was all for the best, as without this tactic the magical site of the Acropolis would have never been constructed.

The site of Ancient Delos itself is huge, and arriving from the sea gives one a full grasp of its enormity. Imagine a city where 42,000 people lived more than 2,000 years ago. The town had two harbours: a sacred harbour to assist with the adoration of Apollo, and a commercial harbour dedicated to supplying citizens with the necessities of life. We docked in the commercial harbour, which has been in continuous use for the last 2,500 years!

Delos was interesting from several points of view. This well-designed town had everything needed by a modern 21st-century city. In addition to the ever-present agora (market place), there were theatres, administrative buildings, a stadium, schools, hotels, baths, shops, bordellos, and private houses for the rich, poor and the middle class. It also boasted sanctuaries and temples built by different member states of the Delian League for the adoration of Apollo. Its excellent sanitation system remained intact in places; the sewers were made of square stones and fresh water ran through clay pipes. Good roads, covered with flat stones, connected the spaciously arranged public buildings.

I was excited to note that the people of Delos lived in a colourful and richly decorated environment surrounded by beautiful everyday items. These items, mass-produced and lovingly decorated, demonstrate that beauty surrounded the citizens everywhere. Even slaves, as they passed walls decorated with frescoes, moved through houses and courtyards adorned with beautifully carved statues, and handled finely crafted household items, thus having opportunities to develop an appreciation of beauty. Beauty, which was defined way back by the Acheans.

The site had a surprisingly small, but nevertheless very interesting museum and it reminded me that we do not often think about the work of archaeologists. Even in this modern age of lasers, satellites and computers, they continue to make their discoveries using the most mundane of tools – a spade and bucket. Sifting through tonnes of soil, they seek items left behind by long-past humans. After unearthing these broken fragments, they painstakingly match and assemble them like an endless puzzle to form buildings, statues, vases or jewellery.

The museum featured a unique presentation detailing how a statue found on the site had been reassembled from broken bits and pieces. As these fragments of yellowish marble, each tinged with red from the Earth, were joined together, a beautiful statue of a male body emerged. Supported by rather elaborate

The tools of an archaeologist's trade, Delos

scaffolding, the fracture lines of this restored statue were not touched up and remained clearly visible. The statue was two to three times the size of a normal human. We admired its gracious form, lightness and perfection. As with all Greek figures, he was delicately balanced with his feet touching the ground with god-like lightness. Looking at it, we completely forgot that the statue weighed several tonnes. An artistic feat combined with superb engineering understanding: this was nothing less than perfection supreme!

Greek statues are so flawless that even the most talented sculptor who ever lived, the Renaissance Michelangelo, refused the request of his mentor, Pope Julius II, to add the missing limbs and head to the famous Torso Belvedere, a fragment of a Greek statue owned by the Vatican. The maestro refused, stating: "No human can ever match the perfection of the statues produced by the Greeks".

In the Vatican Museum, the Torso Belvedere, untouched by subsequent generations, stands as the sublime embodiment of art.

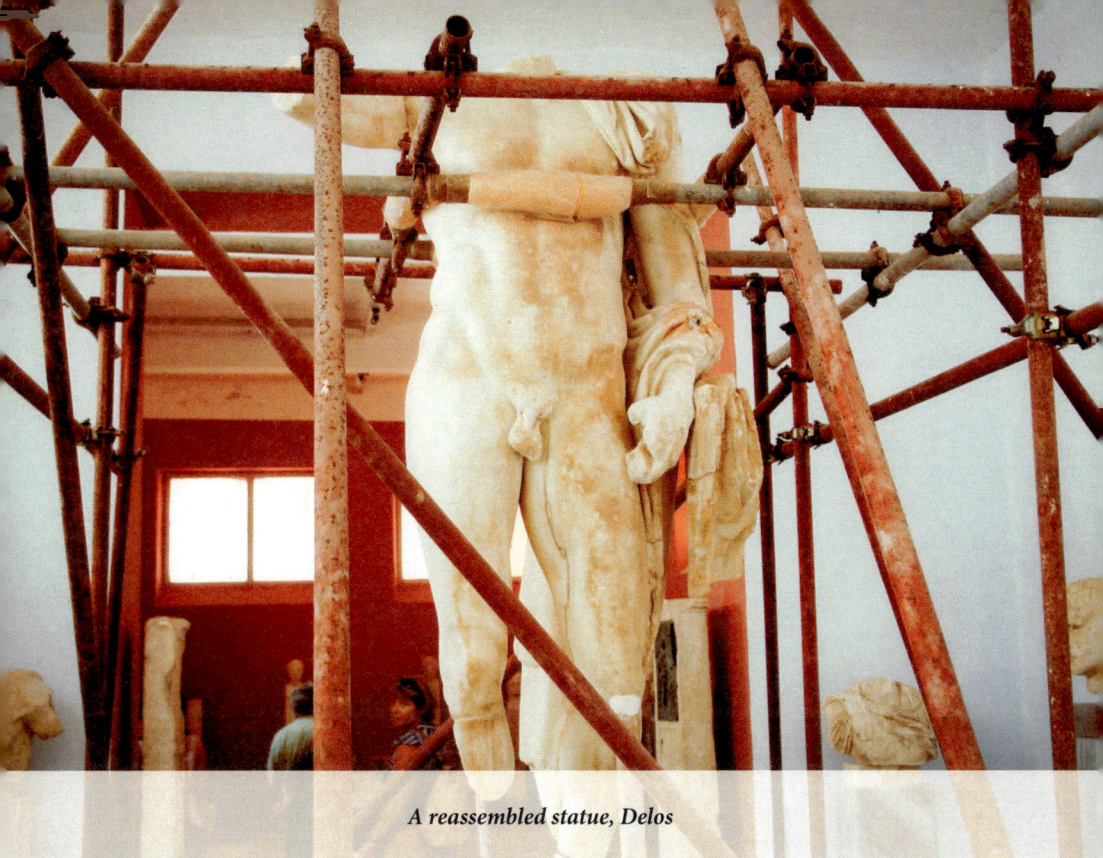

A reassembled statue, Delos

Huge, beautiful and rich in artefacts, the site has unsurprisingly been pillaged for millennia but, as most of the decorations were made from stone, the sheer weight of the ornaments prevented adventurers from removing everything. At the height of their glory, the Venetians even harnessed the efforts of a thousand men to once again lift the fallen 32 m-high statue of the Colossus.

In the end, they just took what they could, including one of the famous lions of the Naxos sanctuary, which was moved to Venice and refitted with a rather ugly head. It became the symbol of Venice; however, to this day, Greeks are keen to point out that the Venetians have far less refined tastes than the Ancient Greeks.

BUREAUCRACY
AT LARGE

2005–2008

T he Greek authorities have devised a bizarre system that requires all boats that sail in Greek waters to register every time they enter an anchorage, harbour or marina within the boundaries of the country. When you arrive at a port, marina or even to a town's anchorage, you are supposed t o visit the port police, where your papers are scrutinised and the details of your yacht, the date of entrance and the intended length of stay are entered in the beautiful handwriting of the officers into the BOOK. To signify the importance of the BOOK I have to write it in capitals. It is a huge A2-sized codex that, instead of giving the words of God, contains the details of all boats that have ever entered into the harbour: small pleasure craft, huge cruise ships, fishing vessels and visiting sailing boats. The only thing it does not contain are the occasional clandestine vessels of people or cigarette smugglers, who are the original raison d'être of the port police. But the last place any smuggler would visit is the port police.

After entering your boat details into the BOOK, your logbook is stamped and from then on the series of stamps are closely scrutinised by whatever official manages to get hold of your logbook. At the time of your departure, you are supposed to return to the port police to gain an exit permit by repeating the same process again. Both times all relevant boat papers are not only scrutinised and entered into the BOOK, but in more advanced stations, they are also photocopied and filed away carefully – never to be found again.

Generally, I am not sure what is more laughable: the strictness of the rules or their lack of enforcement. It really depends on you whether you obtain a logbook and if you register each time you enter a town. The problem with the system is that it was not designed to accommodate the leisure boat industry that gradually emerged from the 1970s onwards – with the thousands of leisure boats sailing the waters of modern Greece, it is not practical or enforceable. If everyone decided to comply, the authorities would be unable to cope. "The authorities" are pompous youngsters outfitted in crisp uniforms, either sporting the white naval look or military blue with heavy boots. Since no one registers for a visit of a couple of days, they have practically nothing to do all day. Actually, strictly speaking this is not true, as there are always some ignoramuses who decide to comply with the regulations to the letter. These people provide endless entertainment and save the officials from death by boredom. One unfortunate morning, under the spell of a bad omen and knowing our plans to leave EU waters, I bravely faced the authorities and registered our entry into and exit out of Cos. It went like dream, and only took half a day. What a waste!

Our sudden compliance was triggered by our plans to visit Turkey: knowing the animosity between Greeks and Turks, we decided it was better to fully comply with the regulations. Turks and Greeks have been fighting more or less from the time of the emergence of the Ottoman Empire, roughly 600 years ago. As recently as 2006, a Greek fighter jet was shot down, and in 2007, the two countries allegedly fought a submarine battle in the narrow Strait of Samos. These skirmishes between two members of the North Atlantic Treaty Organisation do not make any sense unless they are designed to provide entertainment for the tens of thousands of tourists who visit the coastlines and the scattered islands of Turkey and Greece. No better story to take home from your sailing holiday than describing a submarine battle! During the dinner party no one could outdo you. "Has anyone seen a submarine battle?" You could casually drop this line just after the entrée. Those who spent their precious summer break in France or Spain would simply sit humiliated and let the adventurous holiday-makers of Samos get on with their story. I'd consider these clashes between Turkey and Greece childish if they weren't acted out with live ammunition. So, we crossed the Strait of Samos one month after the "battle" a little anxious. But the waters were calm, the breeze perfect and nothing reminded us of the imperfect peace other than the well-hidden observation posts in the mountains.

In spite of all this, both countries are keen on tourist dollars, so there is frequent ferry traffic between the Dodecanese Islands and the western coast of Turkey and trouble-free passport control on both sides. But this did not apply to "yachties".

In Turkey, with its long history as a well-organised, authoritarian, corrupt society, the process of entry has been simplified and no one tried to pretend that it was not a money grab. Upon our arrival, we were kindly requested to hire an agent for a hefty $150 who would take care of everything. Of course, we had the choice of not hiring an agent, but we knew the authorities would do everything they could to discourage this practice. They would simply put our papers at the bottom of the pile and make us wait and walk around from one office to another until we came to our senses and asked for an agent. To save ourselves, the frustration of dealing with this unknown, mysterious bureaucracy, we did hire an agent, ensuring our arrival was trouble-free.

The Ottoman Empire, the predecessor of modern Turkey, ruled Asia Minor and much more from the 13th century until WWI. The memories of an organised, feudal state where the state provided for its citizens in exchange for obedience to its rules remains relatively fresh in the memories of the Turks. The Ottoman Empire trained its citizens well in civic behaviour and the organisational and administrative skills of the bureaucracy were seamlessly transferred to the new generation of public servants and professionals that emerged after the Ataturk revolution. Of course, we should not be mistaken: corruption remains rampant, but at least it is transparent – meaning that you cannot mistakenly think that you do not have "to pay a 'baksis'".

Greece, on the other hand, which by the 1990s had started to fancy itself a European democracy, ended up with a chaotic bureaucracy. On our return from Turkey, we entered Greece at Cos. Following a quick passport check, the "yachties" were instructed to go see the port police, the harbourmaster, etc, which in itself is considered to be quite a normal procedure when one enters a new country. In Greece, everything was complicated, so I approached the port police office with trepidation. It did not help that I have a genuine dislike of uniformed authorities. Indeed, as soon as I entered the building I was stopped behind the entrance door. The watchful receptionist decided not to let me proceed to a room that clearly bore the sign "Incoming yachts". The room was almost empty as far as customers were concerned. There were three guys with serious expressions on their faces, in riot police uniforms, sitting behind their desks and looking at some documents. One customer, standing in front of them with a slightly slouched back, showing his respect for authority, was patiently waiting to be attended to. I was also waiting, but two open doors away, hoping to be rewarded for my good behaviour by admittance to this modern Greek sanctuary. When called upon, I dutifully shuffled through the two doors and handed over the papers we had used for the last five years.

The young office inspected them, looked at them again and announced that the papers were invalid as they were only photocopies of the originals. In our wisdom, we stored the original papers away in a safe to avoid them suffering water damage (in case we capsized) and have been using photocopied copies. The fact that we had been sailing in Greece for three years and that the same office had declared our documents acceptable two months earlier did not bother him whatsoever. So we walked back to *Fenix* to collect whatever proof we could muster to prove that we had not stolen the boat.

He of course knew that he had not made a big catch of detaining a terrorist, an illegal immigrant, a drug smuggler or someone sailing with a stolen boat, but he thoroughly enjoyed our despair. He casually instructed us to return to Turkey, as he couldn't let us enter Greece with such papers. We argued that we had left Greece only a couple of weeks earlier and that we wanted to spend the rest of our holiday in Greece and spend money there, not to mention that our return tickets to Australia were booked from Athens.

After a while, he decided that our case was serious enough to refer it to the harbourmaster himself. For those who are not familiar with maritime rules, the harbourmaster in a harbour is simply the closest equivalent to God himself. Even if he is not God, he is definitely the manifestation of the highest authority as far as pleasure boats are concerned. I can imagine our guy was already seeing himself promoted for his vigilance in protecting the Greek state – perhaps the whole European Union – from holidaymakers with photocopied boat documents. The harbourmaster is always the guy in the crispest uniform. He usually sits behind the biggest desk in a dedicated, pompous office. He was busy as always. However, after a while, his good-looking secretary, also decked out in a crisp white uniform that did not conceal her desirable features appropriate for a harbourmaster's secretary, was handed our papers. She read them with great interest while the officer gave a long-winded list of our sins, which probably also implicated us in some unsolved crimes.

At that point, Steve broke the protocol: instead of talking to our tormentor, he started directly talking to the secretary, explaining that we keep the original boat papers in a safe in Australia as we have a small boat and the papers might get wet or stolen, etc. She looked at us and, in an annoyed voice, instructed our tormentor to provide the stamps and let us go. Obviously, the harbourmaster had more important things to deal with than chasing the originals of some photocopied pleasure craft documents. With that, the secretary made a quick turn and disappeared. Our tormentor, gasping for air, angrily stamped the entry form. At that point, I respectfully mentioned that, by the way, we were leaving that night, so we also needed an exit stamp. That cost us €15 and we were on our way.

Greece remains a strongly male-dominated society. To be instructed this way in front of all the office staff, the waiting unfortunate sailors and fishermen must have been a humiliating defeat for him. I was sorry for the next hapless traveller to reach his desk. You might say, "What is the big deal?" The big deal is that this system is unworkable and in its randomness it does not contribute to the safety or security of Greece. However, the government simply does not have the political will to change it. The unified maritime EU rule might eliminate this useless system in time. Later, we learnt that one way around these sufferings is to hire an agent who, for a ridiculous fee – after all we were in the EU – will sort out the paperwork. I'd hate to think that the young official received some sort of commission from the agent.

Although, Greece has a marvellous past, envied by the rest of the world, it did not exist as a unified country for 2,000 years. Up until the beginning of the 1900s, Greeks lived under Turkish occupation. In this situation, everyone was left to fend for themselves. This resulted in a society characterised by strong families and strong loyalties to the local leaders, respect for immediate authorities and distrust of foreigners. Even today, Greece, a member of the European Union, is characterised by administrative, sometimes social and definitely bureaucratic chaos. People in authority are unreasonably authoritative, like little dictators presiding over their empire, and despite of tourism being a key source of revenue, visitors are considered to be a nuisance.

In many ways, Greece and Turkey both retain a corrupt Byzantine bureaucracy. We came across several instances of little kingpins who simply enjoyed the power that was bestowed on them by a silly rule. They were determined to exercise their power to the fullest over those who were weaker or dependent on them. We ran into these petty officials everywhere. The same type of person ruled the marinas and the ancient sites with a whistle and the same society created the little tyrant who unnecessarily delayed our crossing at the Corinth Canal. This was a shame, as both the Greeks and the Turks are otherwise friendly, easy-going, uncomplicated and helpful. They are ready to talk to or entertain even strangers.

Societies like Australia, with its clear, enforceable rules that people can understand (most of the time) and follow, limit these ambitious Caesars to the playgrounds. Conversely, societies without clear, workable rules easily create corrupt bureaucrats. However, we should not be mistaken: unruly bureaucracy is not a feature unique to Greece or Turkey. These little Caesars spread like pests and they have existed since the formation of the first human cities.

Literature has examined the place of a disenfranchised human being under the power of the aimless bureaucracy. Franz Kafka was the master of describing the hopelessness of the average man in fighting authority in his novels *The Trial* and *The Castle*.

> "Someone must have made a false accusation against Joseph K., for without having done anything wrong he was arrested one fine morning."

With this sentence Franz Kafka opens *The Trial*, a fictional account of an individual's unfortunate encounter with an irrational legal system. Although K. believes the legal system to be fair, predictable and rational, his encounters with that system show the system to be arbitrary and unfathomable.

"'There can be no doubt,' said K., quite softly, for he was elated by the breathless attention of the meeting; in that stillness a subdued hum was audible which was more exciting than the wildest applause, 'there can be no doubt that behind all the actions of this court of justice, that is to say in my case, behind my arrest and today's interrogation, there is a great organization at work. An organization which not only employs corrupt warders, oafish Inspectors, and Examining Magistrates of whom the best that can be said is that they recognize their own limitations, but also has at its disposal a judicial hierarchy of high, indeed of the highest rank, with an indispensable and numerous retinue of servants, clerks, police, and other assistants, perhaps even hangmen, I do not shrink from that word. And the significance of this great organization, gentlemen? It consists in this, that innocent persons are accused of guilt, and senseless proceedings are put in motion against them...'"

Then in *The Castle*:

"Just then the landlord seemed like a child to K. 'The rascal,' said K., laughing, but the landlord said without laughing: 'Even his father is powerful.' 'Come on!' said K., 'You consider everyone powerful. Me too, perhaps?' 'No,' he said, timidly but gravely, 'I do not consider you powerful.' 'Well, you're very observant, then,' said K., 'for, speaking in confidence now, I'm really not powerful at all. And so, I probably have no less respect for those with power than you do, only I'm not as honest as you are and don't always care to admit it.' K. tapped the landlord on the cheek in order to comfort him and to gain his affection. And now he even gave a little smile. He was really a boy with his soft, almost beardless face. How had he come by his stout, older wife, whom one could see through a small window, bustling about with her elbows sticking out? Yet K. did not want to question him any further and risk chasing away the smile he had finally elicited, so he merely signalled to him to open the door and stepped out into the beautiful winter morning.

Now he saw the Castle above, sharply outlined in the clear air and made even sharper by the snow, which traced each shape and lay everywhere in a thin layer."

THE SEVEN
WONDERS OF THE
ANCIENT WORLD

June and August 2007

B y settling in Rhodes and other Aegean islands, the Greeks placed themselves as close as a half-day sail from the civilisations of the East and soon they became acquainted with their achievements. Rhodes and its cities became a crossroad for civilisations, and its alliance frequently changed. While Rhodes remained fundamentally Greek (sometimes allied with Sparta, sometimes with Athens), it tried to assert its independence in several ways. In short, Rhodes tried to develop independent politics. But, being at the crossroads between East and West, it was not easy. Nevertheless, Rhodes developed close trade and political relations with Ptolemaic Egypt. This was something that was frowned upon by other Greek states. Finally, in 306 BC, Antigonus, the Greek-Macedonian King of Syria, sent his famous son, Demetrius Poliorketes (the besieger) to put Rhodes under siege. Plutarch described the siege like this:

> "Now, he made war upon the Rhodians because they were allies of Ptolemy, and brought up against their walls his greatest 'city-taker'. Its base was square, and each of its sides measured at the bottom forty-eight cubits (1 cubit is a length around 45–67cm). It rose to a height of sixty-six cubits, and tapered from base to summit. Within, it was divided off into many storeys and chambers, and the side which faced the enemy had windows opening out of every storey and through these they issued missiles of every sort; for it was full of men who fought in every style of fighting. Moreover, it did not totter or lean when it moved, but remained firm and erect on its base, advancing evenly with much noise and great impetus, and this astounded the minds and at the same time greatly charmed the eyes of those who beheld it."

The Rhodians resisted the capture of the city for a whole year and forced Demetrius to abandon his siege. The great general departed from Rhodes in haste, embarrassed, leaving behind his famous siege-machines. The enterprising Rhodians sold them and the money raised was used to thank the patron of the island, Helios. They commissioned an immense bronze statue of Helios, the famed Colossus, from the sculptor Chares of Lindos. It took 12 years, from 304 BC to 292 BC, for Chares to finish his masterpiece. Inscriptions found near the palace of the Grand Master have allowed us to calculate its height at about 31 m. It is said that Chares cast the bronze limbs of the statue on the spot, one at a time, using huge mounds of soil.

The old myth, that it stood across the entrance to the harbour and that incoming ships sailed between its legs, must, reluctantly, had to be abandoned. Today, we know that it stood on land around the Grand Master's Palace. However, the statue was only a 66-year wonder. A violent earthquake in 226 BC broke its knees and brought it to the ground. The Rhodians, afraid of a curse, did not dare replace it, and it lay where it had fallen for many centuries. At last, in 653 AD, Arab pirates under Moabiah carried the bronze parts to the mainland and sold them to a Jewish merchant. It is said that 900 camels were needed to transport it. Most of the guns that were subsequently used to fight the crusaders must have been constructed from the bronze recovered from the Colossus.

The Colossus was regarded as one of the Seven Wonders of the Ancient World. The others – the Great Pyramid of Giza, the Hanging Gardens of Hammurabi, the Temple of Artemis at Ephesus, the Mausoleum of Halicarnassus, the Statue of Zeus at Olympus and the Lighthouse of Alexandria – may not have had such a tumultuous history, but their constructions were all associated with extraordinary people. The original list put together by the historian Herodotus (ca. 425 BC), and the scholar Callimachus of Cyrene (305–240 BC) at the Library of Alexandria is lost. But in 140 BC, Antipater of Sidon compiled the earliest extant version of a list of seven wonders.

Two of the wonders are tombs. By far the oldest is the Great Pyramid of Giza. It was built by the "pyramid maniac" Egyptian Pharaoh Khufu in 2584 BC. Credit to its builders, it is the only one of the Seven Wonders to survive to date in its full glory. It is recognised as one of the oldest man-made freestanding stone-on-stone structures in the world, though it is a thousand years younger than the temples found on the nearby island of Malta.

The other tomb, the Mausoleum of Halicarnassus, was built by Halicarnassus' grieving sister, who became his wife. Its ruins, or rather the space where it stood, is in modern-day Bodrum.

Nebuchadnezzar II, the ruler of Babylon, is credited with building the Hanging Garden of Babylon to cheer up his homesick wife, Amyitis.

The Temple of Artemis must have been an awesome sight! It was the biggest building in the Ancient World. The temple was a 120-year project started by Croesus of Lydia. Antipater of Sidon, said the following about it:

> "I have set eyes on the wall of lofty Babylon on which is a road for chariots, and the statue of Zeus by the Alpheus, and the hanging gardens, and the Colossus of the Sun, and the huge labour of the high pyramids, and the vast tomb of Mausolus; but when I saw the house of Artemis that mounted to the clouds, those other marvels lost their brilliancy, and I said, 'Lo, apart from Olympus, the Sun never looked on aught so grand.'" (Antipater, Greek Anthology IX.58)

Unfortunately, nothing remains of the Temple of Artemis. What we know is that Artemis of Ephesus was divine and the original temple (to worship the goddess of fertility) was built around 800 BC around a fallen meteorite. In 550 BC, King Croesus of Lydia conquered Ephesus and the other Greek cities of Asia Minor. During the fighting, the temple was destroyed. Croesus proved himself a gracious winner, though, by contributing generously to the building of a new temple. The new temple was the pride of Ephesus until 356 BC when tragedy struck: Herostratus burnt down the temple. The site was so significant that again a new temple was commissioned from one of the most famous sculptors of the day, the architect Scopas of Paros. Ephesus was one of the greatest cities in Asia Minor at this point and no expense was spared in the construction. Alexander the Great offered his contribution to the construction, but the clever, independent Ephesians refused it, saying, "It would not befit a deity like you to build a temple to another deity."

The temple was built in the same marshy place as before, but its size was increased to magnificent proportions. It was the first large building ever built exclusively from marble, and reached a size three times that of the Acropolis in Athens. The statue of Artemis, the great mother of abundance, was refreshingly different from other Greek statues. She was not the perfect sculpted body of a female but her abundant fertility was symbolised by the abstract appearance of numerous eggs on her chest. Unfortunately, an earthquake destroyed the great statue and temple, and today there is nothing to see at Ephesus. When we visited Ephesus, I sadly concluded that I lacked the necessary limitless imagination to see the grassy site as one of the Seven Wonders of the World. I was sorry to see that the same was true for the Mausoleum of Halicarnassus in Bodrum.

The statue of Zeus in Olympus was huge and delicately carved by Phidias from wood and ivory and was gilded in huge amounts of gold.

For me, as a sailor, the Lighthouse of Alexandria tops them all. It guided seafarers to the safe harbour with its mirrors shining day and night.

Most of these monuments were produced by the Greeks or their allies who colonised the eastern coast of the Mediterranean Sea. Today, they are scattered among several modern states. The Mausoleum and the Temple of Artemis are in modern Turkey, the Pyramid and the Lighthouse are in Egypt, the sites of the Colossus and the statue of Zeus are in Greece, and the unknown site of the Hanging Gardens probably lies under the endless sand of the desert in Iraq.

Rhodes

Rhodes is a short distance from Simi and we arrived after an uneventful but most enjoyable day's sail. I knew that getting a place at the Mandaraki Marina would be nothing short of a miracle. The marina is spectacular, with one of the many town walls running parallel with the moored yachts, while the entrance of Mandaraki Harbour is guarded by the modern emblems of the town: two bronze Rhodian deers. I had been talking to the marina staff for a couple of days in advance about a pen, but no luck. So, after fruitlessly searching the town quay for a vacancy, we entered the cruise ship harbour, which led us to the large luxury yacht quay. We were delighted to find a spot! It was late afternoon and we had run out of options to find a safe harbour before sunset. We dropped our anchor and, to the amazement of the crews of the surrounding yachts, started to reverse onto the quay.

By now, of course, we were experts in Mediterranean mooring, so the manoeuvre that had seemed impossible a couple of years ago now appeared to be easy. I have to admit, though, that a healthy dose of adrenaline continued to ensure our alertness. On our starboard, there was a huge British yacht with a shiny, modern hull, and on the port side a beautiful wooden Turkish gulet with faultless varnish. The crews stood by and watched over their vessels with some concern in case we bumped into their shiny craft, but Steve executed a masterful approach to the quay. I was standing on the stern ready to throw my rope to shore when it dawned on me that indeed this quay was designed for much larger vessels.

A stone wall towered above my head. From where I stood, the task of throwing the rope to the shore seemed like trying to harpoon the moon. I tried it a couple of times, and of course the more I tried, the more tired I became, making it less and less likely to happen. Steve was patiently holding the boat steady a metre from the quay, but in the end he abandoned the helm and threw the bundle onto the quay himself.

We made friends with the crews of the neighbouring boats. The captain of the British yacht looked dreamily at our modest craft, saying he wanted to buy a Hallberg-Rassy when he retired. Having established a vital common interest in Hallberg-Rassys, we had a great couple of days talking to each other. We had long chats about the maintenance of luxury yachts, which can be summarised in one sentence: you need a crew of one to five people who do nothing but maintain and shine your craft day and night. Wooden surfaces have to be sanded and re-varnished every three months. I quickly came to the conclusion

The old port of Rhodes

that luxury yachts weren't for me. First of all, sharing the confined space of a craft day and night with someone who is continuously doing something is nothing short of a nightmare. As for me doing it, I have no great interest in shining boats. I am afraid that we will have to be satisfied with a less than perfectly presented craft.

Rhodes is synonymous with the Order of the Knights of St John, who for more than 300 years had their headquarters on the island. The Knights left imposing evidence of their presence in Rhodes. They gave the city the particular character tourists admire to this day: impregnable walls, imposing gates, numerous churches, and magnificent palaces.

The Order of the Knights of St John was founded in 1039 as a charitable brotherhood in Jerusalem by merchants from Amalfi, Italy, to care for the pilgrims visiting the holy city. Later, the Order gained in strength and became more of a military organisation. Members of the Order devoted their time to prayer and military practice to protect the pilgrims. When Jerusalem fell to Saladin, the Knights moved to Acre, in northern Palestine. But the eventual failure of the Crusades drove them out of the area altogether and in 1308 they moved to Rhodes. The Knights' rule in Rhodes was a match made in heaven and both the city and the Knights prospered. After establishing themselves in Rhodes, the Knights even extended their power over the neighbouring islands and, for a considerable time, over Smyrna in present-day Turkey. According to my rationalistic husband, the Knights' ventures were nothing but successful real estate developments. They built fortresses and with their military skill protected the townsfolk who sought refuge in their fort from the endemic piracy of the time.

Eventually, the land within the fortified walls was sold to rich merchants and taxes were collected, making the Knights richer than most kings of the time.

Despite being under the direct authority of the Pope, the Order was a surprisingly democratic organisation, where members had the power to elect their leaders. The number of knights at any time was around 600. They all had to come from decent noble families and were expected to make monetary contributions to the Order. Families were carefully scrutinised before members were accepted into the Order. Once in, the noble men could serve for life or could elect to spend a couple of years with the Knights. The Order divided itself into three groups: the Military Knights of Justice, the Chaplains and the Serving Brothers. The first was devoted to military duties, the second to religious services and the third group's responsibility was to care for the sick. However, they were all well rehearsed in military practice and at times of need they all ran to the walls to defend their faith.

The members of the Order were also divided into seven national and linguistic groups, called "Tongues": Provence, Auvergne, France, Italy, England, Germany and Spain, which was itself later divided into Aragon and Castille. Each Tongue had its own inn and was ruled by a bailiff and a council. Supreme command was exercised by the Grand Master for life, and he was assisted in his tasks by a council of the bailiffs representing each Tongue. The council had legislative and disciplinary powers. The official language for all the Order's documents was Latin, while French was spoken between members of different Tongues. Over the centuries, the Knights' militaristic flair faded away into irrelevance, but their legacy as hospitaliers, is continued by the St John's Ambulance services around the world.

The luxury yacht harbour was in a gorgeous location under the awesome wall of the fortress, and as the setting sun coloured the mighty walls surrounding the harbour first gold then red, we went for a long walk along the fortifications and moats, visited the turrets and slowly, without noticing, entered medieval Rhodes.

The Street of the Knights, Rhodes

By this time it was late, the twilight had turned to deep grey, and most people were leaving the dark, narrow, and winding medieval city streets of the Castle. We walked though a gate with a huge arch disappearing up into the dark sky. Behind the gate, a different world awaited us. On our aimless wandering, we came across a large square decorated with a richly carved fountain encircled by grand buildings.

The shadows of the people hurrying across the square reminded me of the shadow theatre my grandmother used to play on the walls of our cosy bedroom during cold, dark winter evenings when to our amazement shadows of hopping rabbits, flying birds and crawling snakes appeared on the white wall.

Here, something drew us irresistibly towards the narrow streets as we walked deeper and deeper into a medieval world, with our footsteps echoing between the surrounding stone walls. I realised everything was made from stone. No bricks in the walls or roofs, no wood for window and door frames. The buildings themselves lacked any decoration, but the stone frames were richly ornate, with garlands carved from limestone and marble. Here and there, the square was lit with faint yellowish candelabras, giving the impression that they

150

were not electric lights but yellow candles. As we walked further into medieval Rhodes, there were fewer and fewer people, and after passing through a second splendidly decorated gate, we were suddenly alone.

There in front of us was a long, faintly lit street leading into the starry sky. We were mesmerised by this sight and without much hesitation turned into the street. On the left-hand side, there was a long sombre, building with black holes spaced regularly along its facade. They must have been windows at another time, but by night, they looked like the mouths of clowns in an amusement park. This derelict building could have been a community building, prison or a hospital, I thought. I picked up my pace, crossed the narrow street and joined Steve walking on the opposite side.

This side was different: it was more inviting, with one attractive building following another. I felt like knocking on those huge doors to enter uninvited into a party. We passed beautiful houses of up to four stories in height. They formed a hedge along the street, broken only by strangely shaped windows and wide, solid wooden gates. The gates were decorated with carved wood and framed by detailed friezes. Every gate was different and bore Italian, French or Spanish coats of arms and extravagant carvings.

No lights came out from any of the houses, so my aspiration to be invited to a medieval party was quickly squashed. It was quiet. No noise from the 21st century penetrated this silent world. Other than the fluttering of the fine silk flags that adorned the gates, nothing moved. At the far end of the street, I could make out the contours of a large building.

It was almost pitch dark: only the moon shone on the cobblestones, creating a haunted atmosphere. The street was a 500 m-long slope with no alleys crossing it except one almost at the top. I was scared, just a little, which was not totally unreasonable in the eerie darkness. Light gives a false sense of security to humans. This sense of security is an atavism of the cave man in all of us. When darkness fell, scared humans used to gather around the fire, keeping wild animals away. Fire or seeing the light of flames meant company, home and security.

But we are also nasty creatures, and to calm myself, I quickly remembered the story of a man who was lost in the forest. Scared of the night noises, the squeaking trees and the sounds of nocturnal animals moving confidently around him, he was relieved to see a faint light in the distance. He sighed with relief and walked towards the flame, only to find himself at the secret hiding place of a bunch of bandits who duly robbed and beat him. He was happy to escape with his life and the shirt on his back.

I considered the outcome of that last story and bravely continued my walk along the dark street that did not seem to have any connection to the modern world. Suddenly, I heard some rattling noises from behind one of the gates. I became excited and imagined the clattering of armour, the trotting sounds of horses and marching of soldiers. I quickened my pace but was disappointed to see some cats playing with a can at the top of the street. We walked through the narrow alleys for another half an hour or so, without meeting a single soul. By this time I had embraced this medieval existence, its silence and darkness. We felt completely lost both in time and space and it was some relief when an old lady with a curved back crossed the cobbled street. There were some humans around after all!

After a while, we reached what must have been the outside wall and heard and saw the noises and lights of the modern city. We knew that this walk in the enchanted castle was a once-in-a-lifetime experience in our overcrowded world. The next day we learnt that it was no wonder we'd thought we were back in medieval Rhodes, as we had walked through the only completely intact medieval street in Europe. In this mystical place, the Street of Seven Tongues of the Knights of St John, everything was authentic. The derelict building was the hospital, the gorgeous houses were the Knights' inns, and the large building at the top of the street was the Grand Master's palace, infamously but tastefully restored by Mussolini. We visited the street once again in daylight and found ourselves fighting for photo opportunities with other tourists in front of the beautifully restored buildings that today serve as the French and Italian consulates.

The origins of Rhodes reach back to a beautiful ancient myth, which was first told by Homer and passed on by Pindar.

It goes like this: Zeus defeated the Giants and became master of the Earth. After this victory he felt satisfied and generous. To celebrate his victory, he decided to divide his newly acquired treasure among the Gods of Mount Olympus. Somehow Helios, the radiant god, missed out. Helios was very popular as he was not only handsome but also drove the chariot of the sun across the sky each day, bringing light and warmth to humanity. Homer described Helios' chariot as drawn by solar bulls. Was he driving the first solar-powered vehicle?

So, when this popular god complained to Zeus about the injustice done to him, the Father of the Gods suggested he would repeat the draw again. Helios was mortified by the thought of bringing the fury of the other powerful gods onto him! Instead, the wise Helios asked Zeus for the first land which was to rise out of the sea.

As they spoke, something slowly emerged from the bottom of the blue water, glowing with myriad colours due to the flowers covering its fertile surface. It was Rhodes, which had lain hidden beneath the sea. Beaming with happiness, Helios bathed the island with his own radiance and made it the most beautiful and fertile land in the Aegean Sea.

The officials of the luxury quay became impatient with us occupying a prime location and since there was no hope for us to continue to enjoy the hospitality of Helios, after two days we left behind the mysteries of the city of Rhodes. We were sad to leave, as we had just started to get used to the adoring crowds who strolled on the quay every night looking at the impressive, shiny yachts of all kinds. Our little yacht almost disappeared between them, but we did our best and reluctantly shined the steel, washed the deck and placed our best doormat on the passarell to "look the part". I was wondering what the strolling folks thought of our little home proudly sporting its colours. After filling our batteries with electricity, our tank with fresh water and stocking up on what we thought would be enough bottled drinking water, beer, orange juice and wine for the rest of the holiday, we slipped our lines and waved good bye to the crews of the neighbouring yachts.

During our stay, we had been hearing tales about an unfinished marina south of the city of Rhodes. The story of a marina, located somewhere in the unknown, sounded like the tale of Atlantis. Its existence was surrounded by as much mystery as its location. But never say never! Indeed, after a short sail we found a grand entrance surrounded by a huge wave breaker. We entered a bizarre, vast, blue lake-like structure. Someone had built the basic infrastructure, but obviously fleeing from a natural disaster they had interrupted the works in a hurry without laying a single brick. In this waste-land donkeys were grazing along the half-finished quay, a small stone-crushing factory had set up business, some old boats were rotting on the shore, and that was it. The sun was beating down mercilessly, and even if we somehow tied the boat up to an abandoned concrete slab, the only way out was via a rubbish tip. This was not an ideal location for a holiday, particularly as we were expecting a visitor who was going to spend the best holiday on *Fenix*!

I sat down and started to study the charts. It soon became obvious that, beautiful as it might have been, there were simply no friendly anchorages on the island. Its shores were battered by the wind and sea all year round. I found only two other possible anchorages on the whole island.

These were Lindos, a promising little town that appeared to have two natural bays providing shelter from the southerly winds, and the small island group of Nisos Khalki to the north-west. Hugging the shore, we set out for Lindos.

We had a dream sail: the water was blue and warm and when the wind dropped in the early afternoon we stopped for a swim – one after the other! We have a rule that regardless of how still the sea looks and how becalmed we are, one person always stays on the boat. Once you have heard stories of people washed away from their boats, it is actually quite easy to obey this rule.

In 2007, a lifetime adventure for two brothers and their friend came to a sad, bizarre end in the Coral Sea, east of the Australian coast. Like most West Australians, they were experienced sailors (in 1990 one million West Australians owned 60,000 boats), so, confident in their skills, they purchased a catamaran in Brisbane to sail it back through the Torres Strait to their home town of Perth. After *Kaz II* missed its radio-sked for several days, a search operation started. The fate of the men captured headlines around the world after their abandoned craft was found 160 km off Townsville, with the radio on, shorts folded on the deck, coffee in the pot, food laid out on the table and the engine running.

> "With the life-craft and life jackets still stowed, police could find no sign of panic or struggle and believe the torn jib sail – the only sign of damage – probably occurred after the men vanished.
>
> The men were last seen alive 10 days ago when they left Airlie Beach bound for Western Australia. After studying on-board computers and navigational equipment,

Visiting Lindos

police believe the men were somehow thrown from the yacht on the first day of their journey." (The Australian 2007).

Everything was in perfect order on the empty yacht. Speculation was rampant. People talked about battles with drug smugglers, pirates, escaping marriages, secret lovers, etc. For three days, the Volunteer Coast Guard searched from dawn to dusk. Then the search was suspended. The family could not accept the disappearance of their loved ones and hired a plane to search for them on the nearby islands, mangroves, and reefs, anything sticking out of the endless blue water, but to no avail. Then the time came when they had to accept the most likely scenario that, becalmed, the three decided to go for a quick swim before breakfast, not realising that the strong current or a sudden fresh wind could blow their yacht away with them having no chance of ever catching it. It is really surprising that one cannot keep up with a boat moving at barely two knots.

Overseas, the speculation continued as to how sharks had attacked and finished the naked swimmers, but I think they just had a very sad end of simply drowning without any flotation device. That's why I'm always tied to the boat when it's not anchored. I usually carry a long rope that is tied to the push-pit.

We arrived at Lindos in the late afternoon and, after some tricky manoeuvring, entered the anchorage. It was a picture-perfect site and there were only two boats in the whole bay: a real treat in the crowded waters of the Mediterranean. We were going to stay for a week, and anchored in the far side of the bay. Steve checked the anchor while snorkelling as the small bay was surrounded by steep hills and was famous for developing mini-storms of its own. The wind can accelerate down the steep shoulders of the hills, violently moving the yachts and their human cargo down below. There was a makeshift jetty on the left side of the entrance and a small beach next to it. Otherwise, one could only see scattered houses and a glimpse of the Acropolis at the top of the mountain.

The guidebook promised a gorgeous little town. It has been declared a European monument for preservation, and so it has avoided the uncontrolled growth of tourist hotels. Steve went to shore to hire a car, which we needed to pick up my friend who would arrive the next morning, and I enthusiastically started getting the boat ship-shape for her arrival, all the while enjoying the perfect Mediterranean scenery with hidden treasures waiting for me on shore.

In half an hour Steve was back, smiling from ear to ear. He declared that the town was the most exciting and beautiful place we had ever been. He simply could not wait to show it to me, so I dropped my sponge, washed myself and

Relief of a Rhodian trireme (warship)

off we went to discover Lindos. The houses were snow white, the narrow streets covered with ivy to protect the pedestrians from the burning sun and bars served mojitos, my favourite cocktail, on every corner. There was a beautiful bell tower with 10 little bells, churches, shops, cafés and restaurants. And to top it all off, the streets were covered with gorgeous patterns of white and black pebbles that later turned out to be small pieces of mable.

All the houses were white and sparkling clean. Most of them were of medieval origin, and thanks to the city fathers' wisdom, the new buildings melted seamlessly into their environment. These little architectural wonders combined the ultra-modern with the traditional Lindian style. Only pedestrians were allowed, so there were no traffic jams or car fumes!

Lindos is probably the oldest town on Rhodes. It has around 1,000 inhabitants, but every day it sees an influx of visitors many times that number who come to admire the village and its aqua-blue seas. In addition to gorgeous architecture, Lindos has been famous for its ship-building industry and its sculptors. Homer's *Iliad* tells us that Lindos was founded somewhere around the 11th century BC. Lindos was the most formidable city on the island at the and the ships sent to the Trojan War from Rhodes all departed from Lindos.

The impregnable Acropolis was built as early as 700 BC. The city reached the height of its fame in the reign of Cleoboulos, who ruled for more than 40 years. He came up with the idea that public works could be financed by collection from the citizens. There was a tradition that the children of the city went from door to door singing songs written by Cleoboulos himself. Who would dare not to express his appreciation for the ruler's songs by donating some money to the cheerful singers? They raised money from door-to-door collections and, credit to Cleoboulos, the money was used to build the temple of Athena in around 550 BC.

During the Hellenistic period, it was the custom for rich visitors to the sanctuary to dedicate statues to Athena. Despite the number of statues that once stood here, very few were found during archaeological digs. Cassius, one of the murderers of Julius Caesar, was partly responsible for this, as he ordered the fine Lindian statues to be sent to Rome.

On the first level of the Acropolis, there is a magnificent ship relief from 170 BC. The Lindians of the time decided to honour Hagesandros, one of their sea captains, by carving a trihemiolia into the rock. The stern of his ship served as a base for his bronze statue. At the bottom of the relief is a worn inscription: "I the city of Lindos awarded Hagesandros a gold wreath."

The ancient people of Lindos were also known for their beautiful sculptures. The area was not rich in stone suitable for sculpting, but artistic Lindians did not let this minor hindrance limit their self-expression, and became masters in producing bronze statues. And what statues they were! Think nothing less than the statue of the Colossus of Rhodes! Lindian artists have been creating the most impressive bronze statues for centuries and their artistic talent carries on even today. The internal architecture of modern Lindian houses is also outstanding and the quality of the decoration is exceptional.

It was here in Lindos that the first maritime laws were developed and an inscription by Antonius (200 AD) confirms the Lindian origin of Roman maritime laws beyond any doubt:

"I am the master of the world, but law is the master of the sea. Let this issue be judged according to the maritime law of the Rhodians in matters where no law of ours states to the contrary."

Today, Lindos has gracefully resigned itself to the fact that its future is in tourism and provides its visitors with the distinctive experience of small-town life. The town's residents prosper from the short tourist season, which is becoming longer and longer as people seek to avoid the summer peak season. Tourists are treated like kings! Serving customers of a roof is not easy. Regardless, all restaurants had some sort of contraption on top of the flat roofs providing shade. From these prime locations, on one side the visitors can admire the Acropolis, the little bay where St Paul landed to spread the faith of Christianity, and the "large" bay facing east with the patiently floating yachts awaiting the return of their owners. On the other side, there are views of the wide inland plains of Rhodes or the magnificent indigo-blue Mediterranean Sea stretching out towards the shores of Africa.

In the multi-storey buildings, the levels are connected with nothing more than ladders. Customers are warned that only the fittest should climb to the highest level. The view is worth the entire climb, but the real stars of the show are the waiters. They carry trays full of beer mugs, wine glasses, and plates with magnificent Mediterranean dishes from the ground-floor bar and the kitchen in the basement up the ladders to the top of the building. They were like mountain goats on bare rocky cliffs, except that in addition to propelling their own body they also balanced a huge tray in their hands. Their movements were gracious and their legs never seemed to tremble. Their brown calf muscles were those of stallions and their smiles matched the smile of Helios. In Australia, this effort would be simply inconceivable for any hospitality industry worker and would be instantly banned by health and safety officers. Let's hope that the EU safety officers never go on holiday to Lindos and that this great attraction of sheer human strength and agility will remain on display for years to come.

Turkey

We had a big argument with Steve about entering into an Islamic country, as anti-Western sentiment appeared to be increasing there after the Iraq War. As a closet feminist, I find it appalling how women are treated in many Islamic countries. I am also very self-conscious around Muslim men, particularly after the comments of Australia's Chief Mufti during his Ramadan address:

> "In a clear reference to the notorious Sydney gang rapists, Sheik Hilali said in the sermon: 'It is she who takes off her clothes, shortens them, flirts, puts on make-up and powder and takes to the streets, God protect us, dallying.'
>
> 'It's she who shortens, raises and lowers. Then it's a look, then a smile, then a conversation, a greeting, then a conversation, then a date, then a meeting, then a crime, then Long Bay Jail,' he tells his worshippers with a chuckle.
>
> 'Then you get a judge, who has no mercy and he gives you 65 years.
>
> But when it comes to this disaster, who started it?'
>
> In his literature, scholar Al-Rafihi says: 'If I came across a rape crime – kidnap and violation of honour – I would discipline the man and order that the woman be arrested and jailed for life.' 'Why would you do this, Rafihi?' He says because if she had not left the meat uncovered, the cat wouldn't have snatched it." (The Australian 2006).

After I read this, I only could ask: "Is he for real?" Do all Muslim men think like this? Is it the result of living in an isolated community where a couple of old conservative men hold the position of community leaders? In other words, what does a modern Muslim country look like?

So, reluctantly but excited by the promise of visiting cities like Ephesus and Pergamum in a region so famously colonised by the Ionians in 1050 BC, we decided our next destination would be Turkey. To be honest, we also had more mundane reasons. Due to the lack of a marina on Rhodes, we badly needed a good night's sleep without rolling and watching out for anchor drag, our batteries had to be recharged and we were desperately low on water. Tales of wonderful Turkish boat services like chandleries, carpenters, Inox (stainless steel) workshops, upholsterers and electrical and electronic workshops had travelled as far as Australia: these made Turkey an irresistible destination to my husband. In summary, like it or not, I really had no choice but to visit Turkey. So we made the short sail to Bodrum across the narrow strait with anticipation and our arrival in Asia Minor did not disappoint.

Bodrum was our port of entrance to Turkey, and immediately after arrival, the courteous marina staff strongly encouraged us to take care of the paperwork first. While the Greeks have been struggling to build a single marina for the last 15 years, the Turkish coast is serviced by a large number of modern first-class marinas. As a matter of fact, they are the cleanest, best-serviced marinas in the whole Mediterranean. Having sailed on the Mediterranean for more than 10 years, and given my reluctance to enter Turkey, this really is saying something. The attendants were well trained and polite and the facilities were absolutely first-class: always functional and spotless showers; access to water, electricity, and wireless Internet (very expensive but reliable); a laundry service and separate rooms to wash your dishes and clothes; restaurants, supermarkets, car and motorbike rental services; and in some cases even swimming pools. The marina attendants were always courteous, friendly, efficient, kind, and never too busy to help customers. We did not have any of the frustrations so frequently encountered in Greece of looking for non-existent marinas or dealing with over-worked, grumpy marina staff. In summary, the facilities in all the Turkish marinas we visited were absolutely magnificent.

Obviously, Turkey has made significant inroads into attracting tourists away from the traditional Greek destinations. They have not only built hotels and marinas, but have also excavated and carefully restored some of the most magnificent Ancient Greek and Roman sites to the absolute delight of visitors.

However, the most ingenious innovation of the Turkish tourism industry was the gulet. Gulets are wide-bodied wooden boats with two masts, traditional cutter rigging and plenty of space for entertainment. The revival of the boat-building industry has not only provided employment for tens of thousands of impoverished Turks during the winter season in fixing and building this particularly labour-intensive boat type, but has also created a thriving tourist industry. The gulets are reminiscent of the Ottoman era of luxury and indulgence. Huge, soft cushions all over the cockpit ensure a wonderfully comfortable trip. The boat's wide body can hold the water toys of the 21st century and provide up to six comfortable cabins. The crew of four to six provide luxurious service and entertainment. Barbequed and seafood dinners, sumptuous breakfasts with plenty of fruits and light lunches await passengers every day. The meals are prepared while the customers swim carefree in one of the turquoise bays or visit an enchanting destination on shore. There are thousands of gulets of all shapes and sizes sailing around Bodrum. Most of the time, the crew cannot bother with handling the sails so they just motor under a small main sail, but we were lucky enough to see a couple of gulets with all their sails up on a few occasions. They looked magnificent! They were flying across the water with such a graceful elegance. Unfortunately, we missed the regatta in Bodrum. At the end of the tourist season, the Bodrum Cup for wooden gulets is contested by a huge number of vessels and their enthusiastic crews. With all their sails, two masts and cutter rigging, they are hard to handle and they could certainly not match the fast modern boats of the America's Cup, but they are spectacular!

Who are the Turks?

Where did they come from? Can they really be the bridge between East and West, not only in geographical terms but also culturally and philosophically?

For most Europeans, the name "Turks" brought fear into their hearts for centuries. Even today, Europeans find themselves uncomfortably torn between their liberal, tolerant agenda and their suspiciousness of the difference they see in the Turkish people. The Turks, a collection of enterprising tribes from Central Asia, founded the Ottoman Empire that ruled Asia Minor and the Middle East with ambitions to expand into Europe from the 15th century until World War I. Modern-day Turkey, officially known as the Republic of Turkey, is a Eurasian country that stretches across the Anatolian Peninsula in Western Asia and the Balkan region of south-eastern Europe. The largest city is Istanbul, which is stubbornly called Constantinople in Greece. The city famously lies on two continents, Europe and Asia, and is separated by the narrow Bosporus channel. The most vivid description of the place comes from the famous adventure story of Jules Verne, *Around the World in Eighty Days* .

Turkish gulet

In 700 AD, there were two groups of Turks living in Central Asia: the Western Turks, who lived in and around what is now Kazakhstan and Turkestan, and the Celestial Turks, who lived in Central and Western Mongolia, to the south of Lake Baikal. They were probably called "Celestial" because of their piercing blue eyes. It was certainly not because they were virtuous and high minded, for the region was harsh and their lives were arduous and rarely at a level much above that of bare subsistence. Nomadic, preliterate, and contentious, the various Turkish clans began a westward migration around 750 AD, for reasons that are still debated, but that are likely connected to two long famines recorded in China in 720 AD (three years) and 730 AD (two years), and the subsequent pressure of other, more northern, tribes moving down into their territory. The westward migration of the Turkish tribes was at first not an organised march in a vast body, such as the migration of the Huns and Magyars (my ancestors), which took place around the same time. Rather, for the most part a small group of clans wandered beyond their traditional territory into new places where they could feed their animals (mainly camels, sheep, and goats) without too much competition, holding this new territory as their own, and then moving westward again.

Once a significant presence had been established in Asia Minor, the trickle became a flood and the Turks took over Persia, expanded further westward into the Byzantine Empire and occupied Constantinople. As the Turks travelled into southern Russia and northern Persia, large numbers of their clans converted to Islam, so that by the time they reached Anatolia, most of them were Muslims. They maintained the ties reaching all the way back to Mongolia, which helped many Turkish merchants to build wealth for what would become the Ottoman Empire. From the 10th century on, Turks controlled a number of crucial trade routes, most particularly the western end of the Silk Road, the ancient trade route

The evolution of modern Turkey

0   500miles

- ■ 14th Century: After foundation
- ■ 17th Century: At its peak
- ■ 1922-present: Modern Turkey

between China and the Mediterranean, and through that mercantile hegemony, the Ottoman Empire financed the first stages of its major expansion.

By the end of the 13th century, the Bithynian king, a Seliuk Turk named Osman al-Ghazi, a very capable leader with great ambitions, blue-eyed and therefore considered fortunate, founded his empire at Osmanli, the name from which Ottoman is derived. Expansionism remained the cornerstone of the Ottoman Empire for the 700 years up to its collapse during WWI.

The Confrontation

The Turks were a willing interface between Mediterranean merchants and traders of the Far East through Black Sea ports, and they profited from customs and transference fees. They also began a tradition of price-fixing and pilferage and touched all the commerce in which they participated. They were very successful corsairs (state-sanctioned and financed pirates) and were skilful in privateering (privately funded piracy), hoarding the wealth of Western merchants for the Sultan from vessels carrying goods around the Mediterranean Sea. One should not think that this activity was frowned upon as much as is the case today. As a matter of fact, the Venetians, the Genoese, the English, the French and even the holy Knights of Rhodes were expert corsairs. The most famous corsair of all time, Captain Drake, was even knighted for his services by the Queen of England, Elizabeth I.

The confrontation was most intense in Asia Minor, along the shores of the Eastern Mediterranean and the Black Sea, which had been populated by the Greeks since 800 BC. Around 100 BC, the Hellenistic territory was slowly taken over by the Roman Empire. The Romans seamlessly took over the wonderful Greek scientific artistic and governance traditions. The Roman Empire became Christian under Constantine, who founded Constantinople. With the break-up of the Roman Empire, Constantinople became the capital of the Eastern Roman (or Byzantine) Empire. It carried on the Greek traditions and became the bastion of Christianity for another thousand years. Thus the fall of Christian Constantinople in 1453 to the Turks was a terrible defeat for Christianity. The Turks continued their winning streak for another 300 years and slowly took over all the Greek islands, the Balkans and Central Europe, and even attacked Vienna, the capital of the Habsburg Empire, which came under siege twice, in 1529 and 1681.

One of the famous battles that in many ways came to define the future and character of the Knights of St John, or the Knights of Rhodes, was fought between Christians and Turks in Rhodes, at the very castle where we experienced that memorable enchanted walk. In 1522, at the beginning of summer, the Turkish fleet of 400 battleships descended on Rhodes. The Grand Master realised that the Order's fleet was hopelessly outnumbered and withdrew his fleet without a fight to the harbour. Having seen the Turkish fleet, the Rhodians dragged huge chains across the harbour more or less at the location where the Colossus supposedly stood a thousand years earlier. In return, the Turks blockaded the harbour. The Turkish fleet not only had galleys or battleships, equipped with fierce cannons, but was capable of delivering tens of thousands of troops in their carracks. Some reckon troop numbers deployed on Rhodes reached 120,000. This number is disputed by historians, pointing out only 40,000 troops were summoned for the attack on Vienna. However, Vienna was a faraway place, accessible only by long marches on land, while Rhodes was a couple of hours' sail from the Ottoman harbours.

I could not find any data on the capabilities of the Ottoman battleships, but I found that the *Mary Rose*, built in Portsmouth, England, between 1509 and 1510, could carry around 400 people. So, at least in theory, it would not have been a problem to deposit all those fighters on the island. Why would the Turks put so much effort into taking a relatively unimportant island? Maybe the Ottoman generals just wanted to exercise their troops?

The knights and inhabitants of the island courageously defended their island. As usual, Christian Europe promised help that never materialised. The defenders, who numbered around 4,000 under the leadership of the Grand Master Villiers de Isle Adam, fought a fierce siege and repelled continuous attacks for six months. However, in the end, the Christians were defeated, and on 29 December 1522 the city was forced to surrender. The story of the siege of Rhodes reminded me one of my favourite books of my early teenage years, *Eclipse of the Crescent Moon*, by Geza Gardonyi. It is about the siege of Eger and how a handful of Hungarians resisted a Turkish force more than 20 times their size, forcing it to retreat in disgrace. It is an exciting tale of chivalry, romance, love, treachery, bravery, adventures, heroes and villains, and has descriptions of gory battle scenes that would have been played out on all battlefields of the time, like in Rhodes in 1522.

"'Bismillah!' (In the name of God!)

The Turkish cannon and rifles thundered out together. The walls of the fortress trembled and the ramparts cracked apart from the countless cannon-balls that burst on them. Arrows and rifle-bullets rained down on the palisades protecting the bastions. The air became filled with the stench of gunpowder. And mingled with the Earth-shattering thunder came the clamour of drums, bugles and trumpets and the screams of 'Allah!' from a hundred thousand Turks.

The asabs, janissaries, delis, djebedjis and all kinds of Turkish infantry leapt out of the trenches like a swarm of locusts as the smoke from the rifles billowed up in clouds above them.

A forest of siege-ladders floated towards the wrecked walls and bastions, and behind them a hail of arrows whistled in a high curve onto the walls. And on all sides the Turkish military bands struck up.

But a reply came hurtling down from above too. The cannon, aimed downwards, spewed out flame, iron, lead and fragments of glass where the Turks were massed most closely. Hundreds were covered in blood and wavered and fell. But at the same moment hundreds pressed forward over the fallen.,

The stench of sulphur spread inside the fortress too in swirling clouds. The iron hooks of the Turkish siege-ladders crashed into the stone, iron, and beams of the walls, and the mob rose up them almost at a run, shield over their heads a barbed lance in one hand and a dagger held horizontally in their mouths.

Twenty-seven red Turkish banners wove and fluttered, leading the army up the ladders over the ruins behind the palaces.

'Allah akbar! La illa il Allah! Ya kerim! Ya rahim! Ya fetih!' raged the ceaseless cry.

'To the walls! To the walls!' came the cries from up above.

And the walls filled with defenders. Only now did the rain of bombs begin. They were simply thrown by hand: first they spluttered, then they burst into flame and finally they exploded down below. A thousand rumbling, crackling sparks of lightening rained down. Shouts, cries, smoke, explosions, the smell of sulphur, hell. Axes, machetes and cleavers clanged on the grappling-irons of the ladders. Some ladders had twenty men on them when they fell.

'Allah! Ya kerim!'

They crashed down on each other and cut a path through the swarm of men below.

But a minute later their places were taken by a new wave of armed attackers, and a new host of ladders rose beside those that have fallen. 'Allah! Allah akbar! Allah !'

"The siege-ladders are now slippery with blood. And the wall round the tops of them is purple-coloured. Down below there are bloodstained, twitching heaps of dead and dying. But there too ever more regiments of fresh troops press on over the dead, leaping and yelling. Bugles sound, drums roll, military bands bray, and the unceasing shouts of, 'Allah!' , mingle with the battle cries from above, the shouted orders of the yasavuls on horseback down below, the roar of cannon, the crack of rifles, exploding bombs, whinnying of horses, groans of the dying and the creaking and snapping of ladders.

'Come on pasha, come on! Puff!'

Towards noon the battle slowly dies down in other places too. The smoke disperses. The sunshine breaks through. Beneath the walls lie thousands of dead and wounded Turks, blackened and bloodstained. The air is intoxicated with the cries of the wounded. They sound like bleating sheep. The yasavuls have lost their authority; that day they cannot compel the men to continue the attack.

But the square inside the fortress is also full of standing, sitting and lying wounded men covered in blood. All the barbers and women are there, carrying bowls of water, linen, bandages, alum and arnica among the wounded. Some of them groan, others sway and grind their teeth. And they are still bringing men out of the ruins of the tower, some in handcarts, others in blankets."

The bravery of the defenders of Rhodes earned the admiration of Suleiman the Magnificent. Grand Master Villiers de Isle Adam and his remaining Knights were not only allowed to leave Rhodes unmolested, but were also given a ceremonial guard of honour to see them off the island in their own galleys. The Order was defeated but not dishonoured. The immediate problem was to find a new home. Temporarily, they moved into the Covent of Syracuse and then were finally given the islands of Malta and Gozo by the Spanish King Charles V. The Knights of Rhodes became the Knights of Malta and continued their tradition of praying, defending Christian values, tending the sick and hospitality. As for the Turks, they continued their relentless expansion over Europe, sometimes allied with some Christian states against others. I was surprised to learn that the French were Ottoman allies for most of the 16th and 17th centuries. Ottoman rule might have been seen as a disaster in most of European countries, but in Turkey, it was promoted as *Pax Turcica* (Turkish Peace) bringing peace and tolerance among the quarrelling Europeans. A plaque above the entrance of the Bodrum Castle was a memento of this point of view.

Pax Turcica

Modern Turkey

After the final defeat of the Ottoman Empire in World War I, a young general, Mustafa Kemal Ataturk, tricked the supervising powers of the Amritsar and instead of disarming his troops initiated a successful uprising. The Turkish troops defeated the occupying Greeks forces, leading to the renegotiation of the borders of Turkey and the formation of the Republic of Turkey. The result was one of the largest exoduses of people in Europe. All Greeks were expelled from Turkey and all Turks from Greece. The scars of these events are still present even today, even a century later.

Ataturk, who subsequently became the first president of the Republic of Turkey, laid the foundations of a modern state. He had not only the vision but also the political will and skill to force his feudal nation to make a leap into the 20th century. He launched a programme of revolutionary social and political reforms to modernise Turkey. These reforms included the emancipation of women, the abolition of all Islamic institutions and the introduction of Western legal codes, dress, calendar and alphabet, replacing the Arabic script with a Latin one. Abroad, he pursued a policy of neutrality, establishing friendly relations with Turkey's neighbours. One of the famous new laws was the abolition of the fez, the traditional Turkish cap, and banning the wearing of the hijab, the Muslim headscarf, in government institutions. Events of 2007 and 2008 proved that his foresight to firmly and irreversibly lock Turkey into a modern secular state was essential and invaluable for the country that, unknown to him, was going to face an Islamic renewal in the early 21st century.

Bodrum was a great place, and as far as shopping was concerned perhaps the best in the whole of Greece and Turkey. The bazaar, however, was not as colourful as I imagined. Today, it mainly serves tourists, but in the dark alleyways, the locals continued to go about their business of fixing their computers, and buying their vegetables, furniture, bed linen, and modest outfits. There was an endless variety of T-shirts, shorts, jewellery, and designer clothes and the biggest collection of shoes and leather goods I'd ever seen. They advertise the selling of "original fakes"! That's really something.

No matter the price you are willing to pay, you can find copies of Prada, Gucci, Pucci, Fendi, Pierre Cardin and Chanel bags, Oakley and Ray Ban sunglasses and the polo shirt brands from around the world. I guess they manufacture all of these items for the designer brands, so it may not be such a big deal to run the machines for an extra couple of hours after the factory has closed. The shops selling the fakes live together in harmony with those selling the original items for 10 times more. And believe me, there are shoppers for both products! Some people see the difference between the fake and original items and they are ready to pay the extraordinary prices to have the latest fashion. Whatever they do, the copies are always at least a season behind and that does not satisfy the fashionistas. Perhaps this competition helps to maintain innovation and creativity in the leading fashion houses. To make money, they always have to be a step ahead of the fakes.

We visited the Underwater Museum in the castle that dominates the Bodrum skyline. It was underwater in the sense that all the items exhibited were recovered from the bottom of the Mediterranean. Anchors from Greek and Roman times, sunken ships, pottery, china, coins, carafes, and amphorae used for carrying olive oil, grain and wine. From the high walls of the castle, I could observe the heroic efforts of the water planes as they scooped up water from just below the castle, to climb above us within seconds and drop their load on a nearby fire threatening Bodrum.

In the evenings, we wandered into one of the myriad of cafés bordering the calm, balmy sea and tried nargileh, the national pastime of Middle Eastern people. Nargileh is a tobacco pipe smoked through water. You can get natural and flavoured tobacco. Horror of horrors, there were green-apple and strawberry-flavoured nargileh on the menu. Although officially no marijuana or hashish is smoked in nargileh, somehow the tobacco is different: perhaps it was mixed with some narcotics.

Although we were delighted with Bodrum, having spent a week in the crowded marina, we were itching to get away. Such is human nature. We skirted the peninsula and anchored in the lee of Catalada, one of two small islands facing Turqutreis. It was beautiful and peaceful. The bay was well protected from the prevailing wind, had crystal-clear water and was great for swimming and snorkelling. During the day, the bays were full of visiting yachts and gulets, but by night there were only two or three boats left rocking in the summer breeze. We spent two blissfully peaceful days swimming, reading, cooking, listening to music and discussing the problems of the world.

Unfortunately, the forecast was bleak, not only for the well-being of the world but also for the weather. After the wind strengthened to 25 knots, with gusts predicted to reach 44 knots, we departed to the nearby marina of D-marine in Turqutreis. I have already talked about the glorious Turkish marinas, but this one in Turqutreis, in addition to having all those greatly appreciated features I mentioned earlier, also had a great shopping precinct, a few good restaurants and a swimming pool in the adjacent yacht club. Marina visitors had free access to the club. One evening, we had a great candlelit dinner by the swimming pool while a trio of young girls played classical music with understanding and technical skill well beyond their age. The evening, with perfectly laid silver tableware, an ironed tablecloth and excellent service, was a great contrast to our everyday sailing lives.

The food was absolutely delicious: my swordfish arrived on a skewer with tomato, lemon, bay leaves and onion, giving it a unique flavour I had never experienced before. Steve had a lamb casserole, which again had exotic flavouring. How they served a casserole with crispy vegetables remains a mystery. We had a bottle of white wine, which was really dry and cold – exactly the way we liked it. So it was one of those nights that you can describe as perfect. Next, we reminded each other how lucky we were and how beautiful life was!

The following morning, after my morning run, I could not resist the call of the Armani shop hiding in a distant corner of the marina. I walked in without any plans or particular urge to buy anything: I only wanted to look. But when I saw the prices, I decided that I simply had to buy a fabulous Armani suit! Original or not, I did not care. So after my jog, I returned to the boat in the unexpected company of an Armani suit. The jacket was a classic white linen and silk combination. The pants hugged the waist tight but around the hips they evolved into a large wavy skirt that danced uninterrupted around the leg. I think these sort of clothes are called trouser-skirts. I was delighted with my purchase. Now, I just have to find an occasion on which to wear it!

We spent the afternoon wandering a round in Turqutreis. And it did not take long for us to come across the carpet sellers' quarter. Turkey has been famous for its carpets for a millennium and carpet shopping anywhere is about more than buying a rug. It is an all-consuming pastime for both the seller and the buyer. The history of carpet weaving goes back to somewhere between 2000 and 1000 BC. The oldest carpet ever found dates back to about 600 BC, and considering its age, it is in a pretty good shape, sporting still bright colours. Virtually, all carpets are woven on a loom, which is simply a horizontal or vertical wooden frame. It is thought that carpet weaving originated in Ancient Mesopotamia, the birthplace of writing and other essentials of civilisation.

There are three types of carpets. The simplest are the flatweaves or kilims woven just like a tapestry. They are also called tribal carpets. Soumaks carpets are like kilims but include a second set of horizontal threads woven into the carpet over the warp threads. They look like brocades. Knotted (pile) carpets are the best known and the most widespread. The knot is created by tying a short thread around the warp thread horizontally across the loom width, creating something like fur with an intricate pattern. The colour of each knot and thread collectively makes up the design of the rug or carpet (Wikipedia 2012).

We learnt about carpets in our other life, in India. It all happened in Kashmir, "God's own country", where beauty surpasses everything human eyes can ever experience in this world. Salman Rushdie has a beautiful description of the valley in his book *Midnight's Children* :

> "The world was new again. After a winter's gestation in its eggshell of ice, the valley had beaked its way out into the open, moist and yellow. The new grass bided its time underground; the mountains were retreating to their hill stations for the warm season. In the winter, when the valley shrank under the ice, the mountains closed in and snarled like angry jaws around the city on the lake."

Being young and knowing nothing about anything, we fell in love with the carpet that covered the living area – grandiosely called "the saloon" – of our houseboat in Kashmir. We asked the owners whether it was for sale.

Their eyes lit up and said: "Of course, for the right price."

Steve, careful as always, went to town, visited a couple of carpet shops and paid one of the owners to come to our houseboat and have a look at the carpet. That afternoon, everyone on the boat was excited. Even the dog on the shore sensed the excitement and was running up and down out of control.

The carpet shop owner arrived on time and we duly showed him into the saloon. He stopped and asked: "So, where is the carpet?"

He was standing on the damn thing!

We knew straight away that it would be a good idea to spend some more time studying the art of rugs before buying anything but a wall-to-wall carpet from a suburban Carpet Call shop. Unfortunately, Kashmir was not to be the place to learn about carpets: things were becoming tricky and we were advised to leave. Not to mention that our 14-month-old son and our aya (nanny) were eagerly waiting for us in the care of some friends in Bangalore. A month after our departure, six tourists were kidnapped and subsequently beheaded, signalling the start of the unrest that continues today. But we duly learnt our lesson and spent that year talking carpets with people and slowly learning the secrets of the trade.

With the knowledge acquired more than quarter of a century ago, we walked into the Ali Baba carpet shop in Turqutreis full of anticipation – and we were not disappointed. Greeted with a warm smile, we made ourselves comfortable on the corner couch. Within minutes, the shop boy arrived with green-apple teas. In spite of consuming quite a bit of this murky liquid, I still have no idea what green-apple tea is. It was a marginally drinkable hot liquid.

The shopkeeper did not ask about our intention or anything else in particular. We started aimlessly chatting about his hometown, our sailing plans and, while talking, two of his assistants picked up the rolled rugs. They threw them up in the air with a single movement. The rugs unrolled in mid-air and, hanging there for an instant, miraculously landed perfectly positioned in front of us. Slowly, a one metre-high pile of carpets was building up before our eyes. Of course, while seamlessly continuing to chat, our eyes were focused on every one of them, yet without showing interest in any one in particular.

To a superficial observer, the whole piece of theatre would make no sense. The shopkeeper effortlessly played the role of a proud collector showing off his collection of new and old carpets. We sat on the couch and played our role as mesmerised visitors to a museum.

When certain carpets appeared, we paused and stories were told. After a while, almost not noticing, he asked the question.

"So, if you were going to buy a carpet, what would you like?"

At this point, the carpet pile was undone, each of them was lifted and their features described and praised. We were invited to make comments that were not more detailed than:

"Yes, we like this. No, we wouldn't take that even if it was free."

By the time we reached the bottom of the pile, there were only 10–15 rugs in front of us.

Now we were into the real business of carpet-buying! First, we immersed ourselves with the owner into the history of each of the rugs presented to us. We discussed their fine colours, and the differences between all those oranges, reds and browns. We carefully examined whether the makers used vegetable or synthetic dyes. Our fingers searched for the right resistance in the millions of knots, the roughness of the wool, the fineness of the silk. We discussed the intricate patterns, their meanings and the thousand of stories they told. On some old carpets, we could smell the camels they had been used to cover. The owner described the tribal homes some carpets might have come from. We admired the freshness and the bright details of the new carpets.

Then, once again we carefully looked at each rug one by one: criticised their colours, or the lack thereof, the liveliness or the dullness of their patterns, the low number of knots, etc. Now we started to talk prices, too. At this point, he knew we were potential customers and we were presented with another supply of green-apple tea, probably spiked with some secret ingredient to loosen our will. After around two hours of quality entertainment, we walked home with a small old kilim rug that was just perfect for our aft cabin!

We finished our day at a local eatery where women were working the dough before our eyes, making excellent gozmele and pida. It was a family business: the mother and some other women were making the dough, the father was baking the gozmele and the young girl, who was a high school student and spoke excellent English, served the customers. Gozmele is like a pizza with minced local cheese, spring onion and dill topping, while the pida is folded up and conceals some spicy minced meat inside. They were wonderful!

We just could not resist "the call of the rugs" and later, after a similar drawn-out bargaining process late into the night, we also purchased a huge, marvellous soumak carpet from the owner of our small pension at Pamukale. This was an extraordinarily beautiful silk rug on cotton that decorated the wall of the carpet shop in the courtyard. I was uncertain how it would fit the furnishings of our modern apartment as the motifs were ancient. It was decorated with original Mesopotamian motifs of the immortal fire-bird, the animals from Noah's Ark, strange human-like figures and some hesitant signs from the first-ever written text on this Earth. To my surprise, these ancient motifs and the bright colours of the silk made this carpet strangely compatible with our modern home.

After returning to Bodrum, we decided to visit one of the famous beach clubs of the region, Bianca Beach Club. The drive started on a freeway that came to a halt after 20 km. From there, we continued our trip on a narrow bitumen road through interesting countryside of mountains and glimpses of the sea. The village that is home to this famous beach club was caught somewhere between a medieval existence and the 21st century. Goats and sheep were happily grazing in the club's car park, where guards in dark sun glasses with walkie-talkies in hand were patrolling the black four-wheel drives. Once we had paid the ridiculous entrance fee, we found ourselves immersed into full Roman decadence. The place was totally luxurious, comparable or better than its St Tropez cousins. There were sofa beds and huge flat beds with baldachins surrounded by white muslin curtains, wide armchairs, chaises longues and luxurious sofas, all snow-white and decorated with colourful cushions. Small tables were scattered everywhere, and on top of them champagne buckets were sweating in the intense heat! Music relentlessly blasted from the loudspeakers playing the latest European hits. Young girls and boys were sipping alcoholic drinks and cocktails or were nibbling on light dishes, chocolates and fruits while half lying down. Their Turkish voices were mixed with all sorts of other languages. The more intellectual ones were playing board games or reading books. It was all just as it might have been for Anthony and Cleopatra thousands of years ago, before they set sail for the fatal Battle of Actium.

Without too much hesitation, I placed myself on one of the comfortable mattresses and begin reading my favourite book. Later, I ordered a grilled paper-thin veal steak served on a bed of rocket salad. No calories whatsoever, but it looked like a meal! I thoroughly enjoyed it and declared it the best meal of the season! We swam, then had a fruit platter in the bar while watching the sunset. The bar continued the decadent spirit of the place and was decorated with white leather couches, white tables and pink crystal chandeliers.

This place was an extraordinary outfit to satisfy human indulgence. It was an eye-opener to see that, when it comes to lifestyle, the rich of the world, whether they are Muslims, atheists, Christians, Jews or Hindus, have much more in common than one would have thought. They enjoy the same hotels and clubs, drive the same cars, eat the same luxurious food and drink the same insanely expensive Cristal champagne in their segregated sanctuaries all over the world. They have more in common with their fellow rich than with the citizens of their country of origin, who remain unknown and totally alien to them. To be honest, I did not think it was a bad experience, but I was definitely disturbed by the view of the collapsing dwellings nearby and by the sight of skinny goats on the nearby fields trying to find some nutrition on the sunburnt fields.

On Politics of the Time

There were elections held in Turkey on 22 July 2007 and the Islamist party of Erdogan won a majority. The American press cheered what it claimed to be democracy in action. For me, it was frightening to think that apparently all democracy could achieve in Muslim countries was to deliver fundamentalist governments.

I wrote these notes during our first visit, and by the time of our second visit a year later, the election of the new president was also complete, again with a profound victory for Islamist parties. The tug-of-war around the selection of an Islamist president continued for a while and later it was confirmed.

Travelling across Turkey, we saw the revival of Islam everywhere. We saw mosques recently renovated or newly built in all the towns and villages we passed through. I could not believe that this huge investment into Islamic infrastructure was simply the result of the generosity of pious people living there. There might have been an Islamic revival in Turkey, but usually people are reluctant to willingly donate large amounts of their hard-earned wages. We were told that coercion was slowly finding its way into Turkish society, where women are now frowned upon if they expose too much flesh or do not wear the hijab, the Islamic headscarf. Workers who do not pray five times a day are looked at with great disappointment. Those who do not observe Ramadan have to hide while eating their meal.

In addition, fueled by anti-USA/Western sentiment, everywhere defiant young women and men were proudly sporting Islamic outfits, thus visibly differentiating themselves from their parents who wore Western-style clothes. Wearing Muslim headscarves has been increasingly common in Turkey over the past two decades.

My initial response was, "Who cares?", but in the light of Ataturk's effort to lift his nation from medieval times into the modern world by means of his enlightened laws and by the removal of the symbols of backwardness, this clear opposition to his banning the fez and the hijab represented an ongoing resistance to the idea of a modern Turkey. Or did it? Couldn't we just say that Turkey is a mature nation where the symbolism of the hijab should not be considered more important than the kilt for the Scots?

Without doubt, the role of Islam in the secular state of Turkey was being increased in a sneaky and ingenious way. The Department of Islamic Affairs, set up by Ataturk, contrary to its original aim of controlling Islam, had lately been used to promote it. It was reported in a Turkish newspaper that in 2008 the Department had a budget that exceeded that of the top 22 Turkish universities combined. The Department financed the building of mosques, setting up of Islamic schools and Koranic courses. The imams, although government employees, were not expected to comply with a code of conduct and they openly preached against women working and promoted the segregation of sexes and conservative Islamic views. It is believed that some financial aid is being provided by conservative overseas organisations for those who choose to wear Islamic outfits. In Turkey I saw a society at war with itself, trying to determine its future.

Then, I suddenly realised that it is not only happening in Turkey. The major fault line in today's world is not between Islam and Christianity, Judaism and Islam, Catholics and Protestants, gays and non-gays, communists and conservatives, racists and non-racists, Hutus and Tutsis, Hindus and Muslims, North and South, environmentalists and industry, but between fundamentalists and liberals. I consider fundamentalist people to be those who do not believe in progress or in the solution of differences through any other means than conquering the opposition or forcefully silencing them. In its traditional interpretation of the word, liberals believe more in progress and in the possibility of finding a compromise even in the most challenging situation. A recent shocking demonstration of how humans can be easily manipulated into otherwise unthinkable actions was the 1990s Balkan Wars. The misery of the people, living in a country that we used to call Yugoslavia, was unleashed by three people and their mistaken views: Slobodan Milosevic, a Serb; Franjo Tudjman, a Croat; and Alija Izetbegovic, a Bosnian. The Balkan Wars destroyed and broke up a flourishing and potentially prosperous country. By 2006, all three of them were dead, but by inflaming religious and ethnic differences they left a legacy of misery and hatred that will not heal for centuries.

The big issue in the 21st century is that while we recognise that, fundamentally, people want the same things (to bring up their children in peace and prosperity and enjoy life, etc) regardless of race, religion or origin, as humans they also need status, moral guidance and identity. How can we deliver this to each and every human being on this Earth?

Some Other Wonders

With eyes wide open, we walked through something we have never seen before: a functional Roman city. "The present site was established by Lysimachos in 300 BC. Almost everything we see is from the Augustan period, 62–14 BC. It was the capital of the Asia Minor Roman provinces ..." – our guide was saying. Ephesus was nothing like the piles of stones sometimes seen at archaeological sites. No, the site was simply magnificent! On both sides, there were large buildings, temples, baths, monuments, statues, palaces, fountains: all sorts of remains of a well-built city. The buildings were well preserved. It was easy to understand their function and admire their beautiful structures and decorations. The site was ingeniously designed. The main roads – Curetes Street, Marble Street, Harbour Street and Stadium Street – ran through the small valley at the bottom of the hills and conveniently gave good access to the theatres and other large public buildings that were carved into the hillsides. Behind the public buildings, an endless number of terrace houses populated the hillsides. All of them had small gardens and views of the magnificent town. As we reached the end of the road, we arrived at a square facing the beautiful building of the famous library of Ephesus. It was built to honour Celsus, the General Governor of the Province of Asia, in 135 AD. The building was several stories high, made from beautifully carved white marble decorated with numerous friezes and statues of Virtue, Justice, Celsus and so on. Niches were carved into the thick marble walls to hold the 12,000 books or rolls. The library housed not only separate rooms for the storage of Greek and Roman texts but also a separate reading room. Even before the erection of this magnificent building, the city of Ephesus was a famous scholastic place. We know that Hippocrates, Pythagoras and many others studied here. The building stands as a testimony to a period that greatly appreciated art, the sciences and philosophy.

We finished this great visit by walking through the truly majestic Marble Street, and visited the 26,000-seat theatre. Because the sun was going down, the site was closing and we reluctantly said goodbye to the line of marble columns and the library gilded by the setting sun. On the next day, fresh from a good night's sleep, we came back to the site to visit the excavated terrace houses. They were under a truly enormous tent, which protected the houses from further damage by the elements. There were small winding streets connecting the houses to each other and to the main roads. Almost all them were from the Augustan period, 62–14 BC. The place gave the impression that for a relatively small investment one could renovate these almost 2,000-year-old houses and move in. We followed the winding, perfectly preserved water and sewage systems as they moved from house to house. The houses were splendidly decorated by frescos depicting Socrates and Hippocrates and the floors were covered with equally magnificent mosaics. Some of the condominiums were huge, reaching 900 m² per flat. There were marble courtyards, water fountains, private temples, baths, and reception rooms. The decorations were very sophisticated but not ostentatious, a characteristic feature of Western Roman buildings. It was fantastic to peek into the life of everyday people who lived so long ago. I was genuinely surprised that their artistic taste, lifestyle, and pleasures were not so different from ours. They enjoyed good meals, comfortable houses, good theatrical performances, warm baths, sports, reading in the library and parties. They participated in governing themselves, were astute traders and loved meeting with people from faraway places: all in all, their activities were very similar to ours.

Earthquakes and raids by the Goths weakened Ephesus, and its end came slowly after the collapse of trade due to the fall of the Temple of Artemis and the silting of the harbour in around 300 AD.

We jumped into our tiny rented car and drove to Pergamum through chaotic traffic. Having passed the busy town of Smyrna, we reached the fertile plains. Our little car struggled to climb the serpentine road leading to the temple – not that surprising as the simmering heat penetrated everything and slowed down man, beast and engine. To our greatest surprise, we came across a hitchhiking girl walking along the road in the blazing sun. She was a university student from Smyrna and had decided to visit some of the ancient sites around her birthplace during the holidays. I admired her courage, as hitchhiking for a girl in the middle of a newly emerging Islamist movement could be dangerous. She was grateful for the lift and we parted at the top of the mountain where in the distance some shining marble pieces signalled the location of Pergamum.

Pergamum was a huge, majestic site presiding over the surrounding countryside. The climb from the car park was hard but it was worth every puff to get there! The fantastic restoration work effortlessly showed the grandiosity of the site. The name of the city, Pergamum, was derived from the Greek word *"purgos"*, meaning tower. Pergamum sat like a citadel towering above the surrounding plains, valleys and hills. The city's water was supplied via an ingenious aqueduct arrangement from the nearby lower, lush, hilly regions. Eumenes, the King of Pergamum, set out to build the greatest library in the world, aiming to surpass the grand library in Alexandria, Egypt. After a while, the Pharaoh, Ptolemy, reportedly jealous of the growing fame of the library in Pergamum, prohibited the export of papyrus from Egypt, thereby hoping to slow down the growth of the rival library. Not to be defeated, King Eumene set out to produce a superior writing material by improving the already long-established use of animal skins. His scientists developed a new refining technique for sheep- or calf-skin, creating the famous Pergamene paper or parchment. This high-quality skin was superior to papyrus as both sides could be written on and the writing could be erased using a pumice stone. Once clean, the page could be reused. Parchment was first used in 300 BC, and by 400 AD, it had replaced papyrus as the preferred writing material all over Europe. The famous Library of Pergamum contained 200,000 books. It is said that the besotted Anthony, the governor of the near-eastern provinces of the Roman Empire, promised all the books of the library to Cleopatra as a very generous wedding gift.

Unfortunately, over the centuries the library was completely destroyed and the location of the dispersed books is unknown. The imposing site of Pergamum fuelled the imagination of collectors for millennia, so much so that the German archaeologists excavating the Temple of Zeus in the 19th century sent the famous Quadriga, a larger-than-life chariot with four horses, to Berlin, where – although vehemently denied – it is believed to be the statute that stands atop the Brandenburg Gate.

After our land trip, we returned to *Fenix* and sailed back along the coast to our destination where *Fenix* would be spending the winter. On a bright day in the middle of August, we tied up the boat for the last time that season in Marti Marina, just north of Marmaris.

Lessons
in History

In spite of an unpleasant welcome by the authorities, I was glad and excited to be back in Cos. I felt liberated that I did not have to worry about offending the famous Islamic sensitivities and at last I could again wear whatever I wanted. We cheerfully rode the newly built cycle path to Stefano's and indulged ourselves in our favourite Greek dishes of stuffed tomatoes, shrimp saganaki, bacon and liver and grilled lamb. I re-started my ritual morning jog and wanted to visit the Knight's Castle, but unfortunately it was closed.

Heraclitus famously said, "You cannot step into the same river twice." How true! The previous year I had been enchanted by Cos and its history. This time it was different. I was simply unable to recreate the same magical place that had revealed itself before my eyes on our walks last year. Then, I envisaged Hippocrates with his pupils, citizens busily drafting the text for political refugees, craftsmen breaking rock up into minuscule pieces' and converting them into artful mosaics, the Knights of Rhodes in their armour around every corner. Perhaps I had changed and became more observant and critical of the shortcomings of the place. This was not my Cos! This was another Cos – Cos the resort full of noisy tourists.

Steve left the boat for a business trip to Spain and, noisy or not, I was left to spend a couple of days on my own. It was a wonderful, relaxing experience that gave me a chance to forget about equipment failures and endless repairs. Contemplating the world around me, I slowly reconstructed Ancient Cos in my mind and my ancient friends started to talk to me again.

Soon enough, Steve arrived back from his business trip and I became anxious again about the constant equipment failure and the renewed crazy maintenance schedule. We expected dire consequences from badly executed maintenance work in Turkey. In spite of the friendly, efficient marina staff, the boat services in Turkey were substandard and repair work at the famous Marti Marina was a real let-down. So much so that for the first time in our lives we seriously considered suing them for their shoddy workmanship. Indeed, equipment failure, and all the frustrations associated with it, plagued this trip. The Ottoman Empire might have left an efficient administration, but its legacy did not extend to the craft of mechanical services and engineering talent. The workmanship at Marti Marina was simply awful. It was executed by a bunch of lazy country bums who had a total lack of interest in anything mechanical. Their dark, angry eyes carried the boredom of their recent life as shepherds –day after day looking over the horizon in search of their flocks. Their bosses – an English drug addict, washed up from the cannabis and opium trade of the 1970s and his Turkish partner concerned with nothing but his lifestyle – were no better than their workers. They had had a whole year to do some minor maintenance work on *Fenix*, but when we arrived we found a dirty boat full of tools. While waiting for them to complete their work on *Fenix*, Steve decided to install a *Lupolight*, which is an LED three-colour mast-top light. Fenix has a mast that is 17 m high, thus regular bulb changes at the top of the mast are not one of our favourite pastimes. The *Lupolight*, with its promise of never failing, appeared to be an attractive option. Steve put the tool belt around his waist, climbed into the harness, secured the extra rope around his chest and started to climb. We are lucky as *Fenix* has steps all the way up to the mast top and with a professional climbing gear equipped with a fall-arrester, climbing the mast is much easier than on new-style boats. In spite of all this fancy gear, I always keep the brake rope tight using the winch on the mast. Steve reached the top and settled into cutting off the wires to remove the old light. I was standing next to the mast in case I needed to pull up some extra tools. Suddenly, I heard an urgent call: "Juuump!!!!!"

I have to admit that I am not the best crew member. Instead of following orders, I contemplate, rationalise and sometimes even argue. But in this case, perhaps it was his tone of voice, that compelled me to jump all the way back to the cockpit, just in time to hear a bundle of heavy equipment hitting the deck. The *Lupolight* made a big dent on the teak deck, happily bounced up and, crossing the lifelines, fell into the 11m-deep water of our pen, while the other pieces lay scattered as if left by a hurriedly departing crew.

We remained speechless for several minutes, each playing different scenarios in our heads. The end was stubbornly the same. Me, hit with one of the tools on my head, bleeding and unconscious on the deck – hoping for a quick end. The possibility of me having escaped the onslaught of metal tools was so low that it took couple of minutes for both of us to realise that I had actually survived and, at last, we dared to talk.

Are you all right?
Yes. Are you?
Yes. Please come down.

There was nothing else to say. Once safely back on the deck, we silently looked at each other and started to pick up the screw-drivers, hammer, lamp base, screws, measuring tape, electric soldering iron, etc and the tool bag lying like a dead crow with an open mouth. Here it was, the guilty item: the lock had opened, vomiting its contents and letting them follow the laws of physics. We looked into the deep blue water, searching not only for the *Lupolight* but for answers, how to continue. And after half an hour of contemplation, we were back to our old ways. I found a diver who was able to recover the light just before the sun dived into the wine-dark sea. What is the best way to treat shock? Good food and good wine. So, we decided to treat our selves to a well-deserved five-star dinner in one of the restaurants, hidden in the surrounding pine forest.

Repair work on the mast, Marti Marina, Turkey

We had fish baked in salt. The idea is that the fish is covered or rather buried in salt and then baked to perfection in the wood-fired oven. They brought the hot salt sculpture to our table and with a well-aimed blow with a hammer, the sculpture was shattered, revealing its shiny, flavoursome contents of quivering white fish. I was meant to survive to taste for the first time this marvellously prepared food. We enjoyed the starry sky, the singing of the cicadas and the fragrant smell of the pine forest. Yes, it was good to be alive!

Next morning, we installed the *Lupolight*. Our casual approach had changed and I was decked out with a helmet and was winching Steve's security rope from the relative safety of the cockpit. This time, instead of the fancy tool belt, he carried the tools in a strong plastic bag. He installed the lamp and – voilà – we had a mast-top three-colour light.

Once we sailed to Marmaris, our luck changed somewhat. We found a great guy to repair our eutectic fridge and air-conditioner, but he flatly refused to look at the engine-fridge. After years of admiring the beautifully crafted, elegant, soft cockpit cushions on other boats and endlessly yearning for them, at last I had my turn: I had some comfortable cockpit cushions made. Mind you, the whole process was somewhat similar to pulling teeth. Sometimes I found myself wondering who was the paying customer: us or the upholsterers? Considering that we paid good money for their services, the whole situation was quite annoying. But I was proud of my newly acquired luxury. It took almost half of the season to realise that most of the zips did not work and the stitches easily came undone. All in all, as far as boat services were concerned in Turkey, I had no idea what people were raving about. It was slow, badly executed, not particularly cheap and we had to deal with some unpleasant people.

Our plan was to cross the Mediterranean from east to west, so we were going to sail against the prevailing west/north-west wind all summer. I knew that sailing from Marmaris through the Corinth Canal to Sicily would be a struggle, but after all, so many boats had done the same over the millennia that it must have been possible.

From Cos, we sailed to the large, protected bay of the small, uninhabited island of Sperimos. To reach Sperimos, a 25 nautical mile trip to the north-west, we sailed around 40 nautical miles, tacking back and forth all the time. To make things worse, the wind direction changed every half an hour, but it was surprisingly steady for the season: blowing around 20 knots, not that bad after all. We spent two days swimming, sunbathing, just relaxing and trying to forget about the troubles of the world. After that, we sailed to Augusta on the island of Nisos Arkoi. This island is one of the most northerly of the Sporades and not frequented by tourists, who prefer visiting the neighbouring island of Patmos for the religious experience.

The island of Nisos Arkoi was like Greece had been 20 years ago. Crystal-clear waters surrounded a totally barren island with some dwellings scattered among the rocks and some hapless goats roaming the surrounding area. The town had approximately 30 houses. The town quay still showed the signs of freshly poured concrete with new shiny cleats sparkling in the blistering sun. The quay could accommodate around 10 boats. The citizens of the island had pinned the revival of their town on visitors arriving on boats and the business they might bring. There was a lovely town square with a dry well in the middle. The square was surrounded by three tavernas. We picked one on the basis of the décor and tentatively walked in. It was a real Greek family affair. The son waited at the tables, the mother cooked in the kitchen and the father operated the charcoal grill. We had a feast of traditional Greek food: Mama's secret aubergine stack straight from the oven, boiled spinach, saganaki of oven-baked cheese that was interestingly served without tomato sauce, macrella grilled in front of us on charcoal, baby shark with garlic, and sweet watermelon. It was an idyllic moment. I looked up at the sky scattered with shining stars and decided I was in paradise.

Soon enough, paradise expelled me when I woke up at 4 am to check the wind. I was unusually anxious about our 60 nautical mile trip to Mykonos and started to formulate cunning plans to cope with dire scenarios – too much or too little wind, wind from the wrong direction, equipment failure, collisions! Around 6 am, we motored through the narrow strait between the islands and when we turned the last corner and set the sails for our final direction, we started to fly. There was a steady 20-knot northerly wind that propelled us to the west, our speed reaching a respectable 8 knots, more or less the maximum *Fenix* can do. This was simply perfect sailing, a sheer pleasure. I could not believe our luck! This was our wind, the wind this boat was built for. She loved it as she glided gracefully from one wave to the other, leaving frothy water behind her. I microwaved the pasta cooked the previous night for lunch. We had a hearty meal in the middle of the frothy sea. No one cared that we heeled around 20 degrees: we continued to sail effortlessly and we all enjoyed the thrill of speed.

The waves were quite big, around two metres high, and the blueness of the ocean was enhanced by the whiteness of the white horses riding on the top of the waves like cheeky children. We passed to the north of the island of Patmos and to the south of a large desolate island. It must have been an old island, as the rocks were crumbling over a huge barren mountainside and slowly converting themselves into fertile soil right in front of our eyes. On the southern coastline, towards the end of the island, human effort had speeded up the process and created greenery in the middle of the stony desert. A small village was emerging from the wasteland. As we passed the island, the boat made a jerk and tacked without any warning. We looked at the autopilot and noticed it had stopped its marvellous effort and was not cooperating anymore. Since we had only 30 miles to go, we decided to hand steer for the rest of the trip.

By this time, we had a stable 25-knot wind so Steve tied himself to the binnacle and steered for an hour. Then I collected my wet-weather gear and replaced him. First I was somewhat scared: the waves were two to three metres high and the wind was gusting to 35 knots. We reefed the main, which stabilised the boat and made it easier to steer. After a while, I started to "feel" the boat and to enjoy steering. Another 10 minutes and I loved it!

I was Poseidon and a mermaid kneaded into one mystical creature riding the waves! It was only *Fenix*, the sea and me: everything else disappeared. I concentrated and tried my best to steer the boat gently but efficiently, positioning her bow towards our destination: the mountains on the distant island of Mykonos. The speed and controlling the movement was a pleasure only comparable to a wild downhill ski ride. Having been dropped on top of an inhospitable mountain, it is only your skills you can rely on to make your way down; you hope the spirits of the mountain are watching over you. Speed might be dangerous, but I think the human brain is irreversibly wired for the exhilarating feeling of moving our body around much faster than it might be possible using our own legs. Now that I recall seeing dogs travelling in cars with their furry heads out of the window, their ears swept behind and smiling like humans, I do realise that the love of speed is an important evolutionary trait. Regardless of whether the creature is the hunter or the hunted, speed is a huge advantage and it means survival. Our superior brain helps us to create equipment, boats, cars, aeroplanes, kite-surfs, skates, motorbikes, wind-gliders and rockets to move our body around with incredible speed, giving us pleasure and more importantly an unsurpassable advantage when it comes to survival.

On this windy summer day on the Aegean, the world ceased to exist and my brain was rewired for the single task of steering the boat. It was a sheer pleasure driving the boat across the treacherous waters of the sea. Like a roller coaster – up on one wave and down the other – the boat gently lifted itself and surfed down without sudden jerks. Gazing into the distance, I anticipated all the waves crashing onto the deck. Preparing to face the next one, I had a Zen experience. My eyes saw only the mountains in the distance, my hands gripped the wheel and my legs were firmly planted onto the side panels. I was anticipating every wave, every movement of the boat, my face was sensing the change in wind force and direction, and my brain steered the boat in synchrony with nature.

I was really disappointed when we arrived at the anchorage. I wanted it to continue forever. It was a unique experience that I hope to repeat in the future. My father used to say when something bad happened, "Don't worry! You never know what's good or bad." Indeed, the autopilot failure, which later turned out to be associated with a badly installed rudder in Turkey, was a blessing in disguise.

We had got into the habit of using the autopilot during long journeys and hardly ever steered the boat in 20 knots or more of wind. What a mistake! I read several books by sailors who had sailed around the world single-handedly and I was amazed that after being alone on the sea for months they say that just to have some fun they started to steer their boat: something I think I now understand! I guess it is almost unfair to mention my rather self-indulgent sailing experiences on the same page as those of my hero Ellen MacArthur. Ellen is a young woman whose achievements beggar belief. She was the youngest female to circumnavigate the globe single-handedly and the fastest woman ever to do so. She came second in the incredibly competitive 2001 Vende-Globe around-the-world race. I cannot help but include her description of one of the highlights of her experiences in the Southern Ocean :

> "The following day I was on better form and decided I would make the fastest progress I possibly could. I held the genoa up to 40 knots of breeze but hand-steered so as to keep it full. The wind felt incredibly powerful, and Kingfisher just seemed to rally, sailing faster and faster, and surfing for longer and longer as the waves built around her. It was magic sailing; even the sun was out and the blue-water seemed to shine as its crests began to break in a starkly contrasting white. Kingfisher felt alive as I held her helm in my hand, and was loving every minute of it. Our speed went up – 15 knots… 20 knots… 25 knots – incredible, almost like slalom skiing through the waves. I grinned from ear to ear – this was the best sailing anyone could imagine. This was what we had come down here to see, the enormous breaking waves, the wildlife and the feeling of being in the largest open space that exists on Earth. I closed my eyes as we surfed down the massive waves, trying to feel Kingfisher's position, the wind cold and fresh on the side of my face though through it I could still feel the sun. I could hear the humming as her keel flew through the water, probably with a piece of weed on it. After a few hours, I changed down to her solent, then went below to check the weather and sleep a little."

I read her book after our return and it was fascinating to find that she used skiing as the closest thing to describe the thrills of sailing. Mykonos was nice as always; but again I did not have the same magical experience as the previous year. We spent a couple of days there to show our favourite places to my friend, then we set sail to Sounio, approximately 50 nautical miles away.

Sounio

2008 was shaping up as a fantastic year as far as sailing experience was concerned. We had a great sailing day. We only had to motor the last four nautical miles out of 50 to get to the anchorage at Sounio. All the time we had been sailing in Greece, we had never had the privilege to anchor in the shadow of ancient ruins. This time we anchored under the 2,500-year-old Temple of Poseidon, the infamous god of the sea who condemned Odysseus to 10 years of wandering.

The temple looked glorious at dusk with its white marble columns sparkling in the fading light. We had a nice dinner on board and to welcome Poseidon we rose early and motored to shore to climb the mountain and to visit the temple. Previously, we had never been so diligent in our endeavours, but as sailors we had become superstitious creatures and, although not ready to admit it, we were hoping to please Poseidon; after all, he was the god of the sea. We were the

The Temple of Poseidon at Sounio, ~480 BC

first visitors on the site and for our efforts were rewarded by having the entire temple to ourselves. Even the omnipresent guard with his whistle was absent. The temple was as magnificent as only Greek temples can be, with their perfect proportions reaching for the sky and their carefully carved columns glittering in the early morning sun above the blue Mediterranean Sea. Like every piece of rock in Greece, the temple also had a tumultuous history. It was taken by the Persians, then taken back by the Greeks, and later pillaged during the impatient and intolerant medieval times. Today, except for a flock of partridges, the Temple of Poseidon stands all alone and continues to greet the friendly sailors approaching the waterways of Athens or warn the Athenians of any approaching danger.

Hydra

Two of the most beautiful islands of the Saronic Sea are Poros and Hydra. The difference between these two islands could not be greater. Poros, unusually for a Greek island, is covered with green hills and pleasantly inviting and thriving forests that run down the slopes to the water. In contrast, Hydra defiantly emerges from the narrow strait that separates the island from the Peloponnesian peninsula. From the distance there was no sign of life on the grey, rocky mountains reaching for the sky and the island looked as if it was unable to support human or any other vertebrate life form. Wrong! As we sailed closer to Limin Idhras, goats, donkeys and humans became visible. The houses cheekily clung to the almost-vertical mountainside, which, after a moment of thinking, drops straight into the small natural harbour. Entering the small port is not that difficult, but every time we were completely overwhelmed by the smallness of the port and the frequency and variety of boat traffic in it. Small cruisers, hydrofoils, sailing, speed and fishing boats, ferries: all found their way into the small harbour and were desperate to moor. Usually, sailing boats and leisure crafts were rafted in two or three rows, boating accidents were daily events and swimming was prohibited. The police simply

The port of Hydra – packed to capacity

dragged anyone out of the water and banned the offender from the island. One could ask: why would any one come here?

Hydra has an interesting history going back to the Neolithic period (3000–2600 BC). However, in contrast to the extensive written histories of other islands, not much remains in writing. After the fall of Constantinople, large numbers of people from the mainland found refuge in the inaccessible heights of the mountains on Hydra. They were fiercely independent and even during Ottoman times the island remained semi-autonomous. Hydriotes, the people of Hydra, developed an advanced ship-building industry in the 17th century and became fearsome sailors. Their continuous skirmishes with the ever-present pirates made them battle-hardened, and the Hydriot merchant fleet became a formidable force. As traders, they owned the largest merchant fleet (150 ships) in the Ottoman Empire and traded all over the Mediterranean Sea. Their ships even reached America! From 1814, many wealthy sea captains used their vessels as warships in support of the Greek uprising. Their support was essential for the victory of the Greek revolution against Ottoman occupation. There is a small, interesting museum with local artifacts commemorating the heroic efforts of the Hydriotes and showing off their maritime history.

The Greek revolution, as it is known today, was a long, drawn-out process characterised by occasional victories, frequent setbacks, internal fights among the revolutionary factions and foreign interventions. In many ways, the Greek revolution was a forerunner of things to come. Nationalism became the theme of the times and by the middle of the 19th century revolutions burst into flames all over the European continent. In the 1810s, there had been skirmishes with the occupied minorities everywhere in the Ottoman Empire. On 13 March 1821, 12 days before the official start of the War of Independence, the first revolutionary flag was actually raised on the island of Spetses by Laskarina Bouboulina. Twice widowed, with seven children but extremely rich, she owned several ships. On 3 April, Spetsai revolted, followed by the islands of Hydra and Psara, with a total of over 300 ships between them. Bouboulina and her fleet of eight ships sailed to Nafplion and took part in the siege of the impregnable fortress there. Her later attack on Monemvasia resulted in the capture of that fortress. She took part in the blockade of Pylos and brought supplies to the revolutionaries by sea. Bouboulina became a national hero, one of the first women to play a major role in a revolution. Without her and her ships, the Greeks might not have gained their independence. What is less well known is that she was actually Albanian.

"On 14th March, 1821 Nikolaos Soliotis and his troops fired on Turkish tax-collectors in Arcadia and subsequently liberated Kalamata. The revolution gradually spread from the islands to Central Greece, Thessaly and the Aegean islands. The Greeks, led by local heroes like Theodoros Kolokotronis from the Mani, captured the Peloponnesus and formed a provisional government, electing the Phanariot Alexandros Mavrokordatos as president. On 26th April, the Greeks attacked Athens and the Turks of the city were forced to flee to the Acropolis. They were rescued in August by Turkish troops but finally surrendered in June 1822. In the meantime differences led to internal fight among the Greeks in the Peloponnesus. No wonder that by 1826 the Peloponnesus was back in Turkish hands. For a while Athens remained one of only a few cities controlled by the Greeks but on June 5th the Acropolis was lost again. By 1827 the Turks had all of Greece with the exception of Nafplion and a few islands.

But perhaps influenced by public opinion the European powers started to support the Greek revolution. Subsequently, The Treaty of London, backed by Britain, Russia and France declared that the three great powers could intervene 'peacefully' to secure the autonomy of the Hellenes. Following negotiations, the Turkish-Egyptian army left the best part of the Peloponnesus once and for all. In 1828 the assembly of Troezene elected Count John Capodistrias of Corfu (Ioannis Kapodistrias) as the first governor of Greece.

Ioannis Kaposdistrias was born in Corfu in 1776. He was a typical aristocratic man of Europe. He studied medicine in Padua and practised as a doctor on Corfu. Subsequently, he went to work in a Turkish military hospital. During the 2nd occupation of Corfu by the French he left the island and joined the Russian foreign service rising to become the foreign minister of Tsar Alexander I. After his retirement in 1822 he devoted the rest of his life to Greek independence. Kapodistrias wanted to develop a strong centralised government but as a realist he campaigned for Greece becoming a British protectorate with some level of autonomy. He was excellent at enlisting foreign support for the weak Greek government but was unable to quell the squabbling between the various independence fractions. He was assassinated in 1831. The assassination of Governor Kapodistrias by Greek hands put an end to the country's republican dreams for a long time. With the blessings of the leading powers of Europe, Great Britain, France and Russia, Prince Otto of Bavaria was installed as the country's first monarch. Finally, on 31 March, 1833 the Turkish troops, occupying the Acropolis, left.

For the rest of the 19th and early 20th centuries, in a series of wars with the Ottomans, Greece sought to enlarge its boundaries to include all territories inhabited by ethnic Greeks of the Ottoman Empire. The Ionian Islands were returned by Britain upon the arrival of the new king from Denmark in 1863 and Thessaly was ceded by the Ottomans without a fight. As a result of the Balkan Wars of 1912-13 Epirus, southern Macedonia, Crete and the Aegean Islands were annexed into Greece. Greece reached its present configuration in 1947." (Wikipedia, 2012)

It may sound cynical, but the reason the Greek revolution succeeded was because the powerhouses of Europe – Great Britain, France and Russia – changed their policy: they decided that the collapse of the Ottoman Empire no longer meant a major danger to the stability of Europe. By the middle of the 1820s, they started to support the plight of the Greeks. In this change of heart, the educated aristocracy played quite an important role. In England, the movement was perhaps unknowingly lead by Lord Byron, who travelled extensively in the region, from Portugal to Istanbul, at the beginning of the 1800s. He was an enthusiastic beneficiary of the fine Ottoman hospitality and wrote most positively about his experiences to his mother. It is interesting to note his musings on the "rankings" of the different nations and his critical views on the status of the Irish:

Letter, March 17, 1811

"The difficulties of travelling in Turkey have been much exaggerated, or rather have considerably diminished of late years. The Mussulmans have been beaten into a kind of sullen civility, very comfortable to voyagers.

As far as my own slight experience carried me I have no complaint to make; but am indebted for many civilities (I might almost say for friendship, and much hospitality); to Ali Pacha, his son Veli Pacha of the Morea and several others of high rank in the provinces. Suleyman Aga, late Governor of Athens and now of Thebes, was a bon vivant and as social being' as ever sat cross-legged at a tray or a table. During the carnival, when our English party were masquerading, both himself and his successor were more happy to 'receive masks' than any dowager in Grosvenor-Square.

In all money transactions with the Moslems, I ever found the strictest honour, the highest disinterestedness. In transacting business with them, there are none of those dirty speculations, under the name of interest difference of exchange, commission, etc. uniformly found in applying to a Greek consul to cash bills, even in the first Houses in Pera.

In the capital and at court the citizens and courtiers are formed in the same school with those of Christianity, but there does not exist a more honourable, friendly, and high-spirited character than the true Turkish provincial, Aga, or Moslem country-gentleman. It is not meant here to designate the governors of towns, but those Agas who, by a kind of feudal tenure possess lands and houses, of more or less extent, in Greece and Asia Minor.

The Ottomans, with all respect, are not the people to be despised. Equal at least to the Spaniards, they are superior to the Portuguese. If it be difficult to pronounce what they are, we can at least say what they are not: they are not treacherous, they are not cowardly, they do not burn heretics, they are not assassins, nor has an enemy advanced to their capital.

They are faithful to their sultan till he becomes unfit to govern, and devout to their God without an inquisition.

I remember Mahmout, the grandson of Ali Pacha, asking whether my fellow traveller and myself were in the upper or lower House of Parliament. Now this question from a boy of ten years old proved that his education had not been neglected. It may be doubted if an English boy at that age knows the difference of the Divan, from a College of Dervises; but I am very sure a Spaniard does not. How little Mahmout, surrounded, as he had been, entirely by his Turkish tutors, had learned that there was such a thing as a Parliament it were useless to conjecture, unless we suppose that his instructors did not confine his studies to the Koran.

In all the mosques there are schools established, which are very regularly attended; and the poor are taught without the church of Turkey being put into peril.

The Greeks also – a kind of Eastern Irish papist – have a college of their own at Maynoothno, at Haivali; the heterodox receive much the same kind of countenance from the Ottoman as the Catholic college from the English legislature. Who shall then affirm that the Turks are ignorant bigots, when they thus evince the exact proportion of Christian charity which is tolerated in the most prosperous and orthodox of all possible kingdoms?

But, though they allow all this, they will not suffer the Greeks to participate in their privileges: no, let them fight their battles, and pay thief haratch (taxes); be drubbed in this world; and damned in the next. And shall we then emancipate our Irish Helots? Mahomet forbid! We should then be bad Mussulmans and worse Christians; at present, we unite the best of both Jesuitical faith, and something not much inferior to Turkish toleration."

Lord Byron was one of the greatest European poets. He described his adventures across Europe and around the Mediterranean in his famous poem *Childe Harold's Pilgrimage*. The Childe is Byron's surrogate. He is young, privileged and disaffected. He experiences sorrow, projects the image of a desperate future and foresees changes in the make-up of society. The emphasis is on the personality and the sufferings of the individual in the midst of the political struggle. The publication of the first two Cantos delivered instant fame to Byron in 1812.

> "Childe Harold sail'd, and pass'd the barren spot,
> Where sad Penelope o'erlook'd the wave;
> And onward view'd the mount, not yet forgot,
> The lover's refuge, and the Lesbian's grave.
> Dark Sappho! could not verse immortal save
> Could she not live who life eternal gave?
> If life eternal may await the lyre,
> That only Heaven to which Earth's children may aspire." (39)

> "'Twas on a Grecian autumn's gentle eve
> Childe Harold hail'd Leucadia's cape afar;
> A spot he long'd to see, nor cared to leave:
> Oft did he mark the scenes of vanish'd war,
> Actium, Lepanto, fatal Trafalgar;*
> Mark them unmov'd, for he' would not delight
> (Born beneath some remote inglorious star)
> In themes of bloody fray, or gallant fight,
> But loath'd the bravo's trade, and laugh'd at martial wight." (40)

> "Fair Greece! sad relic of departed worth!
> Immortal, though no more! though fallen, great!
> Who now shall lead thy scatter'd children forth,
> And long accustom'd bondage uncreate?
> Not such thy sons who whilome did await,
> The hopeless warriors of a willing doom;
> In bleak Thermopylae's sepulchral strait
> Oh! who that gallant spirit shall resume,
> Leap from Eurotas' banks, and call thee from the tomb?" (73)

Byron went to escape depressing European affairs and rediscover the source of and basis of Europe's most cherished social and cultural ideals in Levant and in Greece. He found that the famous places of Ancient Greece were inhabited by unworthy people: supine Greeks and self-serving Ottomans. He travelled to the islands of Ithaca and Levkas, and visited Lepanto, Thermopyla, Delphi and other major ancient sites. He also used his Mediterranean experiences later in his other poems, *Don Juan* and *Prometheus*. In spite of his upbeat experience during his travels in the Ottoman Empire, by 1820 Byron, like many fellow aristocrats, became an enthusiastic supporter of the new nationalistic revolutionary movements. He became actively engaged with the revolutionary leaders and participated in several nationalist struggles.

He served as a regional leader of Italy's revolutionary organisation, the Carbonari, in its struggle against Austria. He later travelled to fight in the Greek War of Independence. On 16 July, 1823 Byron left Genoa on the *Hercules*, arriving at Cephalonia on 4 August. He contributed £4,000 toward fitting out the Greek fleet. Then he sailed for Messolonghi in western Greece, to join the forces of Alexandros Mavrokordatos. Mavrokordatos and Byron planned to attack the Turkish-held fortress of Lepanto at the mouth of the Gulf of Corinth. Despite his total lack of military experience, Byron decided to act alone. He employed a fire-master and elected to lead his own rebel army into battle. But before the expedition could sail to Lepanto, about 25 nautical miles away, he fell ill on 15 February 1824 he fell ill, and the popular remedy of the time, bleeding, weakened him further. He made a partial recovery, but in early April he caught a violent cold which therapeutic bleeding aggravated further. It is suspected this treatment, carried out with unsterilised medical instruments, may have caused him to develop sepsis. According to some accounts, he simply had malaria. Regardless of the original cause, he developed a violent fever, and died on 19 April, 1824. It has been said that had Byron lived, he might have been declared King of Greece. He was a controversial character who wrote beautiful poems and one of the few who not only preached the importance of freedom but also was ready to sacrifice his life for it. His stanzas below are a clear testimony to this belief:

> "When a man hath no freedom to fight for at home
> Let him combat for that of his neighbours;
> Let him think of the glories of Greece and of Rome.
> And get knock'd. on the head for his labours.
>
> To do good to mankind is the chivalrous plan,
> And is always as nobly requited;
> Then battle for freedom wherever you can,
> And, if not shot or hang'd, you'll get knighted."

Although Hydra played an important role in the foundation of modern Greece, it was marginalised after the victory and by the time of the 20th century Hydriotes were dirt poor. The rugged island, with its striking beauty and harsh conditions, was re-discovered in the 1950s by a group of artists who, as forerunners of the Beat and Hippie movements, were turning away from Western society. The island provided primitive living conditions without electricity, cars and the general conveniences of the 20th century. The idea was that the solitude of the island, away from the rat race and a back-to-basics lifestyle would stimulate the young adventurers' artistic creativity.

It worked for some! Some residents of the artist community became well known, entertaining many millions with their wonderful craft. Filmmakers also discovered the charms of Hydra and used the island for their movies (such as *Boy on a Dolphin* directed by Jean Negulesco and starring Sophia Loren, and *Phaedra* directed by Mihalis Kakoyiannis and starring Anthony Perkins and Melina Merkouri).

One of the artists who lived on Hydra for 10 years and was inspired by the muses and free from the confinements of western city life was Canadian Leonard Cohen. For many years after he left the island, he created wonderful poetry and songs. Cohen described his home to his mother:

> "It has a huge terrace with a view of a dramatic mountain and shining white houses. The rooms are large and cool with deep windows set in thick walls. I suppose it's about 200 years old and many generations of seamen must have lived here. I will do a little work on it every year and in a few years it will be a mansion. I live on a hill and life has been going on here exactly the same for hundreds of years. All through the day you hear the calls of the street vendors and they are really rather musical. I get up around 7 generally and work till about noon. Early morning is coolest and therefore best, but I love the heat anyhow, especially when the Aegean Sea is 10 minutes from my door."

He knew the community had accepted him when he began receiving regular visits from the garbage man and his donkey. He wrote, "It is like receiving the Legion of Honour." He became a cult figure and continued touring until his death, spreading the sometimes confused wisdom of the Beat generation. One of his wonderful songs commemorated the arrival of electricity on Hydra which amazed the local birds, who suddenly found new landing places all around town.

> "Like a bird on the wire,
> like a drunk in a midnight choir
> I have tried in my way to be free.
> Like a worm on a hook,
> like a knight from some old fashioned book
> I have saved all my ribbons for thee.
> If I, if I have been unkind,
> I hope that you can just let it go by.
> If I, if I have been untrue
> I hope you know it was never to you."

I never found out why, but today the people of Hydra are reluctant to remember the artists and I simply could not find a single person who was familiar with the name of Leonard Cohen. Even the owner of the cute little bookshop, who considered himself nothing less than the oracle of Hydra, denied any knowledge of anyone from those days.

In contrast to other places, where the beauty and thrill faded with every return, Hydra remained a place of excitement and admiration for me. We have visited the island at least four times and it has never failed to deliver its magic. The narrow strait between Hydra and the Peloponnesian peninsula works as a wind tunnel that generates an unusually turbulent entrance into the only small port of the island. Every time we have visited the island, the wind was blowing around 15–20 knots, creating excitement among the tiny crew of *Fenix*.

Even during our last visit, when we slowly approached, fighting the wind on the nose, while the tiny port revealed itself in the middle of the most dramatic landscape, the miracle did not fail to happen. The minuscule port of Limin Idhras, fringed around with boats of all shapes and sizes rafted to each other in several rows, cleat to cleat, is an unforgettable sight. Once we had entered, it quickly became obvious that the place was bursting with all sorts of vessels. As usual, at this crucial time of reckoning, both the hydrofoil and the cargo ship started to move, forcing us to execute manoeuvres similar to those of a trapped animal. After some crazy moves, the large boats found their way, and we could finally contemplate our situation. Contemplating your situation was good, but unfortunately no Zen reflection could solve our problem – the total lack of mooring space.

But we soon saw a friendly wave inviting us to raft up to a sailing boat. Interestingly, this tiny, incredibly crowded harbour brought out the best in people. It was a true Babel in the biblical sense where, in spite of linguistic differences, people patiently worked together towards the common aim of securing everyone's yacht. Soon, a rental boat with a Russian crew rafted up next to us, then another Greek craft next to them, creating a floating village like those seen in newsreels from Bangkok. As the sun went down, "Sorry" and "Excuse us" rang out as the crews of the rafted yachts launched themselves onto our boat through the pushpit, walking across our private little home as if it was a boulevard. Never mind: everyone was careful and it all happened in good spirits!

We were lucky, as without too many acrobatics we could simply step onto the next boat. One more step and we were on a wide promenade separating the floating village from the real one. The promenade was full of elegantly dressed people who were taking their before-dinner constitutional.

The promenade is a wide space, the equivalent of an Italian piazza, with the same ancient role of bringing people together, and is crowded day and night. In the early morning, it was occupied by donkeys and donkey-drivers, and later by the coffee sipping locals and tourists, who only disappeared during the siesta from 1–5 pm. After 1 pm, the beaches became the favoured destination for all. Then, around 6 pm, the crowds returned to the port and stayed till the end of the day.

Hydra is a beautiful town where the town fathers made the right decision by banning motorised traffic forever. There are two forms of transportations associated with Hydra: boats to get to the island and to reach the pristine beaches, and donkeys to carry the load of the cargo ship. Everything is carried by mules, donkeys or asses – except lighter items, which are lugged by men pulling or pushing handcarts. Life revolves around the schedule of the hydrofoils and the cargo ship. The first brings the tourists to the island several times a day, the second everything else once a day.

At 7 am, the marble promenade suddenly sprang to life from its short nightly slumber, and I could see that it meant business. Nothing remained of the slow pace of a sleepy island. With unexpected efficiency, a couple of burly guys started to unload the cargo ship straight onto the backs of dozens of donkeys. As their

Morning in the port of Hydra

A donkey driver.

drivers jostled for position, the usual noise of a market place was combined with braying of the donkeys. Everyone – beasts and humans – was busy!

The animals were incredibly well trained. They waited patiently for their turn, usually in pairs or sometimes up to half a dozen tied together with thin strings. Their drivers didn't have to do much other than expertly tie the cargo onto their backs. The donkeys knew their way up and down the steep steps between the town and the port. They carried everything from precious flat screen TVs, suitcases and backpacks to shopkeepers' merchandise of water, vegetables, fruits, meat, toys and colourful flowers. Even the mundane cargo of wooden planks, bricks and bags of cement were expertly tied with ropes to their backs.

Being a donkey driver must be a well-paid, respectable profession in the town. The drivers were intelligent-looking, equipped with proud Greek noses and all were well dressed. They were carried mobile phones, iPods and other trappings of the 21st century while walking next to their animals. Someone sarcastically suggested that they were all employed by the local tourist bureau. Nonsense! This island has simply found the key to human happiness.

The donkey drivers were a cheerful lot – even though they spent at least part of their days picking up the droppings of their animals. In Hydra, we never saw animal dung dirtying the narrow, winding streets. Not that the animals were respectful of the whitewashed stairs or the marble-covered streets, but their drivers immediately picked up their droppings and the spot was even washed with water. There was no presence of the stench that spoiled the air in the beautiful town of Santorini. Hydra was spotless day and night!

Generally, all Greek islands were extremely clean. There was no rubbish rotting in the alleys, in most places no animal dung on the white-washed streets, and, in spite of the fact that almost everyone smoked, there were no cigarette butts on the marble-clad streets. This seemed to me like a miracle, as rubbish bins, so as not to spoil the perfect Greek landscape, were few and far between. Apparently, all smokers must have been ready to make the small sacrifice of swallowing the cigarette butt to keep their beautiful little towns clean. I wish the people on the east and west of Greece would keep their towns similarly clean and not keep good housekeeping within the limits of their threshold.

All this donkey traffic inspired the tourists and even the fussiest forgot to object to the inevitable climb to their hotels. We could see tourists who scaled the endless number of steps around town with smiles on their faces. Their efforts were highly rewarded by the myriad quality shops along the streets and by the chic bars, where tired visitors could find shelter from the sun and cool themselves with a cold beer. The town also had some good restaurants and fantastic, unique rocky beaches, though not comparable to the fine white sandy beaches of Western Australia.

Just outside the piazza, there was a small cave, from the top of which the local boys hurled themselves into the water. After some hesitation, Steve dived into the blue water, not knowing what would come of him. He hit the water and disappeared. Soon he surfaced and, after some vacillation, I also climbed to the top of the cave. I collected myself, timidly crept to the lowest edge and bravely dived in. I hit the water like a bullet, then suddenly everything became quiet. As I sank deep into the crystal-clear blue, the outside world stopped existing. Encouragingly, I could still feel water rushing around my body and I remembered to kick. Soon I floated to the surface and was pleased to hear the noise of the beach goers. As I floated, small, colourful fish swam around me, in and out of the cave. Apparently, this clear blue water was a favourite breeding ground for some local fish. This was quite incredible, as one would think that the large number of swimmers and the heavy boat traffic would discourage any species from selecting this area as a good nursery. But, as Darwin so cleverly observed, nature is very adaptable and it prevails even in the crowded beaches of 21st-century Europe.

In Greece, hydrofoils became my favourite boat type. A hydrofoil is a boat with wing-like foils mounted on struts below the hull. As the craft increases its

Approaching hydrofoil

speed, the hydrofoils create enough lift to raise the hull up and out of the water. Lifting most of the hull out of the water results in a great reduction in drag caused by friction between the hull and the water. A hydrofoil propelled by normal engines glides on the water's surface with incredible speed. We were shocked to see a craft heading towards us in a narrow strait at 38 knots (almost 70 km/h)!

The hydrofoils, coming to the island from Athens and other nearby towns, first emerged on the horizon like dragonflies skimming the water's surface. They fast approached the island, becoming larger and larger. They looked like alien insects with two pairs of legs above the water, dragging their heavy body behind. As they slowed down, the vessel,s slowly lowered themselves into the water, and before our eyes, the alien insects converted themselves into normal ships.

The small town of Hydra has a good-sized basilica, a couple of marble church towers and a bell tower that could successfully compete with that of London's Big Ben in beauty. One of the most charming features of pre-20th-century towns was the sound of the tolling bells marking the passage of time. In those days, the town bells were essential so people could organise their lives. Today, when wristwatches are fashion items and the correct time of the atomic clock can be found in glowing digital numbers on our phones and iPods, no one cares about town bells anymore. Anyway, in most towns the noise of ever-present combustion engines would muffles the sometimes majestic, sometimes playful sound of the bells.

Of course, Hydra was different. The braying of the donkeys and the noisy tourists could not compete with the magnificent sound of the bell tower proudly echoing across the alleys from the shore to the top of the mountain. In the mornings and evenings, at regular intervals, long, complicated tunes were played. First the small bells clanged, then the bigger ones rang, and finally the big ding-dong sound joined in.

We were lucky enough to be present at the celebration of the town's saint. The popular Virgin Mary was the protector of the town and the monastery of the Virgin's Assumption was situated next to the port. On the day of celebration, the bells were overworked all evening. The sound mixed pleasantly with the singing of the priest, celebrating a long, complicated Greek Orthodox Mass. Following Mass, everyone was invited to walk into the monastery's courtyard. We slowly moved forward with the crowd. After some shuffling, we found ourselves in the small courtyard decorated with candles and rosemary branches for the occasion.

The air was heavy with smoke and fragrant from the slowly burning rosemary branches. The bishop, priests and deacons had joined the visitors and were standing at the gate of the courtyard offering slices of bread, which had been blessed during the ceremony. People took some bread and walked away happily munching and chatting. Some of them even took extra slices. Apparently, the blessing would extend even to those who had not attended Mass if they ate the blessed bread.

After the long night of celebration, we contemplated the world in the cockpit when a brand new 65-foot motorboat quietly glided into the tiny port in the early afternoon. It was an impressive sight even to the well-heeled crowd of Hydra. Suddenly all the attention was on the shiny craft and its crew. The captain was on the bridge and the crew, confidently sporting their crisp new uniforms, were all on the foredeck. But after surveying the crowded Hydriot port for a vacancy, their confidence diminished and the captain looked at the busy waters of the port with despair. The port, as usual, was crammed with transport vessels, leisure boats, hydrofoils, and a cargo ship all trying to disgorge their contents onto the already-crowded shores of the town. However, pressure was mounting on the captain as the owners were all on board and some of them were standing next to him, probably giving advice.

Suddenly, they noticed that the sailing boat next to us had started to pick up its anchor and cast off its mooring ropes. This manoeuvre always created some excitement. The anchors were laid in the order of arrivals and more often than not they ended up on top of each other. Since boats did not depart in the same order as they arrived, the sound of an anchor winch brought all nearby boat owners out to the decks. They eagerly watched the unfolding events and readied themselves to untangle the anchors.

Having gone through the procedure a couple of times, Steve became an expert on untangling anchor chains in crowded Greek ports and spent some of his mornings sitting on the bow, distributing advice to the struggling boaties. The sequence was always the same. The struggling winch pulled the anchor to the surface with two anchor chains in its fluke. The most athletic member of the team optimistically bent down with a boat hook in his hand and tried to lift the offending chain off. No luck, it is physically impossible to lift off a chain that is pulling its attached boat towards your own vessel. The only way to deal with the problem is to pull a rope under the chain, secure it to a strong cleat and then lower the anchor 80–100 cm. This frees the anchor so that it can now can be lifted and secured. Subsequently, the chain is released and dropped back into the water.

This time they were lucky; although the old anchor winch struggled, the anchor ran free of any obstacles and comfortably landed on the anchor roller. The skipper accelerated, turned the boat around and they were off. By this time, in spite of my undiminished love for Hydra, we were a little tired of all the traffic and we also decided to leave.

We indicated our intention to the waiting shiny craft and started frantically getting *Fenix* ship-shape. This meant closing all hatches, removing all items from horizontal surfaces and packing them into secure locations, closing the locks on the cupboards, getting the engine keys, changing the rope arrangements so we could easily cast off, lifting the passarell and so on. All done inside, I emerged from the cabin to find mayhem developing. Steve was desperately trying to keep the 65-foot motorboat driven by engines with a couple of hundred horsepower away from *Fenix* using our ridiculously small fenders, which were totally inadequate for the purpose.

Slowly, I worked out what had happened. The captain, under pressure from the owners, ignored the fact that we were just about to leave and decided to squeeze his craft into the much-too-small space left by the departing sailing boat. Without any preparation, he started to reverse his craft onto the quay on our port side. Without its fenders deployed, the motorboat was quite simply crashing into us. Screaming did not help, as the captain was either deaf and blind or was simply ignoring the events unfolding around him. He slowed down, giving us a moment of relief, then, after some hesitation, he continued his destructive work undeterred. By the time I emerged, the motorboat's fenders were within reach and I reached across and started to lower them one by one. The crew stared at me with amazement. They had no idea what to do! Then, from the motorboat on our starboard, a helpful crew member jumped onto our deck. He also, grabbed one of the fenders of the reversing giant and lowered them. Somehow we managed to save *Fenix*.

Between 2003 and 2008, there was an unprecedented bull market on the stock markets around the world. Investment and hedge fund managers made fortunes and average investors also benefited enormously. Generally, as the value of their stocks increased, people felt much richer and went on unprecedented spending sprees. Credit flowed freely. In reality, the affluent lifestyle of Westerners was financed from the astute savings of millions of Chinese and in 2008, it all came crumbling down in the so-called credit crisis, marking the start of a spiralling economic downturn.

But between 2005 and 2008, it was all dancing! The boating industry hugely benefited from this wealth and unprecedented numbers of boats were ordered, produced, and commissioned all over the world, from small plastic fantastics to floating gin-palaces. Very few owners could skipper these new boats, so there was a sudden shortage of qualified sea captains and crew. Adventurous people flocked to the different yachting schools that offered various certificates, and left with qualifications that didn't necessarily match their real practical skills. Unfortunately, we were unlucky to run into one of them.

In this mayhem, our lifeline and one of our stanchions broke. At this point, my dear husband, who can tolerate any personal pain but not a scratch on *Fenix*, was unable to control himself anymore and went into a total rage. Now, squeezed between two giants with my furious husband, our departure seemed impossible. We simply could not move. But there is always a solution, and in the end, we simply waited until the two motorboats on either side were moved slightly apart by the waves then executed a textboook undocking and left, fuming all the way to Nafplion.

Nafplion

The dark clouds and the strong wind matched our mood: we channelled our frustration into sailing. We set and reset the sails again and again, and continued furiously tacking and trimming them all the way across the channel between Hydra and the Peloponnesian peninsula. Once we reached Spetsai, the wind direction had changed and we set the sails to reach and sailed north-west into the bay of the Argolic Gulf. The wind direction required several jibings, a fairly complicated manoeuvre associated with lots of winch work. Having exhausted ourselves with this intensive sailing, our anger duly melted away in the gorgeous bay. We spotted a small island and a bay around five nautical miles from Nafplion in the late afternoon, and after spending five days in bustling Hydra we felt like anchoring. We laid anchor and in the solitude of the bay happily settled into holiday mode, swimming, drinking and eating. As for Steve, he liked doing pleasure-projects – fixing something that looks to take half an hour and ends up being half a day's work.

Next morning, I went to shore to run around the bay. From the comfort of our cockpit, the strange scenery that waited for me hadn't been noticeable. In Greece one gets used to sometimes unexpectedly stumbling over the ruins of ancient civilisations, so the fact there were huge structures in the distance did not bother me, but I was not prepared for what I found on the shore.

The bay, with its crystal-clear waters, was happily basking in the morning sun. In the distance, the contours of low mountains were still slumbering in the morning haze. Some time ago, someone must have liked this location and decided to develop the place into a resort competing with the best of the French Riviera. The whole bay side was scattered with the ruins of this ambition. A reasonable road ran along the sandy beach. Not far from the road was a deep trench that had never been finished and the sandy soil was piled up next to it. Strangely, it provided nutrition for some happy weeds. Big neon lights had been hastily installed but none of them were vertical. Squeaking in the wind, with wires oddly hanging from their long bodies, they looked like abandoned robotic arms. Impressively, the unfinished road was lined with palm trees that had withstood the neglect and continued to flourish in this man-made derelict land. Unfinished parks with thriving eucalyptus trees were scattered all along the bay. Ruins of beach cafés and the enormous concrete structure of a would-be restaurant or perhaps a hotel awkwardly faced the blue sea. The whole beach was covered with rubbish: the ever-present but never decomposing plastic bags and plastic bottles.

In a typical south-eastern European manner, something large, ambitious and spectacular had started. Then, something had happened. The government or the local council had changed and the project was abandoned. No respectable southern government would finish a project that was started by their predecessors. Instead, such unfinished projects are left as testimonies to the previous government's incompetence. An unfinished site is an ever-lasting reminder for the constituents to demonstrate the failure of the party in opposition.

Undeterred, I continued running along the beach and soon I left all the rubbish behind and was running on a very pleasant path carved into the side of the hill, slowly climbing to the top. After about 20 minutes, I reached the top and came across another bizarre construction. It was a hotel on top of the hill overlooking the beautiful town and surrounding bay. Following the previous theme, the grandiose approach continued. It was a huge luxury hotel perched on the promontory, reminding me of storks sitting on their nest raised on top of a chimney. The hotel provided easy access to the beautiful rocky beaches by lifts and a 300 m-long tunnel carved into the rock. It was a wacky sight, totally in contrast with the beautifully refined, marble-covered streets of the Venetian town below. The only reason I could find to explain this wasteful construction was that the designer wanted to recreate the greatness of the town's Venetian fortress and its underground walkways.

On the third night, some unseasonal winds stirred up our calm anchorage. In the morning we decided it was time to reconnect with the world and sailed to Nafplion harbour. The wind remained strong, and after negotiating the narrow entrance, we found ourselves in the outer harbour with strong south-west winds blowing from the side. We motored into the inner harbour, which was filled to capacity with local boats, huge cargo ships and the coast guard. We made an attempt to tie up to the quay, but the coast guard informed us it was not allowed due to the imminent arrival of a cruise ship. Indeed a huge ship duly arrived the next day, casting a shadow over the promenade and the mood of the resident tourists who by now considered themselves locals. But the thousands of passengers who overtook the streets of Nafplion for two days also brought some welcomed business to the cafés, souvenir and jewellery shops and the local restaurants.

We tied up at the outer harbour quay perpendicular to the 25-knot wind. The wind forcefully squashed our fenders against a quay built for much larger vessels. Having previously seen how a surge in the waves can rip mooring lines and physically lift a boat out of the water and deposit it on the quay, we lived in fear not for our lives but for *Fenix*. Steve feels every bang of the quay against the hull of *Fenix* as if he has been hit by a strong punch. So he sat on the bow and observed the conditions for a couple of hours. After some nagging, we went to visit Nafplion and experienced one of the most rewarding visits of our trip.

Nafplion was the harbour of the major Mycenaean city-state of Argos in the 7th century BC. The city was named after Nafplios, son of Poseidon, and was also famous as the birthplace of Palamidis, the local hero of the Trojan War. He had supposedly invented weights and measures, built lighthouses along the bay, invented the Greek alphabet and was the father of the Sophists, a philosophical school. However, it was not a major city during Byzantine times and in 1211 the Venetians took control of the town. The Venetians held the city for the next three hundred years. They fortified the city, including Boúrzi Island in the centre of the bay. In 1540, the Turks reached Nafplion and after a long struggle the mightily reinforced town fell. However, the Turks neglected the city's defences and the Venetians retook it in 1683. Upon retaking the castle, the Venetians built a new fort on the waterfront hill. This castle had eight independent bastions that were linked by hidden passages and walkways. Each one could function on its own if its neighbours were captured. The second Venetian rule held out until 1715, when an army of a hundred thousand Turks invaded the city, pillaging the town and massacring the people after a long siege. After the country's independence was formally established Nafplion became Greece's first capital. The first government did not last long. After four years, southern Peloponnese warlords assassinated the first president, Kaposdistrias, as he was entering the church of Agios Spyrido, for Sunday Mass. The assassins, who were captured and executed, had petty land and power disputes with the government. Unfortunately for Nafplion, the first act of the new monarch, Prince Otto of Bavaria, was to move the capital to Athens, away from the influence of the Peloponnesian warlords. From then on, Nafplion remained a quiet and pretty regional administrative hub of the eastern Peloponnese.

Appropriate to its aspiration to become the capital of Greece, Nafplion was a grand place in its every way. The streets were paved with marble from all over Greece: white, grey, red, brownish marble rectangles perpetually shone in the clear sun all day, and all night in the light of the wrought-iron candelabras. The marble slabs were shiny from centuries of walkers. The large main square was filled with cafés and restaurants, which in itself would not be surprising, but these were cafés more reminiscent of European capitals than traditional Greek joints. In contrast to the cafés of most island towns, they served a quality, modern international menu. I could even find the ever-missing green salad!

But instead of literary discussions, the people congregated around huge TV screens watching their favourite team playing ball games: soccer, handball, basketball, rugby, tennis and whatever else you can think of. And they talked! They screamed! They discussed every move with great enthusiasm, shouting from one table to another. In one of the cafés, there were lovely singing birds in beautifully carved cages. The birds, apparently fluent in Greek, enthusiastically joined in the cavalcade. They sang their songs at the tops of their voices, obviously praising the performance of the Greek team. Vocal chaos is a Mediterranean specialty, but every country along the Sea has its own style. Greek chit-chat is fundamentally different from that of Italy. In Italy, talking is an entirely casual matter. In contrast, in Greece everyone is always intense, and shouting is the preferred and possibly the only recognised means of communication. The society where rhetoric was invented, taught and mastered by thousands is long gone and probably will never return.

A beautifully carved bell tower randomly rang out tunefully in the centre of town. The sound of the bells was probably mysteriously linked to prayer calling. The little bells enthusiastically played their part in promoting Christian belief. However, the churches remained empty, demonstrating that the numbers of churchgoers has decreased among Greek Orthodox believers too.

Traditional Greek towns might be cute, clean and picturesque, but they are never elegant. In contrast, Nafplion was one of the most elegant cities we visited in Greece. The Venetians left an everlasting imprint on the town.

The architecture was impressive, the pedestrians on the streets were elegant, the shops were stylish and artistic flair was present everywhere. The Venetians also had a lasting influence on the cuisine of Nafplion and, most importantly to me, they brought the secret of their magnificent ice cream with them. I could not believe the size and variety of ice creams served. Among the small, stylish shops that populated the narrow streets, another favourite of mine, jewellery shops, were also over-represented. The town had an unimaginable number of jewellery shops filled with a huge variety of necklaces, bracelets, combs and earrings made from every imaginable material and in forms I had never seen before. Sizes varied from metre-long necklaces to hardly visible little pendants. And still there was something that superseded even the numbers and varieties of jewelleries: the variety of worry-beads or komboloi was beyond imagination. They were sold in specialised shops where the walls were covered with beads in a huge range of colours made from all types of stones. I was told by one of the shop owners that, depending on your personality, birth sign and your worries, you choose different types of beads that you use in different ways.

A busy priest

Komboloi worry beads resemble prayer beads, but, unlike the latter, bear no religious significance. They are merely an instrument of relaxation and stress management. Komboloi can be handled in many different ways:

"The most common are a quiet method, for indoors, and a noisier method that is acceptable in public places. The most common quiet method is to start at one end of the thread or chain, near the shield, and to pull the thread forward using that hand's thumb and the side of the index finger until one of the beads is reached. Then the cord is tipped so that the bead falls and hits the shield. This is repeated until all the beads have been tipped and then the user starts over.

The second, louder, method is to divide the beads in to two groups. On one end is the shield and a small number of the beads. On the other end is the rest of the beads. Where the two threads are empty, that space is laid between the index and middle fingers. The hand should be in a position where the palm is facing the torso. Then the end behind the hand is swung up and forward so that it hits the other beads, making a noise. The threads are then switched back into the space between the index and middle fingers by holding the threads between the thumb and the side of the index finger. This is repeated rhythmically, creating a louder clicking noise than the quiet method. An easier and soothing method is to hold all of the kombolói in one hand and roll the beads against each other, creating soft clicking sounds." (Wikipedia 2012).

I loved Nafplion. Its small, elegant streets, the three solemn-looking fortresses surrounding the small town, the beautiful view of the bay, the morning coffees in one of the elegant cafés on the slowly waking, marble-clad main square, but having discovered all the alleys and eaten bucketfuls of ice cream it was time to go.

Spetsai

We set sail and quickly reached our next destination, Spetsai. Spetsai is a beautiful island covered by coniferous forests and surrounded by clear azure water. The sea that washes up to sandy or rocky beaches creates paradise in every nook and bay. Spetsai was known in ancient days as Pitioussa, the island of pines. It barely has 3,000 inhabitants, but the number triples during the summer season. Spetsai has been a summer resort for the prosperous inhabitants of Athens for almost a century. Today, northern Europeans also flock to its beaches.

We arrived in the late afternoon and were disappointed to find that there was no marina or harbour to welcome visiting yachts. So, we simply anchored outside of the harbour in the open water. It was not particularly pleasant as we were rolling quite badly.

Picturesque port of Spetsai

Nevertheless, I was adamant about visiting the island where John Fowles worked and got the inspiration for his first novel, *The Magus*. He abandoned the draft several times and only completed it after the unexpected success of *The Collector*. Thus, unusually, the publication of his second novel, *The Collector*, preceded his first novel. The town remains gorgeous and, in spite of the large numbers of summer visitors, retains something from its past as a sleepy little Greek village. Perhaps it was this sleepiness that inspired Fowles to write his complicated and wonderful story, digging deep into the human mind and heart.

On the surface the story is quite simple. A young Englishman, Nicholas Urfe, takes a teaching position on the Greek island of Phraxos, at the Lord Byron School. The job for him was a chance for different surroundings, and it was also an attempt to escape from his relationship. In real life, Fowles indeed spent two years teaching on the island of Spetsai at the Anargyrios & Korgialenios School of Spetses. The college (which has recently metamorphosed into a conference centre) still exists and remains the only building of significance in the town. At first, Nicholas' life on Phraxos is uneventful and peaceful.

"Phraxos lay eight dazzling hours in a small steamer south of Athens, about six miles off the mainland of the Peloponnesus and in the centre of landscape as memorable as itself: to the north and west a great fixed arm of mountains, in whose crook the island stood; to the east a distant gently-peaked archipelago; to the south the soft blue desert of the Aegean stretching away to Crete. Phraxos was beautiful. There was no other adjective; it was not just pretty, picturesque, charming – it was simply and effortlessly beautiful. It took my breath away when I first saw it, floating under Venus like a majestic black whale in an amethyst evening sea, and it still takes my breath away when I shut my eyes now and remember it. Its beauty was rare even in the Aegean, because its hills were covered with pine trees, Mediterranean pines as light as greenfinch feathers. Nine-tenths of the island was uninhabited and uncultivated: nothing but pines, coves, silence, sea. Herded into one corner, the north-west, lay a spectacular agglomeration of snow-white houses round a couple of small harbours."

But the island not only gives Nicholas the experience of heavenly beauty; his meeting with Conchis, a recluse who owns a huge estate on the far side of the island, changes his world.

Against his will and knowledge, he becomes a performer in the "Godgame" of Conchis. Conchis wants him to get to know himself in full: the little good that is hiding in him and the many dark, horrifying thoughts that continuously lurk inside his head. Slowly, Nicholas realises that the enactments of the Nazi occupation, the absurd playlets after Marquis de Sade, and the obscene parodies of Greek myths are not about Conchis' life, but his own. Nicholas also develops a complex relationship with Conchis' young companion, and consensual and not-so-consensual sex further complicates the story.

The novel is multifaceted and denies the reader the satisfaction of a definite ending. It has a beautiful description of the unique location, the real life of its people and scenes that dig deep into the post-war European mind and soul. For Nicholas, the horrors of the war are not personal. As a young adult, he is a forerunner of the spoilt post-war generations: educated, reasonably well off, flirting with meaninglessness (the favourite slogan of the French existentialist movement) and unable to make commitments in either his professional or private life.

One of the most horrifying descriptions in the book is of the German occupation of the island. It is well known that wars bring out the worst in humanity. Even so, the events of WWII continue to puzzle experts, though they have been studied by hundreds of psychologists, historians and scientists for thousands of hours. Humans from time to time cannot resist their animal instincts and become savages, but it was believed that civilisation helps us to control the beast in ourselves. The cruelty of the German Nazis and the Gestapo during WWII contradicted this belief forever. The same people who enjoyed classical music, could recite the works of Homer, Virgil, Goethe or Byron, enjoyed the art of Durer, Caravaggio or Michelangelo, and admired the genius of Leonardo, built gas chambers and tortured thousands. Recently I learnt that the Nazi regime had a systematic way selecting from its educated population those with animal instincts to serve in the Gestapo and at the concentration camps. An enthusiastic nationalistic youngster would be invited to serve as a guard at a mental hospital for better pay, etc. Then, from time to time the new recruits were required to be very "strict" with the mentally ill patients, sometimes even pushed to execute some patients who "were better off dead". Those who refused to carry out the orders were unceremoniously returned to their previous positions. Those who complied without any hesitation were slowly trained to enjoy cruelty. This was a significant additional piece of the puzzle. Considering the consistent appearance of cruelty in human actions – regardless of race, creed or nationality – it seems reasonable to assume that in any group approximately the same percentage of people are capable of cruelty. However, WWII showed how an insane regime could unleash and use those hidden animal instincts hiding below the surface.

Most Greek islands did not have deep ports thus their strategic significance during WWII was negligible. However, land – even an island that was only a small speckle without fresh water or a natural harbour – was land and the Germans instructed their allies, the Austrians and the Italians, to occupy these unimportant Greek islands in the Mediterranean. From historical accounts we know that once the Germans had taken over the occupation of these small islands they were inhumanly cruel to the local populations. In *The Magus*, there is a heart-wrenching description of how the island of Phraxos sinks into the deepest depths of hell of betrayal, executions, and torture once the German forces take over the investigation of a guerrilla attack. The town's mayor, Conchis, is asked to execute the badly tortured guerrillas in exchange for the lives of 80 villagers who were taken hostage. After some hesitation, Conchis accepts the task and tries to shoot the guerrillas with a machine gun presented to him by the German general.

"'I have tried three times.'

'It will not fire because it is not loaded. It is strictly forbidden for civilian population to possess loaded weapons.'

I stared at him, then the gun, still not understanding. The hostages were silent again.

I said helplessly, 'How can I kill them?'

He smiled, a smile as thin as a sabre-slash. Then he said, 'I am waiting.'

I understood then. I was to club them to death. I understood many things. His self, his real position. And from that came the realisation, that he was mad, and that he was therefore innocent, as all mad people, even the most cruel are innocent. He was what life could do if it wanted – and extreme possibility made hideously mind and flesh. Perhaps that was why he could impose himself so strongly, like a black divinity. For there was something superhuman in the spell cast. And therefore the real evil, the real monstrosity in the situation lay in other Germans, those less-than-mad lieutenants and corporals and privates who stood silently there watching this exchange.

I walked toward him. The two guards thought I was going to attack him because they sharply raised their guns. But he said something to them and stood perfectly still. I stopped some six feet from him. We stared at each other.

'I beg you in the name of European civilisation to stop this barbarity.'

'And I command you to continue the punishment.'

Without looking down he said, 'Refusal to carry out this order will result in your immediate execution.'

And I have said nothing about how I felt this immalleability, this refusal to cohere, was essentially Greek. That is, I finally assumed my Greekness. All I saw in a matter of seconds, perhaps not in time at all. Saw that I was the only person left in that square who had the freedom left to choose, and more important than common sense, self preservation, yes, than my own life was the life of the eighty hostages."

Some of the readers demanded answers from the author. But Fowles refused to help them, as can be seen in his letter below. The book is an intriguing read and remains so 50 years after it was first published.

Dear Tima,

   No, I haven't much spare time and even if I had I wouldn't
spend it explaining my own creation. What one writes is
one's explanation, you see, and if it's baffling, then perhaps
the explanation is baffling. But two approaches - the Magus
is trying to suggest to Nicholas that reality, human existence,
is infinitely baffling. One gets one explanation - the Christian,
the psychological, the scientific ... but always it gets burnt
off like summer mist and a new landscape-explanation appears.
He suggests that the one valid reality or principle for us
lies in eleutheria - freedom. Accept that man has the possibility
of a limited freedom and that if this is so, he must be responsible
for his actions. To be free (which means rejecting all the gods
and political creeds and the rest) leaves one no choice but to
act according to reason: that is, humanely to all humans.

                                        Best wishes

                                        John Fowles
                                        John Fowles

   Due to the impossible rolling of the boat in our open-water anchorage,
we could only spend a day on Spetsai and I never had a chance to visit the
large villa in the pine forest that inspired Villa Bourani. But the small, busy
town of Spetsai bore quite a bit of resemblance to the sleepy village where
Nicholas discovered the borderless imaginative power of the human mind.
I was glad that I had the opportunity to make this short visit.

CROSSING THE
CORINTH CANAL

August, 2006 and July, 2008

We crossed the Corinth Canal twice during our trips. First from east to west at night and once during the day in the other direction. Both were very memorable and the thrill of going through this narrow, hardly 25 m-wide waterway surrounded by limestone walls was unmatched by any other experience.

In 602 BC, the tyrant of Corinth, Periander, who was one of the seven wise men of Greece, was the first to dream about building a canal connecting the Aegean and Adriatic seas. However, the technical difficulties made his idea impossible. Demetrius Poliorkitis, King of Macedon, tried to build a canal in 300 BC. But it was only a half-hearted effort as he believed that Poseidon, God of the Sea, opposed the joining of the Aegean and the Adriatic. The first serious attempt at constructing the canal was made by Emperor Nero, who in 67 AD announced to spectators at the Isthmian Games that he was going to dig the canal that would connect the two seas.

Nero in fact dug the first piece of land out himself, using a golden pick, and carried this first basket of earth and turf on his own back. However, even though Nero had approximately 6,000 slaves working on the canal, the plan was never realised.

The idea for the canal was revived again only in the late 1800s. The Corinth Canal was finally completed, and put to use, on 28 October 1893. The work on the canal was carried out by a combination of French and Greek workmen. The Corinth Canal was actually based on the Panama and Suez Canals, and has often been referred to as the stepchild of these canals. The Corinth Canal is 6,343 m long, 24.6 m wide, 8 m deep and at its highest point is 79 m above sea level.

In 2006, sailing from west to east, we reached Corinth in the blistering afternoon sun with strong winds blowing from the west. We planned to stay for the night and visit Ancient Corinth, but there was no harbour or marina to shelter from the wind. So, after some aimless meandering, we decided to go through. I radioed the canal attendant all excited. After some crackling, an unfriendly voice informed me that our opportunity would come at 9.00 pm and that we would have to pay on the other side.

The canal operator also instructed us to wait outside the breakwater area and informed us not to call again. Typical – "Don't call us, we'll call you". We settled down to have dinner, gilded by the remaining rays of the red sun over the horizon. We waited and waited for the radio to come to life. After a while, we started to worry if we had been completely forgotten. So as not to miss our entry, at 8.50 pm we picked up the anchor and lined up inside the breakwater area, ready for the crossing. In hindsight we should have never done this! The canal operator was outraged by this individualistic action and started to bark (literally): "Go out! Go out!" – in an indignant voice – and then: "Wait for my orders!"

We left the breakwater area and continued our circling at the entrance in the swell. We were waiting and waiting for information – any information – about our situation, but the radio remained silent. After some time, we collected our courage and, defying previous orders, radioed again to ask about the scheduled time of our crossing.

This really infuriated our controller and as punishment our crossing was further delayed to 9.30 pm. Reluctantly, we continued our circling when some small but numerous lights outlining the shape of a sizable ship appeared in distance in the by now pitch-dark Corinthian Gulf.

Then we realised the operator was probably waiting for this cargo ship to open the gate. The wind was blowing furiously as the ship approached the canal's entrance at a snail's pace.

Suddenly, around 10.15 pm the operator barked again that *Fenix* should move quickly to the canal. However, by the time we had put our engine into high revs and started to sprint to the entrance, he unfortunately changed his mind: "No, no! Follow the cargo ship."

That is what we did, and after another half an hour waiting, we entered the canal behind the cargo ship. Of course, the operator had never called us, but we were determined not to miss our opportunity.

All this treatment was totally unnecessary: we could have been told, "Well, mates there will be a little delay as we have to wait for that cargo ship. Settle down for long wait, around two hours, and I will call you when your turn comes."

The informal, reassuring Aussie style that informs you that, yes, you have been noticed, you have been accounted for by a competent professional, was unfamiliar to the canal operator.

The trip through the canal was very exciting. Slowly, we left the canal gates and the lights of the guardhouse behind and we were surrounded by darkness and strange gurgling noises. It reminded me of the scene when Dante passed through the gate of hell: "*Lasciate ogne speranza, voi ch'intrate*", or "Abandon all hope, ye who enter here".

Our slow but steady passage into the darkness of the canal felt like entering into the belly of a huge beast. Other than the faint lights of the cargo ship in front of us, no lights were anywhere to be seen. The huge, dark walls of the isthmus looming on both sides of the canal disappeared into the starless sky. The cargo ship in front of us filled the width of the canal, sometimes scratching the limestone wall. Every so often we thought it might push the walls aside to create a bigger space for itself. Occasionally, we were afraid that it might get stuck between the high walls and the mighty forces of nature would squash it. It was a dark, moonless, starless night, so our only guidance was the small stern lights of the cargo ship. Fortunately, the ship was also slow in this darkness and we had no problems keeping up with it. Sometimes shining beams of light crossed over our heads like comets, an eerie sight. But they were not comets: they were the headlights of the cars crossing high up above our head on one of the bridges. We made a slow progress and our arrival into the Saronic Gulf was nothing less than entry into a new world with a new beginning.

Leaving the narrow intestine of the canal behind, we entered a brightly lit world of restaurants, cargo ships and walkways. In the middle of it all stood the two-storey office of the canal authority on a tastefully arranged little artificial island.

I approached the office clutching our documents and rehearsing my answers to the obviously omnipotent Greek authority. Our documents were a treasure chest of information for those who knew how to scrutinise them. They told who we were, what we were up to, and if we had good or bad intentions. Isn't it interesting that while the majority of mankind spends endless time trying to sort out these fundamental questions of life, as far as the authorities are concerned they know everything, as long as the shapes of the paper, the dates and the stamps on documents are correct? On the Aegean side of the isthmus we had to be examined vigilantly again just in case we had taken on a load of "verboten" items while crossing. Our documents were carefully studied and successfully passed the inspection. They proved beyond reasonable doubt that we were reliable enough to be allowed to cross the canal and pay the exorbitant fee.

In the 21st century, Greece remains a place where East meets West and where authoritarian rule confronts democracy. Greece, as it should be, is the right place for this confrontation. Athens was the birthplace of democracy, but it is less well known that in ancient times an equally successful form of governing was the rule of the tyrants. The struggle against tyranny continues today even at the small outpost of entry to the Corinth Canal. Here a small dictator ruled, with his kingdom limited to a single room and a radio.

Our second crossing took place in 2008 from east to west. After we left Spetsai behind, we day-sailed via Poros to the eastern entrance of the Corinth Canal. It was a nice, uneventful sailing that I spent slumbering on the deck in the gentle, caressing wind. We stopped in the lee of a small island for lunch and a quick swim. It was a perfect day in the Greek paradise: cicadas, blue water, a refreshing swim and a magnificent lunch. We arrived at the canal entry, this time on the Saronic Gulf side and anchored close to the entry for a good night's sleep. In the morning, I headed to the dreaded canal office. Although two years had passed since our first entry, I still approached the office to register our desire to cross and pay with a knot in my stomach. I entered the office where, to my pleasant surprise, a good-looking young man ushered me to sit down in front of his desk. I was unreasonably nervous and could only give some confused answers about our destination. Nevertheless, after he checked our documents, I was simply told to pay. Speaking of payment – I remembered that in 2006 the privilege to cross the canal had not been cheap – but the amount of €216 on this occasion, in 2008, was plain daylight robbery. I paid, and now, armed with the knowledge that we were authorised to cross, I enquired what time we might enter the canal. This was a totally unexpected question for officialdom. I was simply told to keep channel 11 open on the radio. However, an hour or so later, the sharp blow of a whistle indicated that we were allowed to enter – channel 11 never made a sound.

We cast our ropes and entered a wonderland. This time, the sun was shining behind us and the limestone walls were sparkling in the strong light. The noises coming from the canal were those of the sirens inviting us to follow them into the light blue water. Now, we could appreciate and marvel at the vision of the canal builders. The canal is a testament to human ingenuity. It is a beautiful sight for the passing cars above and for the boats crossing on the water. Our travel through this luminous blue water squeezed between two 80 m-high limestone walls was magical! Birds were nesting in the walls and here and there – I guess to the annoyance of the canal operator – shrubs and trees grew in the little nooks.

The canal requires continuous maintenance and is closed every Tuesday. Not only do the crumbling limestone walls require repair and strengthening, but dredging is also a frequent event. Unfortunately, with the emergence of super-sized cargo ships, the importance of the canal has decreased: we did not

Crossing the Corinth Canal.

see too many commercial vehicles lining up at the entrances. But it remains an important waterway for the delivery of local produce between the eastern and western ports of Greece. The trip was phenomenal and it was worth every cent! I am not sure what the future holds for the canal, but it is a spectacle that is worth visiting.

We headed for Corinth and this time, we were lucky to find a place in the local sailing club. We used this opportunity to visit Ancient Corinth, which sits high above its modern-day namesake. The Romans destroyed Corinth in 146 BC and, other than the temple of Apollo, most of the ruins are from Roman times. But the view is magnificent, there is a good museum and considering the importance of Corinth's role in the fortunes of the Greek city-states, a visit to its ancient counterpart is well worth it.

Corinth

The city was founded in the Neolithic Age, circa 6000 BC. According to myth, Sisyphus was the founder of a race of ancient kings at Corinth. It was also in Corinth that Jason, the leader of the Argonauts, abandoned Medea. During the Trojan War, the Corinthians participated under the leadership of Agamemnon.

In 800 BC, the city sent forth colonists to find new settlements along the coast of the Mediterranean. Of these Corcyra (Corfu), Ambracia (Levkas) and Syracuse (in Sicily) were the most important and in many ways defined the destiny of the Greeks.

The first naval battle on record was between Corinth and its settlement Corcyra. In as little as 100 years, Corcyra had become a confident, successful settlement rivalling Corinth itself. In 664 BC, Corcyra revolted against Corinth and allied itself with Athens. Corinth, as before, remained a staunch ally of Sparta. The scene was set for a major showdown between the arch-enemies, Sparta and Athens. But the emergence of a common enemy, the Persians, unified the quarrelling Greek city-states. Corinth was a major participant in the Persian Wars, offering 40 war ships in the sea-based Battle of Salamis (480 BC) and 5,000 hoplites (foot soldiers) in the following battle.

Despite the temporary union, the dispute that stemmed from the traditional trade rivalry between the allies of Athens and Sparta continued. Soon the naval forces of Corcyra, Ambracia, and the other Ionian islands attacked an important Corinthian ally, Syracuse. The Corcyrian forces suffered a devastating defeat. Soon after, in 431 BC, the Peloponnesian War broke out. This war involved all the Greek city-states allied with either Athens or Sparta. The war lasted for almost 30 years and was won by Sparta.

Corinthians were outstanding traders, great seaman and famous for their innovations of black pottery, the trireme, with its unique three rows of oars on each side, and the moving platforms. The city had two main ports, one in the Corinthian Gulf and one in the Saronic Gulf, serving the trade routes of the western and eastern Mediterranean. Both ports had docks for the large war fleet of the city-state. Corinth was built on the isthmus connecting the mainland to the Peloponnesus. Thus it was always in control of trade and the flow of merchandise across the isthmus from east to west and vice versa. The alternative route, a treacherous 200 nautical mile trip around the Peloponnesian peninsula, was too hard to be considered by most merchants. But the riches of the city really started to grow when the *diolkos* was invented and constructed during the rule of Periandes.

First they invented the *olkos,* which was a wheeled vehicle. Ships were lifted onto the *olkos* and taken over land from one side to the other. Not all ships could use the *olkos* due to their size. So in many cases the cargo was taken off at one side, and transported on the *diolkos,* which was a wooden platform that was dragged along a stone path. The *diolkos* and *olkos* ran on a stone path, paved with limestone, which ran along from Schinous on the Saronic Gulf to Poseidonia on the Corinth Gulf. Today, sections of the limestone paving can still be seen.

Around 200 BC, the Corinthians developed the Corinthian order, which is best represented by the gorgeous Corinthian columns that dominated classical architecture and became the favourite architectural feature of the Roman Empire. The Corinthian order was more ornamental and complicated than the Dorian and Ionic orders, showing the accumulation of wealth and the luxurious lifestyle in the ancient city-state.

Corinth was rich and remained so well into Roman times. Horace is quoted as saying: "*non licet omnibus adire Corinthum*", which translates as "not everyone is able to go to Corinth" due to the expensive living standards that prevailed in the city.

From the time of Jason to Roman times, when Corinthians weren't clinching business deals, they were paying homage to the goddess of love, Aphrodite. In a temple dedicated to her, hard-working merchants, sea and military men and ordinary citizens partied endlessly with the temple's male and female sacred prostitutes. The great Christian preacher, St Paul, who successfully converted 5,000 listeners from an audience of 25,000 in Ephesus, was perturbed by the Corinthians' wicked ways and spent 18 fruitless months preaching there.

Delphi

We sailed to the grumpy little town of Galaxidhiou, whose only claim to fame is that it is the closest port to Delphi. We unloaded the motorbike onto the town quay and rode to Delphi. This was the first time that season we had used the motorbike to travel across the countryside. The soft caress of the warm wind on our skin, the blueness of the sea in the distance, the sound of the cicadas and the fragrant scent of the pine trees all made this Mediterranean bike ride unique and unforgettable. We drove through an endless olive grove with trees heavy with ripening green olives. The birds were happily chirping in the grove, singing songs of peace and well-being as they had done it since antiquity. I guess 3,000 years ago anyone walking through this olive grove would have had the same feeling and would have observed that "all was well in the world".

The grove was enormous. It took around half an hour's riding to cross it and to reach the foot of the massive mountain that overlooked it. We rode slowly along the winding road, climbing further and further above the contrasting colours of the azure sea and the pale green of the olive grove. Slowly, the surroundings changed and we entered a different world. We were full of

The majestic view from the Temple of Apollo, 600–400 BC

anticipation and the majestic scenery duly prepared us for our entry into the world of the Greek gods. Suddenly, we reached the unlikely alpine-looking town of Delphi with the intimidating Mount Parnassus looming over us.

We crossed the town and arrived at the Navel of the World. Delphi is the oldest of the old. It was said that gods had been summoned there long before the Olympians ruled the Earth. When the Olympian gods emerged, Zeus, the Father of the Gods, released two eagles. They crossed each other's paths at Delphi, marking the site where mortal humans could communicate with the gods and hear what Zeus had to say about their affairs. Of all the Olympian gods, only Apollo could directly communicate with Zeus. The problem was that a female snake guarded the only spring, Castalia. Then, Apollo killed the snake with his bow and let her rot under the spring; however, absentmindedly he built his altar above the spring. The rotting snake then gave rise to the distinct smell that became part of the legend. The name of the snake was Delphina, from which the name Delphi originates. The first priests of Delphi were sailors from Crete who were hurrying from Knossos to Pylos when the god decided to recruit them. They complained strongly about the place, but Apollo assured them that offerings and sacrifices would take care of all their needs and that they would not need to cultivate anything. In Delphi, Apollo talked to the Oracle, whose words were interpreted by the priests manning the site. In *Sappho's Leap* (Jong 2004), it is described it like this:

> "Everything about Delphi was calculated to fill you with awe. The climb up Mount Parnassus made you so short of breath that you could not help but see gods and goddesses in the mist. The owls' screeching and the hollow footsteps of giants who had come before you intensified the atmosphere of the supernatural. Often, the sky filled with tumultuous black clouds and lighting flashes as if indeed Zeus was hovering near. Then all at once, the skies would open up and radiant rainbows would arc across the mountaintops. The sun would pierce the clouds. You knew that you were in the presence of Apollo.

> Three springs rush through a cleft in the sacred mountain. There at the confluence, where the mist rises almost as thick as fog at sea, is Apollo's chosen spot. Some say it is called ompalos, or navel of the Earth because of the hills that rise around it, trapping sacred mist and intoxicating vapors. Some say Delphi was already a sacred place in days of old, when our ancestors worshipped the Earth goddesses who were later dethroned by Zeus and his children. It feels like a sacred place – as if magic can be worked there. The heart beats faster, the limbs grow cold, you draw breath with difficulty and not only because of the altitude.

> The temple of Apollo is built over this vaporous cleft in the living rock. Apollo's statue – all ivory gold – stands wreathed in mist as if the god himself were there. The Pythia, sits on a tripod over the abyss, crowed in laurel, chewing laurel leaves and raving in fragments of various dream languages. She inhales sacred fumes in a special chamber only priests can enter.

Everyone came to Delphi: founders of cities; would be bridegrooms – no brides, of course, due to prohibition against women; generals who wished to pursues wars against their king's neighbours; tyrants like Pittacus who wished to overtake cities and rule their inhabitants; wise men; stupid men; and stupid wise men."

The Oracle, or Pythia, exerted considerable influence throughout the Greek world, and she was consulted before all major undertakings: marriages, wars, the founding of colonies, and so forth.

Diodorus, the Greek historian explained that the Pythia was initially a young virgin but, as always happens, someone's stupidity ruined it for everyone:

"Echecrates the Thessalian having arrived at the shrine and beheld the virgin who uttered the oracle, became enamoured of her beauty, carried her away and violated her; and the Delphans because of this deplorable occurrence passed a law that in the future a virgin could no longer prophesy, but than an elderly woman would declare the oracles and she would be dressed in the costume of a virgin as a sort of reminder of the prophetess of olden times."

After that, instead of talking to a sweet girl, for hundreds of years those seeking advice had to look at the wrinkled face of an old woman. Nevertheless, Delphi maintained itself as the main spiritual centre of the western world for over a thousand years. In Delphi, wisdom ruled if it ruled nowhere else in the whole civilised world. There are several recorded prophecies of the Oracle, some of which have survived into the 21st century:

- In circa 440 BC, the Oracle is said to have said that there was no one wiser than Socrates, to which Socrates replied that either all were equally ignorant, or that he was wiser in that he alone was aware of his own ignorance. This claim is related to one of the most famous mottos of Delphi, which Socrates said he learned there: *Gnothi Seauton* (Γνῶθι Σεαυτόν), "know thyself!"

- In 336 BC, when the young Alexander the Great, arrived at Delphi to have his fortune foretold, before setting forth to attack the Persian Empire, the Oracle, uncharacteristically remained silent and could not be prompted to say anything, asking him to come back later. Furious, Alexander dragged the Oracle by the hair out of the adyton (inner sanctum of a Greek temple) until she screamed, "Let go of me; you're unbeatable!" The moment he heard these words, he dropped her, saying, "Now I have my answer."

The archaeological site covers a huge area. Modern Greeks have a relaxed attitude to one of the world's most significant historical sites where, prophecies determined the future of nations as well as individuals for thousands of years. For just €3 we could wander around without intervention from overly eager tourist guides. The guards with their ever-present whistles were also missing. Obviously the Greek government assumed that a site ruled by gods wouldn't need any protection from humans.

Delphi is a truly enchanted place and affects young and old, those who know the mythological stories and those who do not. Delphi, overlooked by the awesome Mount Parnassus, retains something of its long-passed spirituality for those who seek it.

As at all Greek sacred places, Delphi had its springs, which were necessary for ritual cleansing before entering the sacred site. The sacred spring of Delphi, the Castalian Spring, lies in the ravine between the Phaedriades cliffs. The preserved remains of two monumental fountains dating from the Archaic period still yield water.

During his visit in 1809, the poet Lord Byron immersed himself into the water of Castalian Spring to be inspired. Judging from his legacy, it worked brilliantly! Unfortunately, I only had a chance to wash my hands…

Why was the site so popular that even the Roman emperors visited Delphi regularly? Why did they seek the help of Apollo and Athena? Why did they ask for the advice of the Delphic Oracle? I have my own simple answer. All humans have the tendency to hear what they want to hear. Visitors to Delphi, with a little free interpretation of the Oracle's words, could strengthen their resolve. Hearing what they wanted to hear gave them confidence and belief in the rightness of their decisions. This gave them strength and helped them to achieve their aims. This help from the gods, Olympian or not, had been invaluable for humanity.

Delphi, the Tholos, ~380BC

Then, around 400 AD, it was declared that the Oracle had lost its power and followers of the emerging Christianity demolished the site. Emperor, Theodosius (347–395 AD) ordered that all pagan temples be shut and banned the Olympic Games.

For the last time in 393 AD, the Oracle prophesied and proved herself right again, by foreseeing her own end. The Oracle declared:

> "Tell the king, the fair wrought house has fallen;
>
> No shelter has Apollo, nor sacred laurel leaves;
>
> The fountains are now silent; the voice is stilled.
>
> It is finished."

Within two years, the Emperor Theodosius was dead. Within 20 years, the Western Roman Empire had fallen to the Visigoths. For the first time in 1,000 years, no further oracular statements were given.

The charioteer, 474 BC

Navpaktos/Lepanto

S omewhere halfway between the Gulf of Patras and the Gulf of Corinth, the small town Lepanto or Navpaktos lies hidden behind the walls of its Venetian harbour. We have visited Navpaktos twice. The first time we launched our Corinth Canal crossing from there, then returned to enjoy the vitality of this small town that etched its name into the history of Europe forever with the Battle of Lepanto, which was fought for the survival of Christian Europe in 1571.

Following an overnight and day rest at Vathi, where we escaped from the huge seas, the 20–25 knot winds and the pouring rain, we started refreshed. Our eagerness to enter the Gulf of Patras was demonstrated by nothing less than a brisk early start at 9.30 am. Many sailors are obsessed with an early start. If they start early, they can arrive at their destination in the early afternoon and spend the rest of the day sightseeing and resting. It has never worked for us. We love the late-night strolls and dinners so much associated with life around the Mediterranean, and enjoy a slow start to the day with visits to the nearby cafés where we enjoy breakfast. In Greece, this was Greek coffee, and cheese pie, the sweet, warm, flaky pastry filled with soft Greek cheese similar to ricotta. Considering its huge calorie content, we consumed it in moderation when it was deliciously crispy and steaming from the heat of the oven. Having gone through the Corinth Canal, the Italian influence was more and more apparent. In Navpaktos, Greek coffee was replaced by the simple espresso, but brioche, the staple offering of Italian cafés, was still absent. The Australian obsession with cappuccino has not reached Europe and this delightful morning drink was not widely available. May I risk my life and say that the best cappuccino in the world is made in Fremantle, not in its birthplace of Italy! So, unless we had a serious agenda, like having to catch a train or a bus, to meet someone or to avoid arriving in the dark at an unknown destination after a two- or three-day passage, we never left the port before midday.

We were fortunate to arrive at the cape of Ithaca, Skhoinos, as a yacht race, with about 30 vessels, was just about to begin. It was a glorious spinnaker start and the huge colourful sails created a spectacular scene as they sailed towards us.

They were much faster than us and soon we waved goodbye to the racers and set our sails towards the Gulf of Patras. Sailing was great across the fairly narrow channel on broad reach, our speed exceeding 7.5 knots. We were never enticed by the industrial city of Patras and were hoping to find something more appealing for an overnight stay. We arrived in the region of Patras in time to take some glorious photos of the huge and at the same time beautiful new European Union-funded bridge basking in the sunset.

After the impromptu photo session, we sailed in the dying sun to Navpaktos. By this time, the wind was blowing a steady 25 knots and we were seriously worried about anchoring in the not-well-protected bay in front of the town. But the small medieval port appeared to be full and we had no choice but to anchor at the entrance to the port. Undeterred, we jumped into our dinghy and went for a visit. The town, protected from the sea by medieval walls, was simply gorgeous, all the more so as it was not one of those protective enclaves but was bustling with small town life. This little picture-perfect town appeared to be the favourite stomping ground of the rich and famous of Patras. There was an endless parade of cars including Ferraris, Audis, Mercedes and BMWs. The flow of cars was occasionally interrupted by one or two motorbikes with roaring engines. The parade was part of the Saturday entertainment as the cars progressed at a snail's pace along the minuscule main road, which was hardly wide enough for the larger four-wheel drives to squeeze through. The drivers chatted amicably with the people sitting in the cafés; obviously everyone knew everyone else. The cafés were filled to capacity by old and young, with extra people standing around those friends who were lucky enough to have a chair.

The Bridge of Rio Antirrio in the Gulf of Patras

After a short walk, we selected the café on the quay of the Venetian port. The quay was still surrounded on one side by the original wall. From our strategic position, we could merrily follow life in the fast lane of the main road on the other side of the water. The tables, in traditional Greek fashion, were positioned as close to the water as possible and squashed up in close proximity to each other. There were no lights and no candles, so we could enjoy the glorious star-filled sky while wondering how and when anyone would notice us and bring some drinks. From the darkness, a guy appeared kitted out with the latest wireless handheld device, took our orders with lightning speed and vanished again.

Soon, a small waitress dressed in skimpy clothing arrived. Defying the laws of physics, she was carrying a huge tray from which she distributed the orders. Then with our ouzo (anise-flavoured liquor) and mineral water, we were politely left to enjoy ourselves as long as we wished. People were merrily sitting and sipping their endlessly diluted ouzos, caffè freddo (neat espresso kept in a fridge/freezer and served as icy slush) or fresh fruit juices for hours, contemplating the world without interruption from the eagle-eyed waiters. It was a great place where the contrast of the medieval castle walls and the technology of the 21st century were enhanced and absorbed by all the visitors. We retired around midnight, leaving the locals partying until the morning.

The next day, we visited the Venetian house of the Botsaris family and the castle. The house was beautifully restored, a real gem. It was built in the 15th century and extended in the 16th century by workers from Venice and Florence. The Ionian Islands had an extremely important role in maintaining clear access from Venice through the Adriatic Sea to the Mediterranean, and the Venetians invested lots of energy and money into maintaining their ownership of the islands. These islands were the key to ensuring the free flow of goods from the East to Venice, supplying Venetian traders with the richness of the world and ensuring the fabulous wealth of Venice. The building was the headquarters of commanding officers for 400 years and after the liberation of Navpaktos from Turkish rule in 1829 it was purchased by General Notis Botsaris. At present it houses memorabilia from the naval battle of Lepanto in 1571.

Navpaktos, or Lepanto, was where Christian forces beat the Turkish fleet, ending years of Turkish dominance of the Mediterranean Sea and bringing Turkish expansionist dreams along the shores of the Western Mediterranean to an end.

By the end of the 16th century, the Turkish occupation of the Venetian empire was real. The Venetians, after the terrible, humiliating defeat at Famagusta in Cyprus, decided to challenge the threatening proliferation of the Turks. They found an unlikely supporter in Pope Pius V, who took the initiative and established the Holy League. After long delays, the League was cobbled together to include the Republic of Genoa, the Republic of Venice, Spain, the Knights of Malta, the Papal States, Tuscany, the Duchy of Savoy, Naples, Sicily and Sardinia. Notably, France was absent. Even back then, the French had other ideas about world affairs. The Holy League was supposed to unite the great naval powers of the Christian Mediterranean against the Ottoman forces. However, like the modern-day European Union, the participants could hardly agree on anything – not least who was going to lead the European forces. After almost a year of bickering, the Spanish King Felipe II named Don Juan of Austria, the bastard son of Charles V, the commander but made sure that he remained under supervision: he had to seek the approval of his senior commanders Doria of Genoa, Barbarigo of Venice, Colonna of Rome and Cardona of Sicily. After lots of delays, the Holy League ships arrived at the island of Corfu in the autumn of 1571 and started to look for the Ottoman navy made up of 274 warships, mainly galleys.

On 6 October, without the Europeans noticing, the Ottoman scouts took the news of the arrival of the Holy League. Ali decided to completely abandon the defence of Lepanto and sailed to meet the Europeans in the Gulf of Patmas. In spite of their bickering, the Europeans managed to put together a potent force of 206 galleys and six galleasses, strengthened by a series of significant innovations. The galleasses had been reinforced by elevated front decks with a heavy cannon pointing towards the bow. Their solders were positioned on the elevated platform of the bow behind the canon, thus they were thus protected and their shots would carry further. All the soldiers – for the first time in a naval battle – carried arquebuses, an early form of the rifle. The Turkish forces were equipped only with bows. Finally, all the European ships were equipped with boarding nets.

"Luck favours the prepared," so the saying goes, and when the wind turned behind the Holy League's fleet the European force got the upper hand. After the loss of the *Sultana*, the Ottoman flagship, and the beheading of Ali early in the battle, the spirit of the Ottoman forces was broken. By sunset, the sea was red not only from the rays of the setting sun but also from the blood of 27,000 people, mostly Turks, and the battle was over. To the surprise of many in Europe, the Holy League won the battle. At long last, the Christian forces had managed to stop the Ottoman expansion into the Western Mediterranean.

After three delightful days, we had to leave and sailed towards the Corinth Canal, which we subsequently went through with some difficulties. But I did not mind, as at last we entered the Aegean Sea, the sea of Greece. In three years' time, on our way back from our Greek adventure, we went through the canal again and sailed in the brisk sea breeze through the Gulf of Corinth.

We were escorted to Navpaktos by some frolicking dolphins. It is hard to believe, but even after millennia of human activities, the Mediterranean Sea is still alive, populated by small fish and the most wonderful creatures of the sea, dolphins. To our greatest delight, at least once a year these intelligent, playful animals find our boat and give us a greatly appreciated escort. Sometimes, we only get a short visit and, after briefly checking out the silly humans, they disappear into the blue depths. Sometimes we get their approval and, they accompany us on our long passages, either just swimming around the boat, now and again performing acrobatics, or surfing in the bow-wave on their sides looking straight into our eyes, searching for something that might connect the two species. It was as if they wanted to bid us farewell at the end of our marvellous Greek adventure. We arrived back at Navpaktos after a glorious sail with a pod of dolphins in tow.

This time, we were eager to experience how it feels to anchor inside the protective perimeter of a medieval port. We were also curious to check out first-hand how good the Venetian naval engineers were. We knew they must have known how to build ports that withstood the continuous battering of the wind, the waves and occasionally the enemy. But was the resulting port safe from unexpected surges? Could it provide sufficient flow of water in and out of the enclosed area? In short, would it have been comfortable shelter for the famous Venetian Arsenal (the navy of Venice)? To answer these questions, we

The medieval port of Navpaktos (Lepanto)

had to tie up inside the port. This time we were lucky or just more confident with our manoeuvres. We bravely entered the port, which had hardly enough space to swing *Fenix* around for the Mediterranean mooring. But we skilfully managed to get everything right the first time and successfully tied up at the medieval town jetty. It was tiny! In exchange for our brave manoeuvring in this narrow space, we were rewarded with the best position to enjoy the scenery Navpaktos had to offer. The port was very well built without any surge water entering and with fresh seawater sloshing in and out day and night. The end result of all this was that the boat did not roll and the surrounding water did not stink, a fate not always achieved by the designers of modern harbours. I bow my head to the superior engineering skills of the Venetians! We sat in the cockpit with the sun setting over the medieval town walls and gilding the main square, which was still confined to its original size by the medieval walls, and enjoyed watching the busy town life.

Nothing had changed during the last three years: the partying relentlessly continued over the weekend. Youngsters filled the cafés to capacity, sipping their frappés from 8–11 pm, then moved onto the clubs and partied till six in the morning. The cafés reopened just in time to serve breakfast to the party crowd. We devised a somewhat less punishing schedule and walked to the Koyzina restaurant, around a hundred steps from our boat. The restaurant was in a two-storey building, but food was also served in the front garden overlooking the port. The quay in front of the restaurant was also scattered with small tables and chairs from where one could choose to enjoy the scenery of the medieval wall or the town square.

The tables were covered with snow-white tablecloths, candles sitting in the middle and surrounded by undersized wrought-iron chairs that were covered with cream-coloured cushions. People casually strolled between the tables, occasionally stopping to greet each other or just chatting. We were very lucky to get a fabulous table by the water, and without too much delay our bread and water arrived. We were in the middle of studying the menu when a glamorous-looking lady in a white linen outfit came to our table and started to talk to us. She was the owner, who later turned out to be none other than the celebrity chef of Greece, Maria Loh. She recommended some dishes and told us some stories about Navpaktos and about her family's long history in the restaurant business. She also revealed that she was born in this town and that she kept this restaurant open to test some of her new creations during the summer when her television duties were less demanding. She loved running a real restaurant in her birthplace. Then she disappeared but did not leave. She continued to supervise the workings of the restaurant from the small balcony on the second floor, where she sat at a tastefully laid-out table with some friends, sipping wine. She might have looked relaxed, but she was keeping an eagle eye on her business, and never missed a beat! From time to time, she came down and greeted important guests and enquired about the service and the food. Lights were on inside the restaurant, where customers requiring more privacy were served. We ordered an exotic-sounding salad and I ordered a moussaka. Moussaka is a much-maligned Greek speciality, made from minced lamb, mashed potato and layers of aubergine. I never ordered it in Greece as it was usually too oily or too dry for my liking. But I reckoned if anyone could cook moussaka in Greece, Maria Loh could. Her customers were not tourists but regulars, returning townsfolk, who came to enjoy the superb food, not the location. I made the right decision, as the meal was fantastic! The meat, the aubergine and the mashed potato created a synthesis of flavours I had never experienced before. The whole meal melted in my mouth and all I could think of was the next forkful of this heavenly creation! They also served a unique rosé wine, which had an underlying slight Muscat flavour while maintaining a fundamentally dry character.

After this memorable dinner, we strolled around the town, then returned to our boat for a catnap before going out partying. However, in spite of the loud music around us, my catnap lasted till 6 am the next day and I found my husband fast asleep next to me. Soon he started to stir and I was quick enough to tell him how great the clubbing was last night. We had a good laugh and made sure that we did not miss at least the next phase of the party life in Navpaktos: around 7 am, we joined the party crowd waiting for the opening of the local cafés. The newsagents also opened at 7 am and I managed to beat the holiday-makers to an English-language newspaper to make this early morning coffee a real treat. Due to our unusual early start, we were on our way to Cephalonia at 8.40 am!

Ithaca?

We reached Ithaca, the island of Odysseus, and made landfall at Frikes, a truly attractive place set in the bottom of a ravine. A stream keeps on flowing even in summer, watering the village's orchards and the colourful bougainvilleas. Dark green conifers and pine trees cover the surrounding steep hills. Frikes is an incredibly tiny town. It has two streets and no more than 20 residents in winter. But during the summer months, more and more visitors arrive at the town by ferry. For the most part, they are holidaymakers attracted by the beautiful scenery and the clean, pebbled beaches, not by the name Ithaca. The majority of those who visit have no idea that it was the home of the first official, somewhat reluctant, adventurer in history, Odysseus.

Ithaca is one of the Ionian Islands on the western coast of Greece. The Ionians go back a long way in history. They are mentioned on the Linear B tablets of Knossos, which makes them pre-Mycenaean, a very ancient culture. We know that the Ionians from the western Peloponnesian islands of Corfu, Levkas, Cephalonia, Ithaca and Zakintos became the first Greek colonisers in recorded history when they moved en masse to the western coast of Asia in around 1060 BC. The move, either by sea only or part overland, must have been a logistical nightmare with their primitive transportation equipment. The sea journey would have required them to circumnavigate the Peloponnesian peninsula and to island-hop through the wind-battered waters of the Cyclades: more than 400 nautical miles (about 800 km) of treacherous water between their old and new homes. Part of the journey could have been made on land, crossing the mighty Olympus on the Peloponnesian peninsula or the even less hospitable regions of the Pindus Mountains. Either way, it was far from a pleasure trip. The cause of the migration is not clear – earthquake, drought, an invasion of the Dorians or some other catastrophic event might have instigated the move, but there is plenty of linguistic and historical evidence that the event took place. We know they established thriving cities like Smyrna on the mainland and other cities on the surrounding offshore islands of Ohyllis and Melamphyllos. After Greece's most recent earthquake in 1953, another mass migration took place: most of the survivors from the Ionian Islands migrated to another island, Australia. Australia might have been a faraway place, but as an island lying in the middle of another endless sea it was an attractive option for the modern-day Ionians. Perhaps the stability of this very old continent, which is not at all affected by earthquakes, made it attractive. Or perhaps it was its enlightened immigration policy that enticed the new Ionian refugees. Whatever the reason, the Greeks made Melbourne in the south-east corner of the vast Australian continent the second-largest Greek city in the world.

Some of those migrants returned to places like Frikes and built attractive B&B facilities and small hotels to cater for the summer invasion. They only stay for the summer and then return to Australia to spend some time with their children, who are irreversibly settled in the new country.

One night, we were enjoying the hospitality of the locals in a seaside taverna, chatting and savouring the regional wine, when suddenly our feet became wet and within seconds the shore was flooded. Without delay, Steve ran to the boat, anchored nearby, fearing that the surge might push it onto the rocks. He was extremely relieved when he saw that our anchor held. But, as he got closer, he could see that our neighbour's anchor had not held and the incoming surge had pushed the boat onto the quay and the rocks, damaging the hull.

When the water level in the taverna passed my ankle, I decided that it was high time for me to evacuate. I arrived at the town quay to find a small crowd surveying the damage and discussing the next step. We helped the terrified family with two young children leave their damaged craft and assisted them in tying up again. Funnily enough, only a couple of days earlier we had been musing about the medieval engineers who had built the safe Navpaktos port. Obviously, their skills had not been handed down to their modern-day counterparts who built the Frikes port: despite the significant breakwater, the surge freely entered into the town port and caused havoc. Breakwaters are independent-minded creatures. According to some engineers, whether they turn out well or badly is due not to the calculations and construction but to "black magic".

Next morning, I had the most spectacular run in the whole of Greece along the rugged coast of Ithaca. On my right there were beautiful steep green hills, on my left crystal-clear, deep blue water and snow-white pebble beaches. The road followed the uneven coastline and wound freely from one hill to another. Reminiscent of another era, a couple of Venetian watchtowers looked over me and I felt alive as never before. If she could see me, one of her humble creatures, Mother Nature would have been pleased with my enthusiasm as I ran with the wind. I could feel my nervous system activating the skeletal muscles in my calves, the cardiac muscles giving a faster and faster rhythm to my heart, the air filling my lungs, delivering fresh oxygen to every inch of my body, all under the control of my alert mind, regulating my steps while listening to the sounds of the water, the chirping of the birds and the cracking noises of the pine trees.

Life starts late in the Greek islands and as usual I did not see a soul during my run. Exhausted by the early heat, I had an irresistible urge to immerse myself in the gentle, cooling waves of the sea. I ran down a series of steps to the shore, threw my clothes off and went for a swim. I swam and swam and it was only when I had finished my strokes and emerged from the sea that I realised that I knew no woman of my age who would have done such a silly thing. Perhaps my darling daughter, who had informed me a week earlier that she had walked a part of the Bibbulmun track (which is an almost a 1,000 km hike between Perth and Albany) alone across a forest recently savaged by bushfires, inherited her adventurous nature from none other than me. So who can I blame but myself for her recklessness and putting herself into potential danger?

Disturbed by the insecure port, with an approaching low front bringing strong winds and possibly a storm, we left around lunchtime. After a short sail, we reached the capital of the island, Vathi. Vathi lies along a huge natural harbour and it provided good shelter from the strong south-south-westerly winds. I remarked that I could not imagine a better place for the Odyssean fleet than the Bay of Vathi. It is protected from the prevailing wind by good-sized mountains and no sea enters with the wind. Stunning lush green hills and evidence of good summer rains surrounded the bay. We also experienced a healthy August downpour that revitalised the countryside from the dusty heat of summer. We stayed for couple of days enjoying the scenery and reading – what else? – *The Odyssey*.

> "I dwell in shining Ithaca. There is a mountain there,
> high Neriton, covered in forests. Many islands
> lie around it, very close to each other,
> Doulichion, Same, and wooded Zacynthos—
> but low-lying Ithaca is farthest out to sea,
> towards the sunset, and the others are apart, towards the dawn and sun.
> It is rough, but it raises good men."

These lines have been driving historians, archaeologists and geologists nuts for at least 2,500 years. The descriptions are precise and geologically correct enough to suggest that the locations where the events of *The Odyssey* took place must have existed, just as the characters were flesh-and-blood individuals. However, to date no island has been identified that fits fully the bard's description of Ithaca.

Strabo (63–24 BC), the father of geography, devotes several chapters in his book *Geographica* to the description of the locations in *The Odyssey* and *The Iliad*. He concluded that Bronze Age Ithaca was indeed the same place as the Ithaca of his time:

> "From these facts, then, it is clear that the country subject to Nestor, all of which the poet calls 'land of the Pylians' extends on each side of the Alphaeus; but the Alphaeus nowhere touches either Messenia or Coelê Elis. For the fatherland of Nestor is in this country which we call Triphylian, or Arcadian, or Leprean, Pylus. And the truth is that, whereas the other places called Pylus are to be seen on the sea, this Pylus is more than thirty stadia above the sea – a fact that is also clear from the verses of Homer, for, in the first place, a messenger is

sent to the boat after the companions of Timomachus to invite them to an entertainment, and, secondly, Telemachus on his return from Sparta does not permit Peisistratus to drive to the city, but urges him to turn aside towards the ship, knowing that the road towards the city is not the same as that towards the place of anchorage.

And thus the return voyage of Telemachus might be spoken of appropriately in these words: 'And they went past Cruni and fair-flowing Chalcis. And the sun set and all the ways grew dark; and the ship, rejoicing in the breeze of Zeus, drew near to Phea, and on past goodly Elis, where the Epeians held sway.' Thus far, then, the voyage is towards the north, but thence it bends in the direction of the east. That is, the ship abandons the voyage that was set out upon at first and that led straight to Ithaca, because there the wooers had set the ambush 'in the strait between Ithaca and Samos.' And thence again he steered for the islands that are thoai; but by 'thoai' the poet means the islands that are 'pointed'. These belong to the Echinades group and are near the beginning of the Corinthian Gulf and the outlets of the Acheloüs. Again, after passing by Ithaca far enough to put it south of him, Telemachus turns round towards the proper course between Acarnania and Ithaca and makes his landing on the other side of the island – not at the Cephallenian strait which was being guarded by the wooers.'

When we visited, the good citizens of Vathi were making an honest effort to keep the Odyssean spirit alive by selling some incredibly horrendous paintings and sculptures of the adventurer and were promoting their island as the home of Odysseus by advertising a variety of tours to Odyssean sites. Port Polis was promoted as ancient Polis, Port Frikes as Reithron, Ormos Pera Pigadhi as the site of the Arethusa spring, and the plateau of Marathia as the home of Eumaeus the swineherd. There is a rocky outcrop on the island that even today is called Korax, or Raven's Rock. However, unfortunately the visitor has to rely on his or her own imagination to see the sites as the home of the greatest adventurer. There is nothing to see and little archaeological evidence to support these claims.

As a matter of fact, several other Ionian islands have been proposed as the home of Odysseus. Many have argued that the geological and archaeological evidence does not support Strabo's claim about the location of Ithaca and that his claim was accepted more on the basis of its antiquity than of facts. In the 19th century, the German archaeologist William Dörpfeld proposed a variety of geographical locations. After sorting out the mess generated by Heinrich Schliemann at the excavation of Troy, Dorpfeld started to dig on the island of Levkas at what he believed was the site of ancient Ithaca. He proposed that Nidri was the site of the city and that Vlicho Bay was the harbour in *The Odyssey*. Digging unearthed large enough Bronze Age walls, artifacts and pottery to suggest that the place was inhabited during that period, but any conclusive evidence remained elusive. Dorpfeld literally devoted his life to his project and after his death he was buried at Vlicho Bay.

More recently (1990), Cees Göekopp published an exhaustive review of all Homeric descriptions of Ithaca. He concluded that present-day Ithaca, called Ithaki, could not be the place described in *The Odyssey* and *The Iliad*. The obsession with finding Ithaca must have run deep in the family, as his grandfather, also a Greek scholar, proposed a hundred years earlier that Cephalonia was the site of ancient Ithaca.

The previous summer I picked up a book while standing in one of the bookshops of Cambridge University Press, in Cambridge. I was present at the launch of a new ophthalmic biology book and, while listening to the accolades to the authors and the publisher, my eyes wandered, scanning the titles on the long shelves. I was casually reading the titles when a book significant weight and size (for airline passengers and sailors these are essential considerations) caught my attention. Unashamedly, the title claimed *Odysseus Unbound*. I started out casually flicking through it, but after couple of minutes of speed-reading I found the writing absolutely engaging. I became totally immersed in the story – so much so that I even missed out on the essential draw-card of all book launches, wine and nibbles. That was it. I simply could not leave the book behind and in spite of its size and weight and the fact that it was a difficult read, I had to have it. By the end of the launch it was a done deal. I paid and carried the 2 kg volume with me and continued to read it in the dorm, at the airport, on the plane and finally in the comfort of *Fenix*.

Odysseus Unbound is the brilliant, entertaining, semi-scientific story of Robert Bittlestone's quest to solve the ancient puzzle: where did Odysseus live? The idea that Cephalonia was the home of Odysseus was not the unique obsession of the Goekopp family: Bittlestone, an economist turned amateur archaeologist, explores the same conundrum and comes to the same conclusion – with a twist.

In this modern age of specialisation, many may think – detailed though it is – that Bittlestone's work is nothing more than summer entertainment for an amateur scholar. But beware! So-called amateur archaeologists and enthusiasts have made some of the most significant discoveries of ancient Greek monuments. Consider none other than the identification of Troy by Schliemann or Knossos by Evans! And Bittlestone is no fool! He recruited two outstanding scholars: James Diggle, Professor of Greek and Latin at the University of Cambridge, and John Underhill, Professor of Stratiography at the University of Edinburgh, and many others, to help him to prove his theory. He has a sharp analytical mind and his approach is more scientific than scholarly. He made use of spreadsheets, statistics and state-of-the-art satellite and radar. To create a coherent history of ancient Ithaca, the authors combine the classical evidence with geological backing. If we accept that the text gives a correct description of a geological location, then we have to accept that when *The Odyssey* was written, around 1174 BC, Same and ancient Ithaca were two separate islands.

"Doulichion, Same, and wooded Zacynthos—
but low-lying Ithaca is farthest out to sea,
towards the sunset, and the others are apart, towards the dawn and sun."

Crucially, "Ithaca is the farthest out to sea". Once we look at the map it is clear that none of the present-day islands satisfy this description. The land mass furthest out to sea is the peninsula of Paliki on the north-west corner of the island of Cephalonia. Bittlestone proposes that in ancient times Paliki and Same were separated by a narrow channel, which he calls Strabo's Channel, that was subsequently filled up over the millennia. In addition to the rock falls that filled the channel, he also suggests that Paliki (Ithaca) in ancient times lay up to six metres lower than modern-day Paliki because:

"17. At some date between the events of *The Odyssey* and the end of the 6th century BC there is a massive earthquake in ancient Ithaca which elevates the island by at least 0.8 m (and perhaps as much as 4 m).

18. Catastrophic rockfall into Strabo's Channel causes it to become partially obstructed and a huge wave rears up on to the western shore of the channel and across the Ithacan coastline. As the rockfall settles, pockets of salt-laden sea water are trapped underground. The two former islands now resemble a single land mass with a low-lying isthmus that still permits the sea to penetrate from time to time...

23. After a period of desertion Cephalonia starts to be repopulated, centred on Cranioi, Same, Pronnoi and Pale. Alalcomenai is also reoccupied or occupied for the first time. No significant attempt is made to reinhabit ancient Ithaca city or the Kastelli palace, perhaps because of the wrath of Poseidon. Same and former Ithaca are now a single land mass and because the occupants were already called the Cephallenians, this name is adopted for the enlarged island.

24. In the 5th century BC Herodotus regards the settlement of Paleon today's Paliki as being part of Cephalonia, not Ithaca."

For me one of the most convincing arguments for this theory was identification of the locations of the ambush:

"And another thing. Take it to heart, l tell you.
Picked men of the suitors lie in ambush, grim-set
in the straits between lthaca and rocky Same,
poised to kill you before you can reach home,
but I have my doubts they will. Sooner the Earth
will swallow down a few of those young gallants
who eat you out of house and home these days!
Just give the channel islands a wide berth,
push on in your trim ship, sail night and day,
and the deathless god who guards and pulls you through

The proposed way home via the ancient canal that disappeared (after Bittlestone)

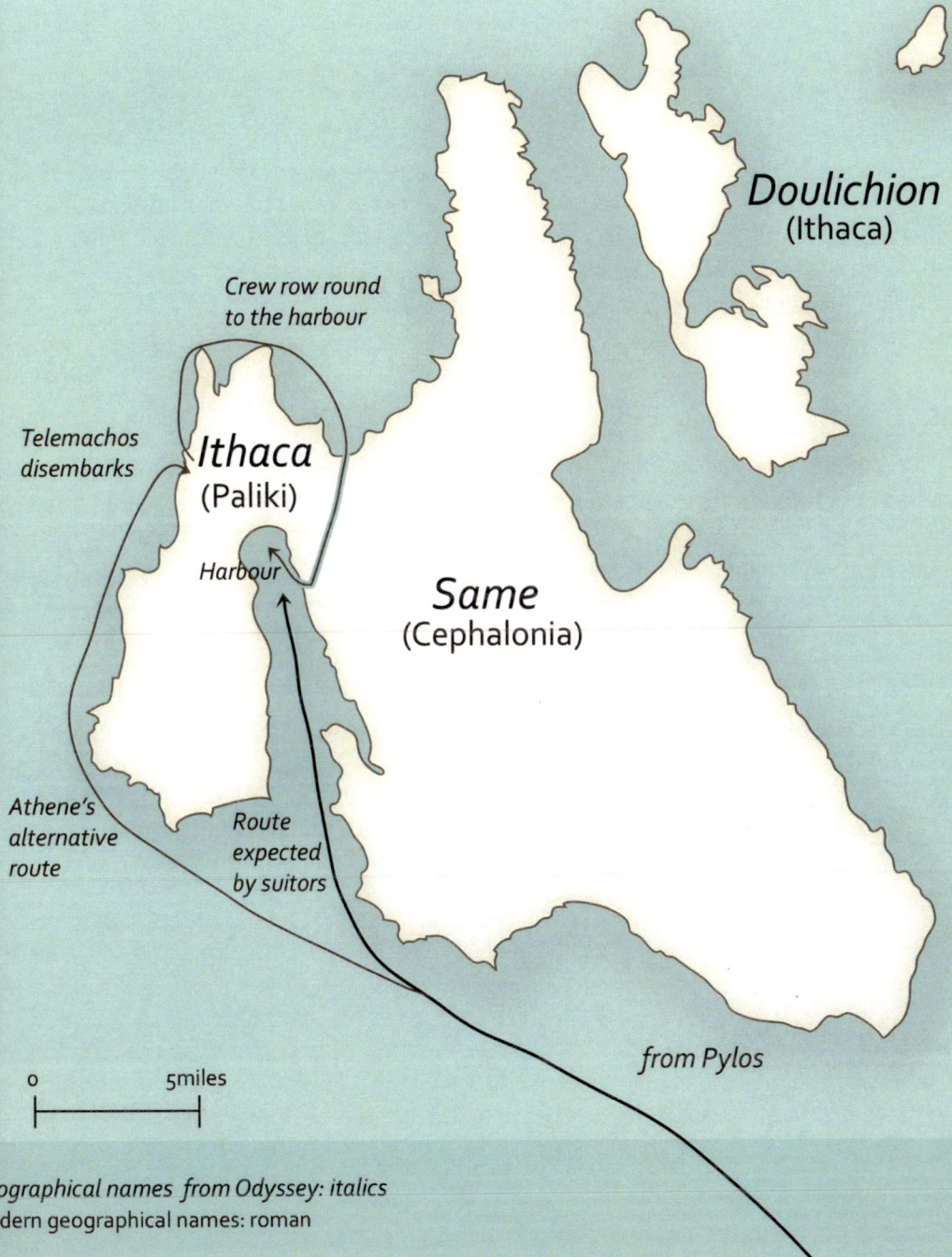

Crew row round
to the harbour

*Telemachos
disembarks*

Ithaca
(Paliki)

Harbour

Same
(Cephalonia)

Doulichion
(Ithaca)

*Athene's
alternative
route*

*Route
expected
by suitors*

from Pylos

0   5miles

geographical names *from Odyssey: italics*
modern geographical names: roman

will send you a fresh fair wind from hard astern.
At your first landfall, Ithaca's outer banks,
speed ship and shipmates round to the city side.
But you—you make your way to the swineherd first,
in charge of your pigs, and hue to you as always.
Sleep the night there, send him to town at once
to tell the news to your mother, wise Penelope —
you've made it back from Pylos safe and sound."

Specific sites from *The Odyssey* – such as Phorcy's Bay (where Odysseus was delivered by the Phaeacians), Asteris, the island where the suitors hid, Ithaca city, Odysseus' Palace, Hermes' Hill, Raven's Rock, Laertes' farm and other locations – have, at least as far as their geological description goes, been identified. Preliminary excavations of the sites have uncovered Bronze Age walls and pottery remains. But as the Bittlestone readily accepts, much more will be required to prove without doubt that Paliki was the site of ancient Ithaca.

So, what were we to do? We decided to sail to Cephalonia and see it for ourselves. It was a windless day and we unhappily motored. Motoring is a contentious issue on *Fenix*. As far as I am concerned, turning on the diesel and putting another nail into the coffin of the Earth is well worth maintaining my sanity. For my irresponsible, selfish thinking people more considerate about the well-being of Planet Earth might think that I deserve a stint in a re-education camp, so efficiently run by the murderous regime of the Khmer Rouge in the 1970s. Steve, on the other hand, is a purist and reckons that we should never use our engine but wait for our luck to turn. So every time the wind stops, a detailed scientific interpretation of the weather conditions is undertaken, followed by delicate negotiations. Whatever the decision is, one of us is unhappy.

After a noisy day on the water, we made our landfall on the island of Cephalonia at the town of Poros. No, this was not the Poros of the Saronic Islands. The Greeks are particularly unimaginative when it comes to naming places. Perhaps the tradition of using the same familiar names again and again to describe geographical locations goes back to the Ionian migration.

According to Iamblichus (140–325 BC), the Ionian leader, Ancauis, received an oracle from the Pythia instructing him, Iamblichus,

"To colonise an island that was called Melamphyllos because of its soil and land, and to call the city Samos, in place of Same in Cephallenia. The oracle said: 'Ancaios, I order you to colonise an island in the sea, Samos, in place of Same. At present its name is Phyllis'".

Reassured by the oracle, the island of Ohyllis was renamed Lesbos and Melamphyllos renamed Samos. Perhaps encouraged by the success of the Ionians, modern Greeks decided to continue this tradition. Therefore, several Mediterranean islands have small towns called Poros, Vathi, Agios Nicolaos or a version of Kalamaki.

Poros on Cephalonia was a miserable town in a great setting. The town planners had no artistic flair and completely lacked any sense of beauty. They successfully proved that in spite of all the splendour of nature, humans could create something truly ugly. Obviously, the lack of imagination in naming the town had carried over to the modern-day town planning.

The next day there was still no wind, but eager to get away we motored to Argostoli, the capital of Cephalonia. Argostoli was completely destroyed by the earthquake in 1953, a story repeated all over the Ionian Islands. But the earthquake destroyed more than Argostoli: it destroyed most of the island's inhabited towns and the spirit of their people. Those who survived left, reducing the island's population from 150,000 to 10,000. Even today, there are only 25,000 permanent residents on the island. But hope has returned, and as far as I could tell from the thriving small hotels and the numerous huge, American-style holiday homes, the migrants were returning in droves to their beautiful green island. Argostoli was a pleasant town, which as far as their harbour showed, appeared to have big plans. Everything was built with grandeur, suggesting the future promise of the busy capital of the island. We put the scooter to shore and I began excitedly to prepare for our trip around the island – however, it was not to be.

We needed to get to Sicily to meet our son who was flying over from Melbourne, Australia to spend a week with us. A real treat for a mother! We had to be in Palermo on a certain date. Depending on the weather and the swell, Argostoli was a two-to-three-day sail from Syracuse, our designated landfall in Sicily. However, because a high was sitting over the Ionian Sea, there had been no or hardly any wind for the last week and I was very worried about our schedule. It is one thing to motor for half a day and quite another to do it for three or possibly four days. We were eagerly consulting the weather reports daily. Finally, we noticed the approach of a low that was going to pass in two days' time. Reluctantly, I had to accept the fact that if Ithaca has been waiting for my visit for more than 3,500 years, it can wait for a couple more, and so we decided to give our trip around the island a miss.

TO SYRACUSE

July, 2008

We stocked up on food and water from the local shops, I cooked two meals for the 270 nautical mile trip, and we checked the contents of the grab bag and all the emergency equipment. I packed the hand-held VHF radio, GPS and EPIRB into the grab bag and loaded them with new batteries. We checked the weather report and after so many windless days we were delighted to see a storm coming through the Ionian Sea between 15 and 17 July. I hate to say this, as wishing for a storm is not something a sailor should ever do. The narrow strait between heel of Italy's boot and the westernmost Ionian Islands of Greece was screaming red. The wind was predicted to come north/north-west, just the right direction to take propel us to the south-west and to our destination in Sicily, Syracuse. The forecast was around 25–35 knots. We decided to prepare for the worst but leave as soon as we could. We reckoned that by leaving the next morning we could run in front of the worst of the storm. We yanked up the storm jib, secured it, applied an extra security rope for the motorbike, cleared the deck and removed anything and everything that could possibly launch itself like a rocket in the cabin. By 10.30 am we were our way, still no wind, so we motored from the town quay of Argostoli towards the head. Then the breeze arrived and we pulled up the sails and set the bearing to 257° towards Syracuse. There was a pleasant 18-knot wind that slowly became stronger. By 11 pm, it had reached 25–30 knots and continued to blow during the night.

We had a wonderful though sometimes scary passage. Even though we ran in front of a storm, the wind got up to 35 knots. So we furled first the jib then a third of the main to keep *Fenix* balanced. The trip was exciting and beautiful. The boat was flying from one mountainous wave to the other and by the morning we were closer to Italy than Greece. Dawn found me on watch and I had the privilege of experiencing sunrise at sea.

On land there are several clues giving away the approaching dawn. Birds start chirping in the darkness, giving a wake up call to the other early risers. Animals that feed at dawn start to stir, making small noises. At sea there were no clues whatsoever. Perhaps the darkness of the night changed, the depth of blackness became less impenetrable. Features that remained invisible during the night started to emerge. This was particularly true for the angrily raging, sea all around us. The darkness of the night prevented me from seeing the huge breaking waves, giving me a false sense of security. Pushed by the front, the water from the Adriatic Sea was rushing down towards Africa and built up in the strait between Sicily and Greece, creating waves up to three metres high. It never failed to amaze me how quickly waves can build up to dangerous heights in the Mediterranean. But *Fenix*, undeterred by the confused sea, was bravely cutting through all those white crests in front of us, giving me confidence in her ability to deliver us safely to shore. After I got used to seeing all those wild white horses around me, I noticed a pale pink on the eastern horizon. The pink became pale orange, then red, and suddenly the first ray of the sun hit the surface of the water, passing a warm welcoming flicker across my face. I hardly had time to adjust my eyes before the sun god Helios in his full glorious brightness emerged to welcome another day.

We continued our passage and made very good time. By dusk we came across some coastal boat traffic and soon we could see the lights of a huge city. The traffic along the coast was extremely busy and approaching the harbour required all our attention. The radar and the recently purchased AIS (Automated Information System: it tells the name, location, bearing and speed of all boats equipped with this instrument, and is compulsory for vessels heavier than 300 tonnes) and our eyesight were all in action to navigate through the busy coastal traffic. We had to avoid the huge tankers travelling parallel with the shore, the unlit vessels of the local fishermen and the passenger ferries. We sailed into the natural port of Syracuse by midnight, lowered our anchor and had a good sleep under the walls of the old town. Next morning, woken by the bells of the cathedral, I could not wait to discover this city where Archimedes designed mirrors to burn the attacking Roman ships. But that is a story for another time.

THE GLORY OF ATHENS

After years of wandering around the islands, we left the shores of modern Greece. Our experiences had mainly been contemporary, with only glimpses of how Ancient Greek ideas have impacted on our modern life. To overcome this shortcoming, in this chapter I intend to discuss the Ancient Greeks' most important contributions to knowledge and understanding of the world. The title of this chapter suggests the supremacy of Athens in Ancient Greece. Depending on your interpretation, this may or may not be true. Ancient Greece was a loose collection of city-states that were scattered around the Mediterranean and the Black Sea. The people were united by speaking the same language and more or less following the same habits or, if you like, the same ideology. Humans have lived in Athens for 7,000 years. The foundation of the city is closely associated with the legend of Theseus and goes back to 1300 BC. Athens' golden age reached its peak around 477 BC, when it became the leader of the Delian League, which consisted of 150 city-states. Around this time, Athens' intellectual and cultural influence became dominant. The spread of Greek thoughts and habits continued during the Hellenistic age (~300 BC–30 AD), when they reached the valleys of the Himalaya, Central Asia, and the Hindu and Persian Empires.

Of course, at the same time there were several similar and in some ways more sophisticated civilisations on this planet. Interestingly, the period around 400 BC was a golden age for mankind when ethics and morality were universally developed. It seems that after thousands of years of a subsistence existence, mankind reached a new level of sophistication in several locations at around the same time. In the highly developed Chinese empire, Confucius resigned as a minister and by wandering around his vast country he started to teach morality, family values, hard work and statecraft that remains a guiding force for over a billion Chinese to date. In the Indian subcontinent, Gautama Buddha, a prince surrounded by wealth and privilege, left it all behind in search of happiness and founded a belief system that even today inspires millions, including many brought up in Western traditions.

So, what are the gifts of the Ancient Greeks that remain universal and should not be limited to people of European origin but cherished by all of mankind? What were these ideas? How can they have such a tremendous effect on people even today?

In this chapter, I extensively relied on information from the Internet.

Human Gods?

Imagine a group of humans living in the wild natural world without their 21st-century city fortresses, without their vision being enhanced by satellites, glasses, binoculars and microscopes for peeking into the distance or seeing more detail, without cars or airplanes or ships to safely deliver their slow, clumsy bodies away from danger, before they learnt to construct strong houses to shelter them from the sun and storms, before myriad natural and synthetic fibres became available to cover their hairless, naked bodies and protect them from cold, heat, sun and rain, before the existence of electricity to push away the fear of darkness, before food came from the much-hated but easily accessible, plentiful supermarkets, before incredibly strong machines were invented to dig, lift, spin, push and pull, challenging even the Titans, before the understanding of illnesses and death, and before printing, radio, television, the Internet and smart phones were invented – the world out there was an awfully scary, dangerous place. No surprise therefore that humans continually turned to religion, asking their gods to help them to survive the brutal forces of nature and to provide some relief from the ever-present fear ruling their existence.

Like it or not, religion has – as far as we can ascertain – been part of human existence from the beginning of time and will be part of it for a long time to come. Humans would not have been able to adapt to cope with fear, frustration and failure, without hope. Perhaps religion is the direct consequence of evolution – though many modern evolutionary biologists would strongly disagree, with the mighty Richard Dawkins leading the charge (Dawkins 2006). However, we cannot exclude that a sort of "faith instinct-hope" emerged in humans, 60–100,000 years ago, when our a big frontal lobe developed and instigated us to ask questions about the surrounding world. Whether we like it or not, our relationship to the gods determines the way we see the world and the way we deal with its everyday challenges. You can tell a lot about a person by the company they keep, but I suspect an even stronger truism is: "show me your god and I'll tell you who you are".

It is not surprising that the gods of primitive societies had to be strong, fearless and immortal. For instance, the Egyptian sphinx, with its head of a human and body of a strong indestructible lion, and the Hindu gods and goddesses with many arms, Durga, Kali and Shiva, all exhibit superhuman qualities. Chinese culture lacks individual gods, but the closest equivalents to supernatural gods or heroes, Nuwa and Fuxi, half-human and half-snake super-human creatures, are worshipped as the ultimate ancestors of humankind.

In the chaotic world of early Greek mythology, the Titans, also known as elder gods, ruled the Earth with iron fists. Cronus was the ruler of the Titans, who in a way reminiscent of human power struggles was de-throned in a violent coup by his son Zeus. The Titans, superhuman in size, behaviour and strength, treated the small, vulnerable humanity as they pleased and their most important role was to punish misbehaviour. But at the same time, there was a kinder, more considerate god also present, Dionysus.

According to some Greek legends, Dionysus was also the child of Zeus and was brought up in the forest under the tender, easy-going care of nymphs. Worship of Dionysus began in prehistoric times and his name already appears in the Linear B tablets of Pylos (1500–1000 BC). The Dionysian cult was associated with the cultivation of grapevines and an understanding of their life cycle. Grapevines were believed to have embodied the living god and the fermentation of wine was associated with the god's essence. Most importantly, however, the intoxicating and disinhibiting effects of wine and the resulting ecstatic dancing were regarded as a sign of being possessed by the god's spirit. Dionysus was celebrated during dedicated festivals that led to the emergence of the Greek theatre.

The people who worshipped the Titans thought that only the omnipotent gods could solve their problems. Perhaps because of the Dionysian cult, the Greeks yearned for more docile, more sympathetic gods. Thus, from this chaotic, aggressive, bleak world of the Titans, the jovial Olympian Greek gods emerged, who afterward cheerfully instructed their worshippers on behaviour and the rights and wrongs of the world until the monotheists' rigid, uncompromising views destroyed their statues, their temples and ultimately their place in the human soul.

The 12 Olympian gods won the battle against the Titans, with **Zeus**, the Father of the Gods, the god of the sky, weather, thunder and storms, becoming the most important. Zeus was able to remain in power because of his intelligence, his sense of justice and his willingness to work with the other gods. **Poseidon** was the brother of Zeus, and after Zeus took possession of the sky, he had to be satisfied with the sea and became the protector of fishermen. Their brother **Hades** became the ruler of the underworld. **Demeter** was the sister of Zeus and was the mother of Earth and crops. The worship of Demeter and her influence goes back to the beginning of agriculture. She was already present in prehistoric Cyprus, Mesopotamia and of course in Minoan Crete. The myth of Demeter and her daughter Persephone was used to explain the reason for the seasons. When Hades, the God of Underworld, kidnapped Persephone, her grieving mother denied the world crops. In the end an agreement was struck between Hades and Zeus such that Persephone spends half of her time with Hades, when there is winter and no crops grow, and half of her life with her mother Demeter, when the world celebrates her return with new growth and the yield of crops during spring and summer. Demeter and Persephone invented the plough and taught humanity to cultivate grain and to till, sow, reap and thresh so that they would be able to sustain themselves through the winter.

Hera, the wife of Zeus and the embodiment of fertility and marriage, had to be very clever to ensure any of her children survived. Thinking about how he gained power, Zeus decided to swallow all his children after birth. However, Hera not only managed to make sure that her children from her union with Zeus survived but, as a forerunner to either immaculate conception or extra-marital sex, she gave birth to the ugly **Hephaestus**, who became the god of technology, blacksmiths, craftsmen, artisans, sculptors, metals, metallurgy, fire and volcanoes.

Although Hera might not have been the perfect faithful wife, Zeus was definitely a philandering husband. One of his encounters with his cousin resulted in her becoming pregnant. Unusually, Zeus did not wait until the birth of this child, but instead swallowed his pregnant cousin. His child clung to life and it was Zeus who ended up giving birth to a daughter, **Athena**, who sprang out of his head in full amour. Athena was wise, incorruptible and invincible and became protector of Attica, Athens, the Acheans, Odysseus, Achilles, Heracles and Telemachos. She was a warrior and promoter of culture and technology. Athena taught humanity not only how to make weapons and ships, but also how to cultivate olives and how to weave.

Aphrodite, the goddess of love, was born from the foam created from the cut-off genitals of her father Cronos. She became the wife of Hephaestus, but marriage did not prevent her from being full of passion for both mortals and immortals. She gave birth to numerous children, including the four muses, Harmony, Deimos, Phobos, Eros and, with Zeus, the gorgeous Adonis. She also had one son with Poseidon, Erykas, who became the King of Sicily. Her daughter Rhodos gave her name to the beautiful island in the east of the Mediterranean Sea, Rhodes.

Ares was the only legitimate son of Zeus and Hera and was born in the rough barbaric country of Thrace. Not surprisingly, he became wild and uncontrollable and embodied tempest and the madness of war without reason. There was continuous conflict between him and Athena, who despite being the goddess of war also embodied wisdom, strategy and reason.

Jealousy was as much a part of the life of gods as that of humans. When Leto, the lover of Zeus, became pregnant with twins, Hera, the jealous wife of Zeus, forbade any place from allowing Leto to give birth. She could only give birth at a place that had never seen the sun. According to the myth, Leto asked her sister Asteria to help, and Asteria became the floating rock of Delos to receive her. There, first **Artemis**, the embodiment of the Moon, was born and then helped her mother to give birth to the beautiful **Apollo**, the incarnation of the Sun. Artemis decided to remain unmarried and lived in the wild mountains hunting wild animals and dancing and playing. When Apollo was born, bathed in light, the barren Delos flowered and bore fruit and produced olive trees with golden leaves. Feeding on nectar and ambrosia, Apollo grew up quickly. Armed with a bow and carrying a lyre, he went to Olympus to announce that he would proclaim the will of Zeus through oracles.

But it took **Hermes**, the youngest child of Zeus, to invent Apollo's famous lyre. According to legend, still a new born baby, he climbed out of his cradle, and, on coming across a tortoise, he killed it, made seven strings from the gut of the animal and thus fashioned the first lyre. Then, he stole his brother Apollo's cows and started the first fire by rubbing a laurel twig against another piece of wood. He butchered and skinned the animals, spitted them and placed them on the fire. When the meat was ready, he divided it into 12 portions, then went back and lay down in his cradle.

When Apollo arrived, he found an innocent child playing. But he did not believe his brother's pretence at innocence. To mollify his brother, Hermes played the lyre and Apollo became so enchanted by it that Hermes gave his lyre to Apollo, who reciprocated by giving him a golden wand. Hermes, the messenger of Zeus, was clever, quick and crafty, but also a thief, playing tricks from his birth. Apollo, on the other hand, became the symbol of order, beauty, light, and thus literature, poetry and the theatre.

So, here they are, the most important gods of the Ancient Greeks cut down to human size. Just like humans, they all have some noble and not-so-noble features; they all embody important activities, or even professions, that became indispensable for the development of Ancient Greece. The gods are said to be similar to humans and to suffer from the same thirst for understanding and knowledge. One of the most important gifts of the Ancient Greeks to the world is philosophy or the love (*philos*) of wisdom (*sophia*), looking for the answers to the eternal questions of, "What am I doing here? Who am I?"

Philosophy

We may not know when it happened the first time, but over the history of mankind probably millions of people have asked these questions. The three most enduring Greek philosophers – Socrates, Plato and Aristotle – were just some of thousands of thinkers. What differentiated them was the way they searched for objectivity and wisdom.

Socrates, the father of philosophy (469–399 BC), was born and lived in Athens. His ugliness and unkempt appearance made him stand out in a city that is considered to be the birthplace of classical beauty. He was the forefather of all those independent academics, dressed in corduroy pants and ill-fitting jackets, these days T-shirts and shapeless jeans, who pride themselves on not worrying about the opinion of their fellow man. Socrates was not rich, but he enjoyed and fully exploited all the rights that the free city-state bestowed upon its citizens. He spent most of his time sitting in his dirty cloak, barefoot, and asking very unpleasant questions of his fellow citizens to find out more and more about morality. This annoying form of investigative method became known as the Socratic Method. To solve a problem, it is broken down into a series of questions, the answers to which gradually distill the answer the person seeks. The development and practice of this method is one of Socrates' most enduring contributions, and is a key factor in his legacy as the father of ethics and political and moral philosophy. He famously summed up something that scientists, including even the most renowned ones, painfully rediscover again and again as they slowly make progress in their subjects: "I only know that I know nothing".

Having said that he had very strong opinions about the world, Socrates made the momentous turn of thought away from speculation towards the liberal questions of morality, justice, virtue and politics. He believed that:

- No one desires evil.
- No one errs or does wrong willingly or knowingly.
- Virtue – all virtue – is knowledge.
- Virtue is sufficient for happiness. (Many would argue with this.)

Somewhere among these assumptions we can discover the roots of our present legal system, with the presumption of innocence, the right to appropriate legal representation and the right to a fair trial. As a forefather of universal education, he put knowledge on a pedestal and urged his fellow citizens to study. He taught us logical thinking, the value of criticism and how to defend our views, to accept the decision of the majority but also to question it. The fact that the majority thinks something is right it does not make it right, but the opposite can also be true.

> "In spite of promoting individual and collective well-being, the Athenians just had enough of his questions and charged him with dishonesty, being a heretic and with corrupting the youth; he stood trial in 399 BC. Mind you, in true Athenian manner he was convicted according to the laws of his city-state. All 550 jurors voted, of whom 360 found him guilty. But the jurors felt that somehow this was not right and he was offered to withdraw his teachings and live in exile. Defiant as ever, he delivered a speech in which he conceded nothing and so became the first person documented to die for his beliefs rather than compromise" (De Botton 2000)

> "So long as I draw breath and have my faculties, I shall never stop practicing philosophy and exhorting you and elucidating the truth for everyone that I meet… And so gentlemen… whether you acquit me or not, you know that I am not going to alter my conduct, not even if I have to die a hundred deaths." (Socrates declared)

But most importantly, all in all, he accepted the decision of the jurors, which was consistent with his views that citizens do have to obey the laws of the state. Thus, he drank the deadly hemlock and died in his bed surrounded by his pupils.

Socrates' most famous and diligent pupil, Plato, gave us via his dialogues not only the views of his teacher but also the perfect description of an ideal state. He also shows us to our dismay how our view of the world is distorted by our limited understanding. *The Republic* was written after the terrible 30-year Peloponnesian Wars that involved all the Greek states on either the side of Athens or Sparta. Plato's main objective was to devise a type of government that could prevent future fighting between Greek city-states. In fact, this celebrated book examines alternative forms of government to democracy. In Plato's ideal state, a wise philosopher king governs with absolute power a communal society where the state intervenes in people's lives, including what they read and how they bring up their children. In 366 BC, Plato was actually invited to Syracuse to set up his experimental republic. But the experiment failed; by 387 BC, the people of Syracuse had had enough and Plato, his followers and his ideas were ousted.

In *The Republic*, Plato compares our limited understanding of the world to someone who has spent his life chained to a cave wall. Socrates is talking to a young follower of his named Glaucon.

> "[**SOCRATES:**] Most people, including ourselves, live in a world of relative ignorance. We are even comfortable with that ignorance, because it is all we know. When we first start facing the truth, the process may be frightening, and many people run back to their old lives. But if you continue to seek truth, you want more!

And now, I said, let me show in a figure how far our nature is enlightened or unenlightened: – Behold! human beings living in a underground den, which has a mouth open towards the light and reaching all along the den; here they have been from their childhood, and have their legs and necks chained so that they cannot move, and can only see before them, being prevented by the chains from turning round their heads. Above and behind them a fire is blazing at a distance, and between the fire and the prisoners there is a raised way; and you will see, if you look, a low wall built along the way, like the screen which marionette players have in front of them, over which they show the puppets.

[GLAUCON:] I see.

[SOCRATES:] And do you see, I said, men passing along the wall carrying all sorts of vessels, and statues and figures of animals made of wood and stone and various materials, which appear over the wall? Some of them are talking, others silent.

[GLAUCON:] You have shown me a strange image, and they are strange prisoners.

[SOCRATES:] Like ourselves, I replied; and they see only their own shadows, or the shadows of one another, which the fire throws on the opposite wall of the cave?

[GLAUCON:] True, he said; how could they see anything but the shadows if they were never allowed to move their heads?

[SOCRATES:] And of the objects which are being carried in like manner they would only see the shadows?

[GLAUCON:] Yes, he said.

[SOCRATES:] And if they were able to converse with one another, would they not suppose that they were naming what was actually before them?

[GLAUCON:] Very true.

[SOCRATES:] And suppose further that the prison had an echo which came from the other side, would they not be sure to fancy when one of the passers-by spoke that the voice which they heard came from the passing shadow?

[GLAUCON:] No question, he replied.

[SOCRATES:] To them, I said, the truth would be literally nothing but the shadows of the images.

[GLAUCON:] That is certain.

[SOCRATES:] And now look again, and see what will naturally follow if the prisoners are released and disabused of their error. At first, when any of them is liberated and compelled suddenly to stand up and turn his neck round and walk and look towards the light, he will suffer sharp pains; the glare will distress him, and he will be unable to see the realities of which in his former state he had seen the shadows; and then conceive some one saying to him, that what he saw before was an illusion, but that now, when he is approaching nearer to being and his eye is turned towards more real existence, he has a clearer vision, – what will be his reply? And you may further imagine that his instructor is pointing to the objects as they pass and requiring him to name them, – will he not be perplexed? Will he not fancy that the shadows which he formerly saw are truer than the objects which are now shown to him?

[**GLAUCON:**] Far truer.

[**SOCRATES:**] And if he is compelled to look straight at the light, will he not have a pain in his eyes which will make him turn away to take and take in the objects of vision which he can see, and which he will conceive to be in reality clearer than the things which are now being shown to him?

[**GLAUCON:**] True, he said.

[**SOCRATES:**] And suppose once more, that he is reluctantly dragged up a steep and rugged ascent, and held fast until he's forced into the presence of the sun himself, is he not likely to be pained and irritated? When he approaches the light his eyes will be dazzled, and he will not be able to see anything at all of what are now called realities.

[**GLAUCON:**] Not all in a moment, he said.

[**SOCRATES:**] He will require to grow accustomed to the sight of the upper world. And first he will see the shadows best, next the reflections of men and other objects in the water, and then the objects themselves; then he will gaze upon the light of the moon and the stars and the spangled heaven; and he will see the sky and the stars by night better than the sun or the light of the sun by day?

[**GLAUCON:**] Certainly.

[**SOCRATES:**] Last of he will be able to see the sun, and not mere reflections of him in the water, but he will see him in his own proper place, and not in another; and he will contemplate him as he is.

[**GLAUCON:**] Certainly.

[**SOCRATES:**] He will then proceed to argue that this is he who gives the season and the years, and is the guardian of all that is in the visible world, and in a certain way the cause of all things which he and his fellows have been accustomed to behold?

[**GLAUCON:**] Clearly, he said, he would first see the sun and then reason about him.

[**SOCRATES:**] And when he remembered his old habitation, and the wisdom of the den and his felllow-prisoners, do you not suppose that he would felicitate himself on the change, and pity them?

[**GLAUCON:**] Certainly, he would.

[**SOCRATES:**] And if they were in the habit of conferring honours among themselves on those who were quickest to observe the passing shadows and to remark which of them went before, and which followed after, and which were together; and who were therefore best able to draw conclusions as to the future, do you think that he would care for such honours and glories, or envy the possessors of them? Would he not say with Homer, 'Better to be the poor

252

servant of a poor master, and to endure anything, rather than think as they do and live after their manner?'

[**GLAUCON**:] Yes, he said, I think that he would rather suffer anything than entertain these false notions and live in this miserable manner.

[**SOCRATES**:] Imagine once more, I said, such an one coming suddenly out of the sun to be replaced in his old situation; would he not be certain to have his eyes full of darkness?

[**GLAUCON**:] To be sure, he said.

[**SOCRATES**:] And if there were a contest, and he had to compete in measuring the shadows with the prisoners who had never moved out of the den, while his sight was still weak, and before his eyes had become steady (and the time which would be needed to acquire this new habit of sight might be very considerable) would he not be ridiculous? Men would say of him that up he went and down he came without his eyes; and that it was better not even to think of ascending; and if any one tried to loose another and lead him up to the light, let them only catch the offender, and they would put him to death.

[**GLAUCON**:] No question, he said.

[**SOCRATES**:] This entire allegory, I said, you may now append, dear Glaucon, to the previous argument; the prison-house is the world of sight, the light of the fire is the sun, and you will not misapprehend me if you interpret the journey upwards to be the ascent of the soul into the intellectual world according to my poor belief, which, at your desire, I have expressed, whether rightly or wrongly God knows. But, whether true or false, my opinion is that in the world of knowledge the idea of good appears last of all, and is seen only with an effort; and, when seen, is also inferred to be the universal author of all things beautiful and right, parent of light and of the lord of light in this visible world, and the immediate source of reason and truth in the intellectual; and that this is the power upon which he who would act rationally, either in public or private life must have his eye fixed."

"Many over the centuries have disagreed with Plato, and in the 19th century, the famous German philosopher Nietzsche simply declared, "Plato is boring". But Nietzsche also built on the Greek idea of agonistic spirit. Agon means contest. The notion that contest is at the core of life is really a central Greek idea that influenced all parts of Greek society. There were theatrical contests, rhetoric contests, poetry contests and athletic competitions, all in honour of Zeus. After years of contemplation, Nietzsche concluded that for humans to be happy they have to struggle. He liked the idea of comparing human life to climbing a mountain, where the sweet reward of the view on the top compensates for the strenuous climb." (De Botton 2000)

I prefer the comparison to sailing, which according to some cynics is "the fine art of getting wet and becoming ill while slowly going nowhere at great expense". When I travel on a vessel that is hardly capable of supporting human life – I guess the majority of people would agree that small sailing boats are not suitable for travelling great distances on open oceans – and struggle with the waves, the constantly failing equipment, the weather, facing the enormous difficulty of finding my way without any visual clues, I really get an immense pleasure out of exercising my judgment and my muscles and from performing complex activities, all the while relying on my big brain given to me by a freak moment in evolution hundreds of thousands of years ago. The success of arriving at a destination is made sweet by the effort and the adventures that led to it.

Today's Western society has unknowingly become a "Schopenhauer fan club". Schopenhauer is another 19th-century German philosopher who declared: "those seeking happiness should try to avoid anything that might require effort."

In Western countries, we live in a "take it easy" society where satisfying yourself with easily achievable, instantly gratifying aims has become the norm. While our society gradually turns away from hardships and people become more and more influenced by ideas preaching the futility of individual effort, like Hinduism (reincarnation – why bother, next time you might be born as a prince) and Buddhism (Nirvana – not wanting anything is the perfect state of existence) (these are cynical interpretations), in the developing world literally billions from China to Brazil are rediscovering the two main driving forces of the Ancient Greeks – contest (*agon*) and personal excellence (*arete*) – to further their own fortunes.

The Birth of Sciences

A lthough the gods were very much present and were consulted in the everyday life of the people of Ancient Greece, they did not condemn the inquisitive nature of humans. Thus, the Greeks, armed with Socrates' teachings, the quest for knowledge, and encouraged by their gods, were not limited in their discovery of the world around them. Not surprisingly, this led not only to a series of inventions but also to the establishment of all modern scientific disciplines.

Astronomy

Until the Industrial Revolution in the 18th century, human life around the globe was dominated by agriculture. Of course, all cultures, even those that did not develop into influential civilisations, have been awed by the skies and have made observations. The people of the Pacific Ocean used the stars to navigate their rickety boats from island to island and all the major ancient civilisations, starting with the Mesopotamians, made detailed descriptions of their observations using the constellations. Astronomy was clearly a subject of major practical importance in creating a rudimentary calendar to sort out dates for the beginning of harvest, and other activities related to agriculture. To this end, the accumulated observations required better analytical methods. Astronomy was not what it is today, but it was a combination of mathematics, physics and philosophy and it was practised by a wide variety of people (there are around 30 astronomers documented in different Greek writings). In *Works and Days,* Hesiod (750–650 BC) gave this advice:

> "When the Pleiades rise it is time to use the sickle, but the plough when they are setting; 40 days they stay away from heaven; when Arcturus ascends from the sea and, rising in the evening, remains visible for the entire night, the grapes must be pruned; but when Orion and Sirius come in the middle of heaven and the rosy fingered Eos sees Arcturus, the grapes must be picked; when the Pleiades, the Hyades, and Orion are setting, then mind the plough; when the Pleiades, fleeing Orion, plunge into the dark sea, storms may be expected; 50 days after the sun's turning is the right time for man to navigate; when Orion appears, Demeter's gift has to be brought to the well-smoothed threshing floor."

To get organised and follow these instructions, people needed a good calendar to tell exactly what 40 or 50 days meant. The early effort of 12 months and 30 days did not work well, as the Moon got out of phase very quickly. Oenopides proposed a 59-year cycle calendar where a year was 730 months. Surely a year was longer than the average lifetime. The ancient astronomers were helped by two pieces of equipment, the *parapegma* and the Antikythera mechanism.

The *parapegma* was a stone tablet with movable pegs and an inscription to indicate the approximate correspondence between, for example, the rising of a particular star and the civil date. Because the calendar had to be changed regularly to keep it in phase with the astronomical one, the *parapegma* had movable pegs, which could be adjusted as necessary. The *parapegma* also contained meteorological forecasts associated with the rising and setting of the stars. *Parapegmata* were not only made out of stone but were also written on papyri.

The Antikythera mechanism was the pinnacle of Ancient Greek science and technology. More than a hundred years ago, an extraordinary mechanism was found by sponge divers at the bottom of the sea near the island of Antikythera. It astonished the whole international community of experts on the ancient world. Was it an astrolabe? Was it an orrery or an astronomical clock? Or something else? For decades, scientific investigation failed to cast much light on it and relied more on imagination than the facts. However, research over the last half-century has begun to reveal its secrets. The machine dates from around the end of the 2nd century BC and is the most sophisticated mechanism known from the ancient world. Nothing as complex is known for the next thousand years. The Antikythera mechanism is now understood to be dedicated to astronomical phenomena and operates as a complex mechanical "computer" which tracks the cycles of the solar system.

Here I provide a list of the Ancient Greeks' major contributions to astronomy that have survived the test of time:

- They identified that the apparent path of the Sun's motion made an angle of 24° with the equator.
- They recognised that the Earth is a sphere.
- They identified that Venus as an evening star is the same as Venus as a morning star and that it is actually a planet.
- They devised a model that correctly identified that the apparently complex motions of the heavenly bodies did indeed result from simple circular motion.
- Pythagoras proposed a beautiful mathematical theory of concentric spheres to describe the motion of the heavenly bodies.
- They named most of the constellations of the northern hemisphere and gave some planets names that are still used today.
- They measured the ratio of the distances to the Moon and to the Sun and showed that the Sun is much further from the Earth than the Moon. The fact, that the Sun was the largest of these three bodies, Earth, Moon and Sun, led to the heliocentric theory. However this Sun-centred universe found little favour with the Ancient Greeks, who continued to develop more and more, sophisticated models based on an Earth-centred universe.

- Ptolemy (150–90 BC) developed a system that predicted the movement of the planets with good accuracy, definitely within the range of measurements of the time. His monumental work, the *Syntaxis Almagest*, the only surviving ancient astronomical work, contained the *Handy Tables* that presented a useful tool for astronomical calculations. The *Handy Tables* was in essence a *parapegma* that tabulated all the data needed to compute the positions of the Sun, Moon and planets, the rising and setting of the stars, and eclipses of the Sun and Moon. In this system, the movement of epicycles on a deferent explained the retrograde motion and changing brightness of the planets. The Christian Church adopted this incorrect Earth-centric universe and it became a doctrine for more than 1,500 years.

Highly developed astronomy took place in all the courts of the ancient world, from Greece to China, South America and India. Greek astronomy was influenced by Babylonian astronomy and, to a lesser extent, Egyptian astronomy; in turn, it influenced Indian and Arabic-Islamic astronomy. Regardless of its origins, all astronomy provided detailed descriptions of the cosmos on the basis of the observed movements of planets. The observers all relied on their senses and tried to describe the universe as they saw it, i.e. that everything revolved around the Earth. However, in addition to this, Greek astronomy also set up a framework that enabled scientists who came later to re-examine the truth of earlier statements. These were two important theories:

1. The idea in Pythagorean philosophy that all complex phenomena must reduce to simple ones. One should not underestimate the importance of this idea, which has proved so powerful throughout the development of science, being a fundamental driving force for great scientists such as Newton and particularly Einstein.
2. The Greek element theories, which claim that things are made up of minute ultimate parts that usually do not look like the parts that are big enough for us to see. Element theories build on the idea that reality is hidden, and direct experience is in some ultimate sense not real (Plato). We usually refer to this fundamental claim as appearance vs. reality.

It was only in the 15th century that Copernicus developed the solar-centric system describing how the planets move around the Sun on fixed orbits. Subsequently, a German monk, Kepler, calculated and developed the system we use today, i.e. the planets move around the Sun on elliptical orbits with changing speed. The star of the show has always been Galileo Galilei. Born in Pisa and educated in the free-thinking Renaissance towns of Pisa and Florence, he became a well-known mathematician, physicist, astronomer and philosopher, later working at the University of Padua. Thanks to the involvement of the Church in science (in fact many of the Christian monks were highly qualified scientists) he got into a scientific argument with one of the scientist-monks. The debate, which was marginally about whether the universe was heliocentric or not, subsequently caught the attention of Pope Urban VIII. Galileo defended heliocentrism, and claimed it was not contrary to Scripture passages. However, the Catholic Church was in trouble. The Reformation Movement was gathering strength in the north, and in the south, there were loud calls to widen the Spanish Inquisition. In this environment, the simple scientific argument became blown out of proportion. Galileo was suspected of heresy and was charged by doubting the Scriptures. He was put under house arrest and he died in his villa Il gioiello in Arcetri, near Florence. His last words were supposedly, "And yet it moves." It was not until 1992, after 350 years of consideration, that Pope John Paul II officially conceded that the Earth was not stationary and moved around the Sun. One cannot say that the Catholic Church did not give a serious deliberation to this matter.

Geometry

On the basis of their astronomy, I think the Ancient Greeks must had reasonably high-level knowledge of calculus, but the great invention of the zero is attributed to the Babylonians. On the other hand, the contribution of two giants, Pythagoras (570–495 BC) and Euclid (~300 BC) to geometry proved to be timeless. The Pythagorean theorem says (see also Samos) that in a right-angled triangle the sum of the squares of the right-angled sides will always be the same as the square of the hypotenuse (the long side): $a^2 + b^2 = c^2$. This famous theorem has stood the test of time and more than 350 proofs show that it is an immutable fact. The theorem has been continuously taught at schools for more than 2,500 years. Euclid, the Alexandrian mathematician, summarised the mathematical knowledge of the Greek world in his work *The Elements*. Although earlier mathematicians had described many of the subjects before, Euclid was the first to show how these propositions could fit into a comprehensive deductive and logical system. The contents of *The Elements* are no less than what is today taught as algebra and geometry in secondary schools.

The Euclidian system is based on axioms. Axioms are statements that are accepted as true. Euclid believed that we couldn't be sure of any axioms without proof, so he devised logical steps to prove them. Euclid divided his 10 axioms, which he called "postulates", into two groups of five. The first five were "common notions", because they were common to all sciences:

- Things which are equal to the same thing are also equal to one another.
- If equals are added to equals, the sums are equal.
- If equals are subtracted from equals, the remainders are equal.
- Things which coincide with one another are equal to one another.
- The whole is greater than the part.

The remaining five postulates were related specifically to geometry:

- You can draw a straight line between any two points.
- You can extend a line indefinitely.
- You can draw a circle using any line segment as the radius and one end point as the centre.
- All right angles are equal.
- Given a line and a point, you can draw only one line through the point that is parallel to the first line.

The Greek philosopher Proclus records that when King Ptolemy asked if there was an easier way to study geometry than *The Elements*, Euclid replied; "Sire, there is no royal road to geometry" – which remains true even today.

All these scientific efforts did not stand alone but were translated into technical and engineering achievements. Archaeologists have found remnants of pipe organs, diving bells, showers, cannons, cannon pulleys, vending machines, and aqueducts, which, seen in conjunction with myriad everyday items, demonstrate that Ancient Greece was a highly developed technical society.

Medicine

Initially the Greek approach to healing was not significantly different from similar therapeutic practices administered to mankind all over the world. From the Kalahari Desert to the Chinese Tao temples and the indigenous people of South America, healers asked for divine intervention. In Ancient Greece in around 500 BC, medicine took a leap forward. This progress in medicine, as in philosophy, is a good example of the restless intellectual activity of the Greek mind. The Ancient Greeks successfully struggled to free their thinking not only from magic and superstition but also from more subtle a priori systems of philosophical thought, where knowledge is independent of experience and theoretical deduction is favoured over direct observation. Thus, as with many other modern pursuits, the experimental scientific method was also born in Ancient Greece. Changing from a priori thinking to proof-based observation was and remains one of the most significant contribution of the Greeks to mankind: it has irreversibly changed how man looks at the surrounding world. As Goethe observed:

> "The writings that have come down to us under the name of Hippocrates present the model of how man should view the world and record what was seen without intruding himself into it."

To our knowledge, this change happened first in the Asclepeion of Cos. The miracle-driven, religion-based healing process was converted into a scientific method, based on memory, observation, categorisation and diagnosis, followed by rigorous therapy and treatment. Thus, the foundations of Western medicine were established. Today, many people when they are at their healthiest turn away from Western medicine, but are usually quick to change their mind at the earliest signs of sickness. After all, the medicines developed by rigorous scientific tests give the best chance for any treatment to succeed. Modern medicine that aspires to understand the disease and treatment processes would not be ours today without Hippocrates, who lived around 460 BC and changed healing forever.

The aforementioned Greek element theory combined with the Pythagorean philosophy determined Western thinking about the world. The idea of breaking down an apparently unsolvable problem into small steps served science well. In my own profession of medical science, it is still practised every day. However, it has its limits. Here is an example: The discovery that diabetes can be treated with the administration of insulin and that insulin can be produced on an industrial scale has improved the quality of life and extended the life span of millions. However, at the same time, this approach has failed to address the cause of type II diabetes, which despite having a genetic component, is mainly associated with a sedentary lifestyle.

Thus, though diabetics live longer, the rate of obesity and associated heart and kidney disease, neuropathy and blindness continues to soar. These changes are slowly pushing the iconic Western state-funded healthcare system into bankruptcy. To solve these problems, perhaps it is time again to pull out the old Socratic method and have a good critical look at our healthcare system.

Geography

The first geographical description of a place and anything that resembles something like a map originates from the 6th century BC. But people must have been using maps forever. The Australian aborigines have described their wanderings in an oral tradition, the famous "songlines", so precisely that even after thousands of years the tribes were capable of following the same routes again and again, giving them the highest chance of survival in the inhospitable Australian desert.

Still, the key figure in ancient geography remains Strabo (63 BC–24 AD), who in his 17-volume work *Geographica* described the history and the look of places around the Mediterranean with so much precision that even today amateurs and professionals alike rely on his descriptions.

History

I understand that traditionally history is categorised as a subject belonging to the humanities. It has been said that "history is written by the victors", but here I would like to make an argument for history, based on facts and impartial assessment, becoming part of the sciences.

The world's first historian was Herodotus (484–425 BC), born in Halicarnassus. He was the first known writer to collect his materials systematically, test their accuracy to a certain extent, and arrange them into a well-constructed, logical narrative. His work *Histories* has been called by many names, "a universal history", "a history of the wars between the Greeks and the barbarians", and "a history of the struggle between Greece and Persia". His aims were laudable and I wish present-day historians provided us with as precise descriptions of modern-day events as Herodotus did almost 2,500 years ago.

> "Herodotus hereby publishes the results of his inquiries, hoping to do two things: to preserve the memory of the past by putting on record the astonishing achievements both of the Greek and the non-Greek peoples; and more particularly, to show how the two races came into conflict."

But Herodotus was not alone in preserving the stories of people. Around the same time in China, people started to write down the stories of dynasties, giving an accurate record in chronological order of their rulers. Although Chinese recorded history is not longer than that of Greece, and is definitely shorter than that of Mesopotamia, it gives us more precise records than anything else from the period. The meticulous nature of these accounts gives the impression of the existence of earlier records, the existence of which unfortunately has not been substantiated by archaeological evidence to date.

Thucydides (460–395 BC) has been dubbed the father of "scientific history", because of his strict standards of evidence-gathering and analysis in terms of cause and effect without reference to intervention by the gods, as outlined in his introduction to his work.

The History of the Peloponnesian War is considered to be one of the greatest texts from antiquity. It breaks off in 411 BC, although Thucydides lived on to see the final defeat of Athens in 404 BC.

"The old form of government was hereditary monarchy with established rights and limitations; but as Hellas became more powerful and as the importance of acquiring money became more and more evident, tyrannies were established in nearly all the cities, revenues increased, shipbuilding flourished, and ambition turned towards sea-power.

The Corinthians are supposed to have been the first to adopt more or less modern methods of shipbuilding, and it is said that the first triremes ever built in Hellas were laid down in Corinth. Then, there is the Corinthian shipwright, Ameinocles, who appears to have built ships for the Samians. It is nearly 300 years ago (dating from the end of this persistent war) that Ameinocles went to Samos. And the first naval battle on record in the one between the Corinthians and the Corsyraens; this was about 260 years ago…

And in the Hellenic states that were governed by tyrants, the tyrant's first thought was always for himself, for his own personal safety, and for the greatness of his own family. Consequently security was the chief political principle of these governments, and no great action ever came out of them – nothing, in fact, that went beyond their immediate local interest, except for the tyrants in Sicily, who rose to great power. So, for a long time that state of affairs everywhere in Hellas was such that nothing very remarkable could be done by any combination of powers and that even the individual cities were lacking enterprise.

Finally, however, the Spartans put down tyranny in the rest of Greece, most of which had been governed by tyrants for much longer than Athens… From the time when the. Dorians first settled in Sparta there had been a particularly long period of political disunity, yet the Spartan constitution goes back to a very early date, and the country has never been ruled by tyrants. For rather more than 400 years, dating from the end of the late war, they have had the same system of government, and this has been not only a source of internal strength, but has enabled them to intervene in the affairs of other states.

Not many years after the end of tyrannies in Hellas the battle of Marathon was fought between the Persians and the Athenians. Ten years later the foreign enemy returned with his vast armada for the conquest of Hellas, and at this moment of peril the Spartans, since they were the leading power, were in command of the allied Hellenic forces. In face of the invasion the Athenians decided to abandon their city; they broke up their homes, took their ships, and became sailors. It was by a common effort that the foreign invasion was repelled; but not long afterwards the Hellenes – both of those who had fought in the war together and those who later revolted from the King of Persia – split into two divisions, one group following Athens and the other Sparta."

The above short selection tells us that even back in that time piracy was a problem, and that the survival of the alliance between the Spartans and the Athenians against the Persians was short lived, not that different from the alliance between the Soviet Union and the USA during and after WWII. It turns out that as far as its citizens were concerned, the Spartan society was for a long time more egalitarian than that of most Greek city-states. Sparta was actually as developed as Athens in every sense, but it has had a bad press for a long time. People loathe the idea of bringing up children away from their parents and hurling babies with birth defects from a big mountain to an abyss – just some of the most abhorred rules of Sparta.

Finally, everyone knows about the marathon, the popular long-distance running event (42.195 km) that is hosted by most large cities nowadays. But very few people know that the distance they run is actually the distance between the dusty fields near the town of Marathon, where a battle was won against the Persians, and Athens. As the fable goes, following the Greek victory, a soldier, Pheidippides, ran all the way to Athens to spread the good news in the city. Thus, running the marathon in the world's big cities in many ways is a very appropriate way of commemorating the event and an individual's superhuman effort.

Arts and Agon?

Architecture

With the fast development of agriculture, urbanisation became widespread, attracting sometimes thousands of people to favoured locations, usually along coastlines and major rivers. These settlements first developed haphazardly, then, with the accumulation of wealth and the emergence of ambitious rulers, the ramshackle buildings were converted into stately towns. Thus, the world's first urban design was probably made sometime around 2500–3000 BC in Mesopotamia. The earliest signs of urban design are visible in several locations – in Ancient Egypt and the Indus Valley civilisations (2000 BC) and in Chinese town planning (1400 BC). We know quite a bit about Chinese town design, which was based on numerology and applied the Lo Shu square, which is essentially a grid of nine squares, arranged like the well-fields plots into a large square. Chinese town planning confirmed the importance of cosmologically based philosophies such as directional orientation (feng shui) and symmetry based on a hierarchical structure of districts, temples, places and streets connecting at right angles in its capital cities during the Zhou dynasty (1122–221 BC).

But it was the ever-boisterous Greeks with their expanding colonies who were perhaps the first to realise the importance of unified town planning for identity. Hippodamus of Miletus (498–408 BC), the Ancient Greek architect, urban planner, physician, mathematician, meteorologist and philosopher (never let it be said that the Greeks did not receive a rounded education), is considered the father of urban planning. His plans of Greek cities were characterised by order and regularity. He devised a plan for the "ideal" city to be inhabited by 10,000 men (free male citizens) in which the overall population, including women, children and slaves, would reach 50,000. His diamond-shaped grid plans consisted of a series of broad, straight streets, crossing one another at 45° and 135° angles. A wide central area was kept unsettled, to evolve into the agora, or market place, which was the centre not only of the city but also of society too. Neighbourhoods of 240 m² blocks were constructed and small groups of two-storey houses erected. Incidentally, the quarter of an acre (~1,000 m²) block of the family home that was considered "ideal" for in Australia is nowadays being replaced by 250 m² blocks in the main cities. The plan uses complicated mathematical formulas like, addition, subtraction, multiplication, and whole number exponents, which were used to instruct how to set out the plumbing infrastructure.

The Parthenon is the most recognisable Greek creation and is considered the pinnacle of Greek civilisation. Of course, there are many great monuments in the world built both before and after the Parthenon. Some of them, like the Great Pyramid of Egypt, are still with us, while others have been destroyed by unappreciative descendents or conquerors of the land they were built on.

The Parthenon was built on the hill of the Acropolis at the zenith of Classical Greece (460–430 BC) and it is the best representation of the Ancient Greeks' aspiration for beauty and perfection. Like almost all glorious pre-industrial structures, it is a temple. In fact, during the Golden Age of Athens, several temples were constructed on the Acropolis, but the Parthenon was built specifically to house the statue of Athena the Champion. As with everything they did, the Greeks went to extremes to create a conceptual approach to define the meaning of a beautiful building. The result was the development of the golden ratio.

From an architectural point of view, the golden ratio is represented by a rectangle where the longer side is of the length a and the shorter side is of the length b. When this rectangle is placed, adjacent to a square with sides of length a, it produces a similar rectangle with the longer side a+b and the shorter side a. The big discovery of the Greeks was that this ratio produces an aesthetically pleasing form – so much so that it has been observed and followed for millennia, even by modern architects like Le Corbusier. The golden ratio itself is a mathematical formula (a + b:a = ~1.6180339887), which is an irrational mathematical constant.

The Parthenon's design was so renowned that it has been copied for centuries. The Romans and incorporated it into the design all of their public buildings. A good example of this can be seen in the Roman library at Ephesus.

The Parthenon was part of an ambitious building campaign on the Acropolis that began around 450 BC. A generation before, the Athenians, as part of the Delian League, an alliance of Greek city-states, had led heroic victories against Persian invaders. This alliance would evolve into a de facto empire under Athenian rule, and some 150–200 cities across the Aegean began paying Athens huge sums of what amounted to protection money. Basking in glory, the Athenians planned their new temple complex on a lavish, unprecedented scale – with the Parthenon as the centerpiece. Surviving fragments of the financial accounts, which were inscribed in stone for public scrutiny, have prompted estimates of the construction budget in the range of around 340–800 silver talents – a considerable sum in an age when a single talent could pay a month's wages for 170 oarsmen on a Greek warship.

"Built by the architects Ictinus and Callicrates under the supervision of the sculptor Phidias the Parthenon is the most stunning example of Doric order (the oldest Greek architectural style). The rectangular building (measured at the top step of its base to be 30.88 m wide by 69.53 m long) was constructed of brilliant white marble, surrounded by 46 great columns, roofed with tiles, and housed a nearly 12.19 m tall statue of the goddess Athena. The Cella was 29.8 m long by 19.2 m wide, with internal Doric colonnades in two tiers, structurally necessary to support the roof. On the exterior, the Doric columns measure 1.9 m in diameter and are 10.4 m high. The corner columns are slightly larger in diameter. The Stylobate has an upward curvature towards its centre of 60 mm on the east and west ends, and of 110 mm on the sides. The statue, known as Athena Promachos, Athena the Champion, was made of wood, gold and ivory and could be seen from a distance of many miles.

Optical refinements reached their extreme in the Parthenon, where not one 'straight' line was exactly straight. To the eye, a vertical column appears to be narrower in the middle than at either the top or the bottom. To counteract this, the each exterior Parthenon column has a very slight bulge in the middle. Also the upper diameter of each is slightly narrower than its base diameter, a practice called entasis. Additionally, these columns slant inward, so that they would meet, were they extended one mile into the sky. The four outside corner columns slant inward diagonally. No architectural manuals survive from the Classical Greek era, but today's experts suspect the temple builders could add curves and inclined angles with a few relatively simple surveying tricks." (Wikipedia 2012).

In the town of Didyma rises one of the most impressive relics of the ancient world, the Temple of Apollo. University of Pennsylvania scholar Lothar Haselberger recalls, "All of a sudden I spotted a series of circles that corresponded precisely to the shape of a column base, the very one at the front of the temple." He realised he had discovered the ancient equivalent of an architect's blueprint (Hadingham 2008):

"Then, just above the outline of the column base, Haselberger noticed a pattern of horizontal lines with a sweeping curve inscribed along one side. Could this be related to entasis, also evident in the towering Didyma columns? After carefully plotting the pattern, the answer became clear: it was a profile view of a column with the vertical dimension— the height of the column—reduced by a factor of 16. This scale drawing must have been a key reference for the masons as they carved out one column segment after another. By measuring along the horizontal lines to the edge of the curve, they would know exactly how wide each segment would have to be to create the smooth, bulging profile.

Haselberger also traced a labyrinth of faint scratches covering most of the temple's unfinished surfaces. The lines proved to be reference drawings for everything from the very slight inward lean of the walls to details of the lintel structure supported by the columns. There were even floor plans, drafted conveniently right on the floor. As the temple's stepped platform rose, each floor plan was copied from one layer to the next. On the topmost floor, the builders marked out the positions of columns, walls and doorways."

Nowadays when we come across Greek temples, most of the time there is not much to see – nothing is left but the columns. The collapsed roof tiles and wall blocks were a convenient source of building materials for the locals and were used to build fortresses, houses and churches. But the columns, reminders of an everlasting Greek presence in the world, were too heavy to be moved by their inferior pre-industrial technology and so they defiantly withstood the passing of time. They are sometimes found lying on the ground in pieces, but sometimes they remain erect. Columns were extremely important in Greek architecture and it is surprising that only three different styles were used over their thousand years of dominance. Perhaps because they were architecturally so important – after all, they bore the huge weight of the building – few people dared to modify their proportions. Alternatively, it may be the case that many were built, but, like in evolution, all those that were not strong enough simply collapsed, were used for other less glorious buildings and ultimately disappeared.

There were three styles of columns: Doric, Ionic, and Corinthian. The Doric column is the oldest, dating back to around 600 BC. The Doric column was placed directly on the temple floor without the addition of a base. These columns are simple and only have the absolutely necessary features, like a fluted shaft tapering toward the top and a capital upon which sits a square block holding the weight. But their proportions and simple slender shapes make them look beautiful. They represent a significant improvement on the sturdy Minoan and enormous Egyptian pillars.

The Ionic column was developed in the late 500s BC. Ionic columns are taller and even more slender than Doric columns, and are topped by capitals that resemble scrolls. The Ionic column sits on a clearly defined base, with carved mouldings. On the whole, the look of the Ionic column is more graceful than the Doric.

The Corinthian column evolved during the 2nd century BC. Its capital is further embellished with a single or double row of stylised acanthus leaves. The base is similar to the Ionic but more refined. The Corinthian column is the celebration of architectural splendour and natural beauty. Every column is a representation of a gigantic tree with a small crown of beautifully carved leaves.

Not surprisingly, the richly decorated Corinthian column continued to be a popular element in Roman architecture. In spite of all the modern trends towards simpler and simpler forms, the influence of Greek architecture funnily enough lasted well into the minimalist 21st century. Many public buildings, like the US Supreme Court, the French Parliament, the British Museum, the Reichstag in Berlin and the New York Stock Exchange, feature columns and tympanums reminding workers and visitors of the legacy of the Ancient Greeks. If you look around in 21st century suburbia, more ambitious owners adorn their houses with columns in one of these three styles, not so much to pay homage to the genius of the Ancient Greeks but to stand out from the suburban monotony.

Sculpture

In many ways, for the art-fanatic Greeks building the Parthenon and other temples was not so much for the purpose of worshipping the gods but rather, I'd suggest, clever excuses to provide a decent place to display their incredible talent for sculpture.

Not surprisingly, initially Greek sculptors took their cues from the easily accessible Egyptian monumental sculptors. The *kouroi*, or full-size or larger-than-life statues of young men, all followed a strict pattern and showed the statue in an upright position making a rigid movement forward. It was the philosophical, human-centred development of Greek sculptors that led to the abandonment of the *kouroi* and the movement towards sculpting more human-like figures.

The sculptor Polykleitos (~400 BC) was the first to create works with true naturalism and balance. He used ideas of scale and mathematical proportions to produce perfectly proportioned figures. These proportions were later referred to as the "Polykleitan Canon of Proportion".

However, anyone who has attended basic art classes can testify that creating realistic proportions is not sufficient to create life-like figures. A perfectly proportioned figure still looks unnatural if it is presented in a rigid and unrelaxed pose. To remove this unnatural rigidity, sculptors started to chisel figures intended to be seen from multiple angles. The results were more interesting sculptures in natural poses. Although there were hundreds, perhaps thousands, of sculptors working in Greece at that time, it was probably Praxiteles who finally cracked the secret of sculpting perfect, life-like human figures. To the best of our knowledge, he was the first to sculpt nude female figures. Perhaps sculpting beautiful female bodies inspired him to create fluidity within human poses by changing from the conventional parallels of the shoulders, hips and knees to sloping angles called the "Praxitelean curve", thus completing the quest for perfect sculptures of the human body.

Some time in the 2nd century AD, Galen wrote about the perfect visual expression of the Greeks' search for harmony and beauty, which is rendered in the perfectly proportioned sculpted male nude:

> "Chrysippos holds beauty to consist not in the commensurability or 'symmetria' [i.e. proportions] of the constituent elements [of the body], but in the commensurability of the parts, such as that of finger to finger, and of all the fingers to the palm and wrist, and of those to the forearm, and of the forearm to the upper arm, and in fact, of everything to everything

else, just as it is written in the Canon of Polyclitus. For having taught us in that work all the proportions of the body, Polyclitus supported his treatise with a work: he made a statue according to the tenets of his treatise, and called the statue, like the work, the 'Canon.'"

The face, so expressive, is the most important manifestation of anything human. Not surprisingly, at the same time as the sculpted human form was liberated from rigid poses, the sculpted face experienced a transformation. The sculptures lost the frozen smiles of the *kouroi* and increasingly expressed the vast range of human emotions. I am not sure if it was the Greeks who devised the rules for drawing the perfect human face, but considering their obsession with conceptualisation I would not be surprised. To draw or sculpt a perfect human face, the ellipse should be divided horizontally into four equal quarters. The first marks the hairline and the second the forehead, while at the top of the third sit the eyes and at the bottom the nose, and in the middle of the fourth sits the mouth. These ratios represent universal beauty. It is not surprising that, regardless of race, people we consider beautiful possess facial features very close to these ratios. The classical Greek period was the first time in human history that the human body was studied for its aesthetic value, was treated as an autonomous universe and became the universal definition of beauty.

This humanist aesthetic was spread not only across the Mediterranean, but also, through the conquests of Alexander the Great, to the East. Alexander the Great single-handedly changed the nature of the ancient world in little more than a decade:

"Alexander the Great was born in Pella, the ancient capital of Macedonia in July 356 BC. His parents were Philip II of Macedon and his wife Olympias. The philosopher Aristotle educated Alexander. Philip was assassinated in 336 BC and Alexander inherited a powerful yet volatile kingdom. He quickly dealt with his enemies at home and reasserted Macedonian power within Greece. He then set out to conquer the massive Persian Empire. Against overwhelming odds, he led his army to victories across the Persian territories of Asia Minor, Syria and Egypt without suffering a single defeat. His greatest victory was at the Battle of Gaugamela, in what is now northern Iraq, in 331 BC. The young king of Macedonia, leader of the Greeks, overlord of Asia Minor and pharaoh of Egypt became 'great king' of Persia at the age of 25.

Over the next eight years, in his capacity as king, commander, politician, scholar and explorer, Alexander led his army a further 18,000 km, founding over 70 cities and creating an empire that stretched across three continents and covered around two million square miles. The entire area from Greece in the west, north to the Danube, south into Egypt and as far to the east as the Indian Punjab, was linked together in a vast international network of trade and commerce. This was united by a common Greek language and culture, while the king himself adopted foreign customs in order to rule his millions of ethnically diverse subjects. Alexander was acknowledged as a military genius who always led by example, although his belief in his own indestructibility meant he was often reckless with his own life and those of his soldiers. The fact that his army only refused to follow him once in 13 years of a reign during which there was constant fighting, indicates the loyalty he inspired. He died of a fever in Babylon in June 323 BC." (Wikipedia 2012).

Alexander the Great's empire-building ambitions coincided with the spread of Buddhism (Gautama Buddha, 563–483 BC). With Alexander's conquests, the Greek sculpting skills spread across Asia and were quickly taken up by the Buddha's followers, resulting in the emergence of Greco-Buddhist sculptures.

Up to this point, only the Buddha's footprints were worshipped (incidentally, recently I saw one of these footprints in Japan). The Greco-Buddhist sculptures were the first representations of the Buddha in human form. Thus they have defined the artistic presentation of the Buddha until the present day. The earliest Buddhas look at us with calm, reflective Greek features, wavy hair, drapery covering their shoulders, shoes and sandals, and leaf decorations. It is interesting to think that without the representation of the Buddha in human form, Buddhism might have never inspired all those millions who became followers of his teachings. This wonderful meeting of the most complex civilisations of the time – the Greek, the Hindu/Buddhist and the Chinese – resulted in a new burst of creativity, producing the brilliant, refined Hindu and Buddhist carvings. Greco-Buddhist art flourished in India and Central Asia (roughly today's Afghanistan, Pakistan, Iran) between 250 BC and 700 AD, spreading via China as far as Japan. But, following the Islamic conquest of Central Asia in 700–900 AD, it started to decline. It is sad that over the centuries the majority of the sculptures from the period were deliberately or inadvertently destroyed, but it is simply criminal that the fundamentalist Taliban government of Afghanistan in 2001 ordered the destruction two of the most outstanding examples of Greco-Buddhist art to have withstood the bloody history of the region. The Two Buddha, as they are known (one 50 m high, the other 35 m), were carved into the sandstone face of the mountain at Bamyan by Buddhist monks, thousands of whom once lived in the caves and grottoes. The sculptures, which date from 300–700 AD, with their flowing Greek robes draped over the familiar look of sub-continental Buddhas, were a sublime fusion of Buddhist imagery and Hellenic influence.

Greek sculptures like Nike, Venus de Milo, the Jockey of Artemision, Laocoön, and the famous friezes of the Pantheon are the most admired and recognised art pieces in the world. They have been present with us through literature and the arts, used as symbols and company logos, reinterpreted in movies, cartoons and pop music, and have featured on YouTube, Twitter and in thousands of photos posted on Facebook. Incidentally, Steve's first company, based on his invention of a distributed intelligence of small control units forming a network, was also called Laocon. Using the image of Laocoön desperately trying to disentangle his sons from the grip of a huge snake resonated well with his customers: they were also untangled from their myriad wires.

The classical Greek sculptor was more of a magician than an artist. While there can be countless arguments about who first discovered and introduced this or that technique, providing endless work for archaeologists and historians, there can be no argument that Greek sculpture was the first and the only in human history to present the human body as the ultimate object of beauty. In the process, the sculptors reversed thousands of years of artistic tradition when they shifted the focus from the supernatural and unknown to more earthly matters without a metaphysical preoccupation.

Following the rediscovery of classical Greek art during the Renaissance era (14–17th centuries), the human-centric and high technical standards of Greek sculptures inspired generations of artists. Well into the 19th century, the classical tradition derived from Ancient Greece dominated the art of the Western world.

It lasted up to the 20th century, when artists started to move away from the life-like presentation of humans and natural objects towards new art forms. These new artistic movements reflected more the imagination of the artists than their straightforward ability to create perfect human and natural objects. Thus, different "isms", e.g. cubism, expressionism, surrealism, Dadaism, futurism, etc, emerged. Perhaps, the development of photography was to blame for abandoning descriptive art, as there was no need anymore to painstakingly reproduce the characteristics of the subject matter. By the end of the 19th century, an accurate reproduction could be easily achieved with the click of a button.

Pottery

Due to nature of the media on which they were done, there is not much left of Ancient Greek paintings. In Ancient Greece, most paintings were done on either papyrus or wooden tablets, and thus they perished. Although we know that the majority of the Greek buildings were richly decorated, the plaster crumbled away over the centuries, leaving small piles of coloured dust behind, blown around the sites like small, man-made rainbows before vanishing. However, demonstrating that Greek painters were not much inferior to their sculptors, we still have magnificent Greek pottery. I have to admit that as much as the pottery drawings and paintings are striking and skilfully executed, they cannot match the almost supernatural, sublime beauty of the sculptures.

The story of pottery goes back into the depth of human history. Little statuettes could have been the first non-essential possessions of the nomadic Homo sapiens. During the march of humanity "Out of Africa", staggering across continents, such statuettes could have been clutched in their rigid fingers with stubborn determination. Or they could have been the only artistic attempts of the brute Neanderthals – a last majestic contribution of their 200,000 years of existence before being pushed out by the smarter Homo sapiens, which has subsequently been relentlessly populating and changing the world since 80000 BC. Pottery has definitely been present longer than agriculture and longer than human settlements and, with the exception of cave art in Europe and Australia, it represents the very first artistic and technological attempts of humanity. The earliest figurines are from the Gravettian period of 29–25000 BC (Czech Republic) and the first pottery vessels date back to 16000 BC (China).

Greek pottery was high-quality and widely used, but not exceptional. Its uniqueness lay not so much in the fine hardened clay or, intricate shapes, but in its splendid decoration with scenes from the life of the Titans and gods, heroes in battle and every-day life. The Greek pottery reads like the history of mankind. Due to its widespread use, large numbers of potteries have been found in ruins and the Romans, who appreciated and loved everything Greek (except the people), widely used Greek pottery as ornaments. As a matter of fact, the use of Greek clay pots, pitchers, containers, jugs, vases, and amphorae (those exceptionally useful large storage vessels) was so wide spread across the ancient world that Greek pottery pieces found at digs are used as "milestones" by archaeologists to identify the exact age of the find. The art of Ancient Greece pottery started in around 900 BC and is usually divided stylistically into four periods: the Geometric, Archaic, Classical, and Hellenistic. Greek vases are the most extraordinarily objects ever created. Loads of poems, literary pieces and paintings refer to the beautifully descriptive scenes of the sulking Achilles, the heroic Odysseus, Athena's birth and Apollo playing his lyre and the everyday lives of people. The greatest artists, from Caravaggio to Picasso, followed their composition. Without Greek vases, Western art as we know it would not have been possible.

Sport

"What would the world be without the agon – the agonistics of one man against another – to show everyone the order of precedence among men, just as no two other things on Earth are alike? How could any of us alive know quality if competition and personal combat did not let all the world know who embodies excellence and who merely manages mediocrity?" (*The Odyssey*).

The main and ever-present Greek ideology from the earliest times was *agon*, contest. The *agon* spread to every aspects of life, be it physical or intellectual, including athletics, horse racing, music and literature. I am sure the Greeks must even have had beauty pageants. But the unquestionable pinnacle of the physical contest was the Olympic Games, where athletes competed for the Olympic Wreath.

According to legend, it was Heracles who first called the Games "Olympic" and established the custom of holding them every four years. A legend persists that after Heracles – better known as Hercules – had completed his 12 labours, which were his punishment for unwittingly killing his family, he built the first Olympic stadium to honour Zeus. The most widely accepted date for the inception of the Ancient Olympics is 776 BC. The Ancient Games featured running events, a pentathlon (consisting of a jumping event, discus and javelin throws, a foot race and wrestling), boxing, and equestrian races.

In the beginning, the events were strictly limited to citizens of Greek states. In a twist of history, a forebear of Alexander the Great, who became the most famous ambassador for Greek culture and established the Hellenistic period, was not allowed to participate in the Olympics because he was Macedonian.

For 1,200 years, every four years wars were suspended and executions delayed, and athletes and spectators descended on the ancient mountain of Olympus to compete for the most coveted prize. Of course, one might expect that the prize for which these athletes trained hard for years would be one that would promise fame and wealth for the rest of their lives. But surprise, the most coveted price in Attica was an olive wreath that was placed on the head of the winner. The winner was invited to walk up to the altar honouring Zeus, and stood above the adoring crowd, waving with joy and standing on the podium. Thus, amateur sport was born.

In 394 AD the games were declared pagan and were banned by the Christian Byzantine Emperor. It was not until the 19th century that, after a long campaign, Frenchman Baron Pierre de Coubertin convinced European governments to restart an international sporting contest in the spirit of the Ancient Games. Thus the first modern Olympic games took place in 1896, fittingly in Athens. Since then, with the exception of the years during WWI and WWII, every four years thousands of amateur athletes from all over the world have competed for Olympic medals.

Theatre

However, *agon* was not limited to physical competition: it also extended to intellectual activities too. There were regular competitions in poetry, rhetoric, singing and drama. A good symposium – a long dinner enhanced with good wine and food – was not complete without cheerful but serious poetry contests, clever repartee or playing fine music. Writing a good epigram was the key to an invitation. Of course, this was not that unique to Greece. Every court, from past to present, aspires to invite fine entertainers, but in Ancient Greece it was a prerequisite for an invitation to be competent in these art forms. All participants had to participate. Well, that's the meaning of the word, isn't it?

Like everywhere in the world during that time, pagan, shamanic practices were wide-spread in the region. By 800 BC, the Dionysian cult was established in Attica (later called Athens). Drama was a significant aspect of the cult, and from 512 BC, every second year there was a competition for the best drama. From then on, in quick succession, three dramatic genres developed: tragedy, comedy and satire. Clever as always, in order to promote a common cultural identity, Athenians exported the festival to their numerous colonies and allies. And successful it was! The event was converted into an annual competition that could be contested by anyone, rich or poor, from any corner of the Greek world. The successful spread of Greek culture far beyond Athens meant that competitors came from as far away as the Black Sea. According to the records, the first competition was won by a man called Thespis – and today we call people with an interest in theatre "*thespians*".

Dionysius I, the tyrant of Syracuse, was an accomplished playwright and his biggest disappointment in life was that he had never won the competition. Had he managed to win, perhaps he would have been a better ruler. On one occasion, his chief advisor, Dion, annoyed him so much that he sentenced him to forced labour in the famous Syracuse stone mines. After a while, the tyrant changed his mind and Dion was allowed back to court. Dionysius dedicated his latest play to his advisor. But Dion got bored during the recital and stood up to leave. "Where do you think you are going?" – roared Dionysius. "Back to the stone mine," – Dion is said to have answered. When it comes to the arts, even tyrants had their critics.

In many ways, the theatre in ancient times was like today's Facebook, Twitter and YouTube. The comparison might sound bizarre, and unfortunately our contemporaries do not measure up to Greek standards in rhetoric, composition or language use, but just like their ancient counterparts, these websites are collections of views of what the respective societies stand for. The theatre summarised not only the ethical, political and artistic views of the

Greeks, but taught them to look at the world with critical eyes and learn to laugh at themselves.

The form of the theatre building that emerged from cutting rough stone seats in a half circle into the hills of Epidaurus became the model for not only every theatre in the world but for all our stadiums, which can now accommodate a hundred thousand people.

We know of about 10 significant Greek playwrights and approximately 100 comedy writers. Aeschylus, Sophocles and Euripides were famous for writing tragedies and Aristophanes is an example of a comedy writer.

Sophocles first won the prize for tragic drama in 468 BC, defeating the veteran Aeschylus. He wrote over 100 plays for the Athenian theatre and is said to have won the first prize at the City Dionysia 18 times. Only seven of his tragedies are now extant. Before Sophocles, two characters and the chorus dominated Greek theatre. In many ways, the chorus was more important than the conflict between the two characters, as the chorus provided not only the background, but sometimes also the judgment. Sophocles introduced a third actor, thus reducing the role of the chorus. Euripides, the other giant of Greek theatre, who lived in a cave on Salamis, introduced the concept of the "cage". In the "cage", the "imprisoned" men and women destroy each other by the intensity of their loves and hates. These fundamentals of human relations continued to be examined by future generations of playwrights, including Shakespeare, Ibsen, Strindberg, Beckett, Brecht, Ionescu and many others. Although Shakespeare did not read Greek, he would have been familiar with Greek drama via Latin translations. Several of his plays are reminiscent of Greek tragedies or comedies.

Music

The Greeks viewed music as being capable of healing the sick, working miracles and changing human hearts, and also as basic to the pursuit of truth and beauty. Music in the ancient world was essentially an oral tradition; the 40 or so fragments we have today were written down on tombstones and clay tablets. Greek music was similar to Eastern music: chant-like, monophonic or a single melody with no harmony or accompaniment per se; the voices and instruments sang and played the same pitches at the same time. But music was omnipresent. The Greeks recognised the power of music to heighten the expressive meaning of words and large parts of many dramas were apparently sung. Euripides wrote the tragedy *Orestes* in around 408 BC, and it is also possible that he composed the music that his Greek-chorus sang during the course of the play. The chorus stood in the semicircular space between the edge of the stage and the spectators' benches.

> "At the heart of 'the Greek view of music' was the 'doctrine of ethos' based on Pythagoras' view of music. Music was seen as a microcosm of the cosmos, a system of pitch and rhythm that was ruled by the same mathematical laws that governed the whole of the universe. Pythagoras discovered that notes that sound harmonious together have similarities between their frequencies. He was deeply struck by how, on the Greek seven-stringed lyre, harmonious notes were obtained when the lengths of those strings was proportional to whole numbers, e.g. 2:1, 3:2, 4:3. This is the Pythagorean 'diatonic' scale, or an octave, which has become the basis of Western music." (Wikipedia 2012)

The Romans adopted Greek music as their own, and being more superficial, with hedonist tendencies, they concentrated on celebrating life and its pleasures. A good example of Roman music is *The Epitaph of Seikilps,* a drinking song from the 1st century that was found carved on a drunkard's tombstone.

After the fall of the Roman Empire, the hundred years of darkness from which the Greeks suffered so badly, was not only repeated, but lasted for a thousand years. Europe became the Christian battleground for the souls of human beings. The monuments of the Greek gods were destroyed; culture as such disappeared from everyday life and was replaced by piety. However, the ancient texts were preserved and silent monks continued to study them in Christian monasteries. Then, from the 14th century, at first hesitantly, the revival of Ancient Greek culture began. Not only were ancient texts, mathematical formulas and astronomical and geographical maps read again and heroic poems recited, but the Greek theatre, with its tragedies and the chanting chorus, was also revived. The appreciation of anything from Ancient Greece reached its pinnacle during the Renaissance in the 16th century in northern Italy.

In Florence an intellectual club, the "Florentine Camerata", met regularly to discuss Ancient Greek works of art. They concluded that Greek tragedy must have been sung. They argued that this was the only way the Ancient Greeks could have possibly derived the powerful emotional experience that they claimed from their drama. Furthermore, the Camerata believed that the power of Ancient Greek music could be attributed to the fact that "it consisted of single melody that could affect the listener's feelings since it exploited the natural expressiveness of the rises and falls of pitch, and register of the voice and of changing rhythms and tempos." (www.oocities.org).

Thus, opera, the ultimate musical art form, combining stage acting and music, was born. Even today, the opera follows the structural arrangements of the Greek theatre. The only modification is the introduction of the orchestra, this marvellous collection of string, woodwind, brass and percussionists with a conductor, which replaced the chorus in front of the stage. Now, the location is fittingly called the orchestra pit and the chorus accompanies the actors on the stage and participates in the lively action.

Epic Poetry

I discussed the two giant Greek epic poems, *The Iliad* and *The Odyssey,* earlier and provided short summaries of the poems. After reading them in the context of our trip, like thousands before me, I also came to the conclusion that these two pieces from the distant past basically determine how all people receiving a "Western-style" education think. *The Iliad* and *The Odyssey* have been copied and translated for millennia. They have been continuously taught by scholars and read by millions of students for almost 3,000 years, with a break of couple of hundred years during the medieval period. Slowly, they became the fabric of our world, having an immense effect on our thinking. The Romans, who modelled their successful empire on Greek ideology, admired the Greeks and spread their views all around their empire. Subsequently, Greek ideas had immense influence on Judaism and so on the teachings of Jesus. In *Sailing in the Wine-Dark Sea: Why the Greeks Matter,* Cahill says that the heroes of these two poems taught us how to fight, feel, party, rule, think, love and – last but not least – how to see (Cahill 2004). In this section, I use the guidance of Cahill with my own comments to explain how these two epic poems shaped our way of thinking about ourselves and about the world around us.

These two poems are unique for their human-centric view. This unique human-centric thinking was the foundation of Greek society that was inspired to test its own limits.

The idea of freedom is deeply rooted in these poems. Although divine intervention is present, the heroes, in spite of temporary setbacks, remain in charge of their own destiny all the way through. They initiate their own actions; they are smart, even cunning and innovative. We read in *The Odyssey*:

> "'So, you ask me the name I'm known by, Cyclops?
> I will tell you. But you must give me a guest-gift
> as you've promised. Nobody – that's my name. Nobody –
> So my mother and father call me, all my friends.'
> But he boomed back at me from his ruthless heart,

'*Nobody*? I'll eat Nobody last of all his friends
I'll eat the others first! That's my gift to you!'

With that,
he toppled over, sprawled full-length, flat on his back
and lay there, his massive neck slumping to one side,
and sleep that conquers all overwhelmed him now
as wine came spurting, flooding up from his gullet
with chunks of human flesh – he vomited, blind drunk.
Now, at last, I thrust our stake in a bed of embers
to get it red-hot and rallied all my comrades:
'Courage – no panic, no one hang back now!'
And green as it was, just as the olive stake
was about to catch fire – the glow terrific, yes –
I dragged it from the flames, my men clustering round
as some god breathed enormous courage through us all.
Hoisting high that olive stake with its stabbing point,
straight into the monster's eye they rammed it hard –
I drove my weight on it from above and bored it home
as a shipwright bores his beam with a shipwright's drill
that men below, whipping the strap back and forth, whirl
And the drill keeps twisting faster, never stopping –
So we seized our stake with its fiery tip
and bored it round and round in the giant's eye
till blood came boiling up around that smoking shaft
and the hot blast singed his brow and eyelids round the core
and the broiling eyeball burst –

its crackling roots blazed
and hissed –

as a blacksmith plunges a glowing ax or adze
in an ice-cold bath and the metal screeches steam
and its temper hardens-that's the iron's strength –
so the eye of the Cyclops sizzled round that stake!
He loosed a hideous roar, the rock walls echoed round

and we scuttled back in terror. The monster wrenched the spike
from his eye and out it came with a red geyser of blood –
he flung it aside with frantic hands, and mad with pain
he bellowed out for help from his neighbour Cyclops
living round about in caves on windswept crags.
Hearing his cries, they lumbered up from every side
and hulking round his cavern, asked what ailed him:
'What, Polyphemus, what in the world's the trouble?
Roaring out in the godsent night to rob us of our sleep.
Surely no one's rustling your flocks against your will –
Surely no one's trying to kill you now by fraud or force!'
'*Nobody*, friends' – Polyphemus bellowed back from his cave –
'*Nobody's* killing me now by fraud and not by force!'
'If you're alone,' his friends boomed back at once,
'and nobody's trying to overpower you now – look,

It must be a plague sent here by mighty Zeus
And there's no escape from that.
You'd better pray to your father, Lord Poseidon.'"

Heroes of epic poems are free to choose and as a result to suffer the consequences of their choices, but they are also free to enjoy the fruits of their achievements and the recognition and respect of their peers. It is not the forgiveness of the gods they seek. The heroes of these poems have an uncanny capacity for using liberty. Welcome to the birth of Western liberal thinking and the idea of freedom!

"Liberalism emphasizes individual rights. It seeks a society characterized by freedom of thought for individuals, limitations on power (especially of government and religion), the rule of law, the free exchange of ideas, a market economy that supports free private enterprise, and a transparent system of government in which the rights of all citizens are protected. In modern society, liberals favor a liberal democracy with open and fair elections, where all citizens have equal rights by law and an equal opportunity to succeed." (Wikipedia 2012).

All these ideas and many more are hidden within the ancient lines of *The Iliad* and *The Odyssey*.

The Iliad is the earliest example of participatory leadership. The Greek troops participate in the development of the battle plan and actively comment on the strategies to be followed. Among the Greeks there are lively discussions about the personal limitations of Agamemnon, their supreme leader, and there was vigorous discussion about everything, including the best time to attack Troy.

"But the swift runner Achilles broke in sharply:
'Field marshal Atrides, lord of men Agamemnon,
produce the gifts if you like, as you see fit,
or keep them back, it's up to you. But now –
quickly, call up the wild joy of war at once!
It's wrong to malinger here with talk, wasting time –
Our great work lies all before us, still to do.
Just as you see Achilles charge the front once more,
hurling his bronze spear, smashing Troy's battalions –
so each of you remember to battle down your man!'

But Odysseus fine at tactics answered firmly.
'Not so quickly, brave as you are, godlike Achilles.
Achaea's troops are hungry: don't drive them against Troy
to fight the Trojans. It's no quick skirmish shaping,
once the massed formations of men begin to clash
with a god breathing fury in both sides at once.
No, command them now to take their food and wine
by the fast ships – a soldier's strength and nerve.
No fighter can battle all day long, cut-and-thrust
till the sun goes down if he is starved for food."

Management by participation of course has become the mantra of the modern corporate organisation in the Western world. An interesting example of the benefits of independent thinking in today's world is the impeccable track record of Qantas Airlines, which is famously the only airline in the world that has never crashed. (I often fly Qantas, so I hope it will remain so.) This track record is thought to be the result of the quick independent thinking of the crew who are not hesitant or shy to participate in decision making or, God forbid, point out if the captain has made an incorrect decision.

This participatory attitude is in sharp contrast with the cultural characteristics of Asian societies. Although respecting your elders and their opinion is part of all human societies, respect became the fundamental principle of Confucian (551–479 BC) philosophy. It has survived practically untouched into the 20th century in most parts of Asia, including China and Japan. For example, I read recently that the most advanced democratic Asian country, Japan, was planning to introduce the jury system. The participation of jurors is an integral part of trials in the West, so much so that it was even maintained, in a corrupted form, by Eastern European communist regimes. However the new jury system was widely dreaded by the vast majority of Japan's citizens (*International Tribune* 2007):

> "For the system to work, the Japanese must first overcome some deep-rooted cultural obstacles: a reluctance to express opinion in public, to argue with one another, and to question authority. To win over the sceptical public Japan's courts have held about 500 mock trials across the country. On these mock trials the jurors preferred directing questions to the judges. They never engaged one another in discussions. Their opinions had to be extracted by the judges and were often hedged by the Japanese language's rich ambiguity. When silence stretched out and a judge prepared to call upon a juror, the room tensed up as if the jurors were students who had not done the reading. In one case during the discussion on repentance, hoping for some response the judge waited for 14 seconds, then said, 'on this point, what does everybody think?' Nine seconds passed. 'Doesn't anyone have an opinion?' After six more seconds one woman questioned whether repentance should lead to a reduced sentence."

Obviously, these people did not grow up on the verses of *The Odyssey* and *The Iliad* and have never been exposed to the inquisitive mind of Socrates.

Essentially, *The Iliad* is a poem about the heroic values war imposes on the participants. The often-misrepresented word "honour" is frequently used to justify war and injustice. The heroes are frequently no more than savages, something that appears to resonate well with today's audiences, as the success of the movie *Troy* (2004) demonstrated. But in *The Iliad*, ultimately the sufferings of the victims and the joyful celebration of the victors are evenly balanced, suggesting Homer took a neutral position.

"War – I know it well, and the butchery of men.
Well I know, shift to the left, shift to the right
my tough tanned shield. That's what the real drill,
defensive fighting means to me. I know it all
how to charge in the rush of plunging horses
I know how to stand and fight to the finish,
twist and lunge in the War-God's deadly dance."

The poems set down the fundamentals of generosity, fair play, bravery and valour, which centuries on would metamorphose into the driving force behind medieval knighthood. In *The Odyssey*, Homer puts it as follows:

"His tale was over now. The Phaeacians all fell silent, hushed,
his story holding them spellbound down the shadowed halls
until Alcinous found the poise to say, 'Odysseus,
now that you have come to my bronze-floored house,
my vaulted roofs, I know you won't be driven
off your course, nothing can hold you back
however much you've suffered, you'll sail home.
Here, friends, here's a command for one and all,
you who frequent my palace day and night and drink
the shining wine of kings and enjoy the harper's songs.
The robes and hammered gold and a haul of other gifts
you lords of our island council brought our guest
all lie packed in his polished sea-chest now. Come,
each of us add a sumptuous tripod, add a cauldron!
Then recover our costs with levies on the people:
It's hard to afford such bounty man by man.'

The king's instructions met with warm applause
and home they went to sleep, each in his own house.
When young Dawn with her rose-red fingers shone once more
they hurried down to the ship with handsome bronze gifts,
and striding along the decks, the ardent King Alcinous
stowed them under the benches, shipshape, so nothing
could foul the crewmen tugging at their oars.
Then back the party went to Alcinous' house
And shared a royal feast."

Perhaps, for the first time in the history of mankind, forgiveness replaces revenge (something that would become the fundamental teaching of Jesus). In *The Iliad* Achilles, who has demonstrated all the best and the worst characteristics of man, listens to the wise words of Odysseus and concludes that there is limit to hatred. Forgiveness has to replace rage. People have to get on with their lives. He promises not to forget his old friend Patroclus and finally gives the body of the brave Hector back to his father to be properly buried:

"'Feel no anger at me, Patroclus, if you learn
Even there in the House of Death – I let his father
have Prince Hector back. He gave me worthy ransom
and vou shall have your share from me, as always,
your fitting, lordly share.'
So he vowed
and brilliant Achilles strode back to his shelter,
sat down on the well-carved chair that he had left,
at the far wall of the room, leaned toward Priam
and firmly spoke the words the king had come to hear:
'Your son is now set free, old man, as you requested.
Hector lies in state. With the first light of day
you will see for yourself as you convey him home.
Now, at last, let us turn our thoughts to supper.'"

We find a similar idea in *The Odyssey*:

"Royal son of Laertes, Odysseus, master of exploits,
Hold back now! Call a halt to the great leveller, War
Don't court the rage of Zeus who rules the world!'
So she commanded. He obeyed her, glad at heart.
And Athena handed down her pacts of peace
Between both sides for all the years to come."

There are endless descriptions of beautiful people, nature and human creations in these poems. The people of *The Iliad* and *The Odyssey* are held together with a common sense of beauty. The appreciation of nature and, above all, life is omnipresent. I suspect that our ideal man and woman are still crafted after the description of Homeric heroes and beauties, where physical beauty and intelligence merges into perfection. We know from detailed descriptions of Greek symposia that physical strength and beauty was only appreciated if it was accompanied by similar intellectual wit and wisdom. In *The Odyssey*:

"Great Odysseus bathed in the river, scrubbed his body
Clean of brine that clung to his back and broad shoulders,
scoured away the brackish scurf that caked his head.
and then, once he had bathed all over, rubbed in oil
and donned the clothes the virgin princess gave him,
Zeus's daughter Athena made him taller to all eyes,
his build more massive now, and down from his brow
she ran his curls like thick hyacinth clusters
full of blooms. As a master craftsman washes
gold over beaten silver – a man the god of fire
and Queen Athena trained in every fine technique –
and finishes off his latest effort, handsome work,
so she lavished splendour over his head and shoulders now.
And down to the beach he walked and sat apart,
and the princess gazed in wonder...
then turned to her maids with lovely braided hair:

'Listen, my white-armed girls, to what I tell you.
The gods of Olympus can't be all against this man
Who's come to mingle among our noble people.
At first he seemed appalling, I must say –
now he seems like a god who rules the skies up there!
Ah, if only a man like that were called my husband,
Lived right here, pleased to stay forever…
Enough.
Give the stranger food and drink, my girls.'"

The poems give a memorable description of the richness of human emotions and behaviour and they represent the first-ever forensic description of a human's feelings. In The *Odyssey* again:

"Dawn soon rose on her splendid throne and woke
Nausicaa finely gowned. Still beguiled by her dream,
down she went through the house to tell her parents now,
her beloved father and mother. She found them both inside.
Her mother sat at the earth with several waiting-women,
spinning yarn on a spindle, lustrous sea-blue wool.
Her father she met as he left to join the lords
At a council island nobles asked him to attend.
She stepped up close to him, confiding, 'Daddy dear,
I wonder, won't you have them harness a wagon for me,
The tall one with the good smooth wheels…so I
Can take our clothes to the river for a washing?'"

They taught us how to love and protect our family and appreciate the comfort of our home. The idea of, and yearning for, his homeland is the driving force behind the adventures of Odysseus:

"I am Odysseus, son of Laertes, known to the world
For every kind of craft – my fame has reached the skies.
Sunny Ithaca is my home. Atop her stands our seamark,
Mount Neriton's leafy ridges shimmering in the wind.
Around her a ring of islands circle side-by-side,
Dulichion, Same, wooded Zacynthus too, but mine
Lies low and away, the farthest out to sea,
while the others face the east and breaking day.
Mine is a rugged land but good for raising sons –
and I myself , I know
Than a man's own native country.
True enough,
Calypso the lustrous goddess tried to hold me back,
Deep in her arching caverns, craving me for a husband.
So did Circe, holding me just as warmly in her halls,
But they never won the heart inside me, never.
So nothing is as sweet as a man's own country,
His own parents, even though he's settled down
In some luxurious house, off in a foreign land
And far from those who bore him."

The first description of love of a married couple is the description of love between Hector, the Trojan hero, and his wife, Andromache, in *The Iliad*. It precedes the Hebrew *Song of Songs* or any other Chinese or Mesopotamian love poetry. It not only describes the love and desire felt by Hector towards his wife but his loving thoughts of his baby son:

> "In the same breath, shining Hector reached down
> for his son – but the boy recoiled,
> cringing against his nurse's full breast,
> screaming out at the sight of his own father,
> terrified by the flashing bronze, the horsehair crest,
> the great ridge of the helmet nodding, bristling terror
> and his mother laughed as well, and glorious Hector,
> quickly lifting the helmet from his head,
> set it down on the ground, fiery in the sunlight,
> and raising his son he kissed him, tossed him in his arms,
> lifting a prayer to Zeus and the other deathless gods
>
> So Hector prayed
> and placed his son in the arms of his loving wife.
> Andromache pressed the child to her scented breast,
> smiling through her tears. Her husband noticed
> and filled with pity now, Hector stroked her gently,
> trying to reassure her, repeating her name: 'Andromache,
> dear one, why so desperate? Why so much grief for me?
> No man will hurl me down to Death, against my fate.
> And fate? No one alive has ever escaped it,
> Neither brave man nor coward, I tell you –
> it's born with us the day that we are born.'"

Since ancient times, these words or their equivalent have been sadly repeated in hundreds of languages by millions of soldiers leaving for the battlefields.

In *The Odyssey*, the first nuclear family unit is described. Odysseus and his wife Penelope live separately from his father and he runs his family and land (kingdom) independently without the interference of Laertes, his father, who lives not far away across the hill.

> "Our ship lies moored off farmlands far from town,
> Riding in Rithron Cove, beneath Mount Nian's woods.
> As for the ties between your father and myself,
> we've been friends forever, I'm proud to say,
> and he would bear me out
> if you went and questioned old lord Laertes.
> He, I gather, no longer ventures into town
> but lives a life of hardship. All to himself –
> off on his farmstead with an aged serving-woman
> who tends him well, who gives him food and drink
> when weariness has taken hold of his withered limbs

from hauling himself along his vineyard's steep slopes.
And now I've come – and why? I heard that he was back."

The poems have a clear distinction between right and wrong and clearly understood the meaning of ethical behaviour. One could say they invented ethical thinking. The poems also give us examples of how to respect our elders, how to be fair to others, how to share hardships with our comrades, how to be patient and impatient, when to be honest and cunning, how and when to obey the laws, how and when to challenge them, how to love, and how to enjoy life. They provide a perfect guide for human existence.

In my opinion, the most unique and formative contribution of these poems is that they invite us to think, to scrutinise, to question, to experiment and to experience. They initiated everlasting social and technical changes in our society driven by human curiosity and independent thinking. These attributes are in stark contrast to the teachings of most religions, including the three monotheist, religions (Judaism, Christianity and Islam), which require total obedience in following the Scriptures.

Sometimes, even worse, a particular interpretation of the teachings of the sacred texts is enforced mercilessly. While religions have enormously enriched the human mind and culture, they have also caused a great deal of suffering – to mention just a few: the Reformation in Europe; the fights between Catholics and Anglicans in Northern Ireland; the ongoing fight between Jews, Christians and Muslims; and more recently the conflict between Shias and Sunnis in the Middle East. This is not to suggest that God – or rather gods – did not play an important role in Ancient Greece. But in contrast to the omnipotent God of the monotheistic religions, the Greek gods were full of human inadequacies. The wide-spread reference to God in all human cultures is not unexpected, but in his brilliant book *The God Delusion*, Richard Dawkins squarely rejects an innate need for God.

We can only hope that, with the spread of independent thinking, pointless fights fuelled by religious dogma will become more and more infrequent. However, if anything, recent developments in the world do not give too much hope on this front.

Lyric Poetry

Having seen the enormous influence of epic poetry on our culture, one would think that there is nothing to add. But for the humanist Greeks, lyric poetry describing their emotions was just as important. Fragments of lyric poems have also been found on tombstones, on clay tablets and infrequently on papyrus, showing that there were plenty of poets following in the footsteps of Homer. Their list is long and my selection does not in any way do justice to the variety and expressive power of Greek poetry. They are everlasting and we do not need a long introduction or even a very vivid imagination to appreciate their beauty even after all this time. The magnificence of these poems captured my imagination.

Pindar: Victory Ode (Pythian 8)
"Creatures of a day! What is a man?
What is he not? A dream of a shadow
Is our mortal being? But when there comes to men
A gleam of splendour given of heaven,
Then rests on them a light of glory
And blessed are their days."

Plato: The Greek Anthology VII
"You're star-gazing, my star?
I wish that I could be the Sky
With all those eyes to look at you."

Sappho: (fragment)
"What is beautiful lasts only as long as it looked upon
But what is good will soon also be beautiful."

Sappho: Words of Love
"By the cool water the breeze murmurs, rustling
Through apple branches, while from quivering leaves
Streams down deep slumber."

On Women

The generally accepted view on the social position of Ancient Greek women is that they could not participate in society. Some anthropologists have suggested that their social status was just above that of the slaves. Fathers often treated their daughters as commodities with which they could buy influence. Does this ring a bell? If we think we have left many of the unsavoury habits of the ancient world behind, we should remember that in the majority of Islamic countries, in India, in Africa and occasionally in China this practice is still alive.

We know that in Athens, the law required all inheritances to go through the male line and limited the amount of property women would own. Again, it was only in 2011 that the law in one of the most developed countries in the world, Great Britain, was at last changed so that now it is the first-born child not the first-born male child who inherits the British throne. A woman's status in the ancient world was determined by that of her father and then later by her husband's. A recent find in which DNA evidence suggested that a sister and a brother were buried together in a lavish grave only offers weak evidence that women in Ancient Greece held certain positions of power by right of birth.

From a feminist perspective, Sparta was a paradise. In contrast to Athenian women, Spartan women could inherit on equal terms with their brothers. There was no law that forbade them from owning property. Formally, a daughter inherited half of what a son inherited, but if we take the dowry into consideration, they ultimately ended up with an equal share of the estate. According to records, over two-fifths of the land in Sparta was owned by women in 400 BC.

In Sparta, men stayed in barracks until they were 30. Thus, not surprisingly, Spartan women had to take more responsibilities in public life and were encouraged to improve their intellectual skills. They were educated and able to go out in public unescorted, and also to participate in athletic contests. Spartan women had a reputation of being bold and daring. They wore short, loose tunics that gave them as much freedom of movement they wanted. Girls exercised at the same time as boys and, just like boys, did so in the nude.

Kyniska, daughter of King Archidamos of Sparta, was the first woman to be listed as an Olympic victor in antiquity. She was the owner of the chariot which won in the four-horse chariot race in the 96th and 97th Olympiads (396 BC and 392 BC respectively). In the Olympic Games, it was forbidden for women to be present. But as the owner of the chariot, Kyniska attended to receive the victory wreath, or *kotinos*. But we should not fail to notice that while today female jockeys race against their male rivals as equals, there was not even a hint of female participation in the Ancient Olympics.

Many anthropologists have argued that life in Ancient Greece has been first reinterpreted by the Christian Church and then by generations of male archaeologists; thus women in Ancient Greece need to be seen in a new light. Some have even gone as far as to suggest that men and women were of equal status and had equal power. Of course we cannot tell for sure whether this was true or not, but the frequency of female subjects in Greek art suggests an important, even if not an equal, role for women in Greek society. The women sculpted and drawn on the vases are not fainting violets but strong, wilful humans who, like their male counterparts, are ready to face challenges and to triumph. There is some evidence that, at least in the Hellenistic age, girls were encouraged to learn to read and write; there were certainly plenty of women who could read and write, and vase paintings suggest that they frequently gathered together. Our best idea of how the Greeks viewed women comes from Greek drama. Turning back to where it all started – *The Odyssey* and *The Iliad* – we find that the female characters, including Helen of Troy, Penelope, Nausicaa and so on were not idealised, perfect human beings but suffered from numerous shortcomings. They were real flesh-and-blood individuals, full of initiative and ready for action, not papier-mâché figurines. The female characters were further developed in the Greek tragedies. There, women often became major players, providing a better insight into how women were treated and thought of in society. Many well-known Greek plays contain several well-described, complex females. There are marvellous, sometimes contentious, female characters in Greek literature: Medea, who killed her children when Jason abandoned her – in Apollonius of Rhodes' *The Voyage of Argo* and in the play by Euripides; Phaedra, who took her own life when she was spurned by her stepson – in the play by Euripides; Electra, a heroine who plotted to revenge her father Agamemnon's murder – in plays by both Sophocles and Euripides; and the wilful Antigone – in the play by Sophocles.

Antigone was the greatest Greek heroine who openly defined power. Following a decree by the king that one of her brothers should be left unburied, Antigone took it upon herself to bury her brother, committing "a holy crime". She asked her sister to help her but her sister refused, saying,

> "We who are women should not contend with men; we who are weak are ruled by the stronger. Pardon me if I obey our rulers since I must."

Antigone might defy the rules of society, but these lines clearly describe the expectations of society towards women. Antigone decides openly to rebel against her fixed position in life. She may be a heroine, but she cannot win; thus as a true hero she chooses to take her death into her own hands.

To the best of my knowledge, I do not know of any female playwright. However, Sappho (630–570 BC), who was described by Alcaeus in 385 BC as "violet-haired, pure, honey-smiling Sappho", certainly wrote some of the most beautiful lyric poems in the ancient world. Her works were "best-sellers" and she was well known and admired throughout antiquity.

Unfortunately, today, only fragments survive, but we know that Herodotus, Strabo, Atheneus and Ovid admired her poetry. The clarity of her language and the simplicity of her poems are astounding. Here are two of the most beautiful love poems. Whether they were describing her longing for a male or female lover is not clear. But does it matter at all?

> "At mere sight of you
> My voice falters, my tongue
> is broken.
>
> Straightaway, a delicate thin fire runs in
> My limbs, my eyes
> Are blinded and my ears
> Thunder.
>
> Sweat pours out a trembling hunts
> me down. I grow paler
> than dry grass and lack little
> of dying."
>
> "Your body is all grace
> Your eyes…honey
> The love flows into
> Your longed-for face."

Greek women of course were admired for their beauty and adorned themselves with astonishingly beautiful jewellery. They were in charge of running their households and were greatly respected for it. They were also lovers, entertainers, prostitutes and mothers and, until the emergence of Christianity, highly respected priestesses. Sometimes they had to be brave and become leaders.

Just to prove that courageous brave women really existed in ancient societies, here is the lovely story of Artemisia as told by Herodotus:

> "Artemisia lived Halikarnassos (Bodrum) in the 5th century BC and was the daughter of Lygdamis. Her father's family was from Capadocia and her mother's side came from Crete.

Artemisia married the ruler of the Carian Empire but her husband died leaving her with a small son. Unexpectedly but not unprepared she became the ruler of Halikarnassos, Kos, Nissiros and Kalymnos. She was enterprising, fearless and intelligent. The area she governed was one of the busiest and most strategic in the Aegean; a fertile peninsula where Anatolia met the sea, the route of many trade ships, and it was rampant with piracy. Governing this union of islands was not at all easy but she became one of the most respected rulers in the region. She was keen to keep her islands independent from the ever-expanding influence of Athens so she became the ally of the Persian king, Xerxes."

Herodotus described in detail the events in both camps before the battle of Salamis in 480 BC. When Xerxes asked his commanders and allies if they supported him in his decision to go into a battle:

'Yes of course; we will win,' they answered as one. But there was just one dissenting voice.

Artemisia said: 'Tell this to the king for me, Mardonius. I, who in the fight near Euboia was no less useful than your soldiers, nor the weakest of your commanders, know it my binding duty to tell you my thoughts about what I think is the right course for you. Because of this I say: Don't enter your ships into battle. The sailors here are as superior to your sailors as a man is superior to a woman. What's the necessity of war at sea? The main reason for this campaign is Athens, but aren't you the master of that city anyway?"

After informing Xerxes that she thought he shouldn't go to war at sea, Artemisia made a point that few commanders would dare to: "The best men have inferior slaves under their command, but bad leaders have good slaves. You are the most superior man in the world, but your servants are worth nothing. Don't expect good from them."

The king appreciated her frankness, but the majority would sway the day and preparations for the battle began. According to Herodotus, the Carians prepared 60 ships, of which five were commanded by Artemisia. The sailors on her ships were second only to the sailors of Sidon.

Imagine the scene in the Aegean off the coast of Salamis in 480 BC. The Persian and Athenian ships were fighting fiercely at close quarters. A Greek trireme cornered Artemisia's ship. Unfortunately, another vessel fighting on the side of Xerxes and commanded by the Calyndian King, Damasithymos blocked her escape. Without hesitation she rammed and sank the allied vessel:

"For when the captain on the Athenian ship saw her attacking an enemy vessel, he supposed Artemisia's ship was either Greek or was a deserter from the enemy cause who was fighting for the Greeks. He changed course and made for the rest of the enemy ships. For, according to the story, the king was watching and saw that it was her ship that made the attack. What is more, one of the people with him said, 'Master, do you see how well Artemisia is fighting? She has sunk an enemy ship.' When the king asked whether it was really Artemisia who had done so, they confirmed it was because they recognised her vessel's flag clearly and assumed that she had sunk an enemy ship. As far as the rest of the story goes, the incident turned out to her advantage because no one from the Calyndian ship survived to bring a charge against her. Xerxes is said to have replied to the news, 'My men have become women and my women, men.'"

After the war, Artemisia advised the king to return to rule his country. This time Xerxes listened to her.

Before he left, he sent Artemisia to Ephesus, asking her to keep an eye on his sons. Heroic though Artemisia might have been, in the end, after fulfilling her role as a warrior, the king sent her back to do womanly duties. This confirms that after all there was a presumption in ancient society about what women were supposed to do and how they should behave. Although, she stands alone with her success at sea, the world would never forget its first female admiral.

And finally some wisdom from those who seek wisdom (Plato):

"[**SOCRATES:**] Yesterday my main object was to describe my view of the ideal state and its citizens.

[**TIMAEUS:**] And your description was much to our liking, Socrates

[**SOCRATES:**] We began, did we not, by separating the farmers and the other craftsmen from the defence forces?

[**TIMAEUS:**] Yes.

[**SOCRATES:**] And we assigned to each class, as being natural to it, a single appropriate occupation or craft. Those whose duty it was to defend the community would be its sole guardians against threats of injury; whether external or internal; they would be gentle in aiming at justice to their subjects, who were their natural friends, and tough in fighting battles against external enemies.

[**TIMAEUS:**] Certainly.

[**SOCRATES:**] And to ensure the appropriate gentleness and toughness in their behaviour to each, we said that the character of the guardians must combine the spirited and the philosophic to a rare degree.

[**TIMAEUS:**] Yes.

[**SOCRATES:**] And for their upbringing they were to be trained physically and mentally in all studies suitable for the purpose.

[**TIMAEUS:**] Of course.

[**SOCRATES:**] Having been so brought up they must never, we said, regard gold or silver or anything else as their own private property, but earn as a garrison a modest wage, sufficient for their simple needs, in return for the safeguard they afforded to those under their protection. They were to abate all expenditure and live a common life together, devoting their attention wholly to excellence, freed from all other preoccupations.

[**TIMAEUS:**] That was what we said.

[**SOCRATES:**] And we had something to say about the women, too. Their characters were to be moulded similarly to men's, and they were to share the same occupations both in war and in the rest of life.'

[**TIMAEUS:**] We said that too."

If we believe that philosophers like Socrates and Plato influenced the behaviour of Greeks, this conversation suggests that there were no religious or ideological boundaries preventing women from participation in society. However, there is no point of denying that without the modern inventions of tampons and, more importantly, contraception it was difficult for women to participate in society. In a world that relied so much on physical strength, pregnancy, child bearing and their complex emotional effects would have limited the participation of women, not to mention the fact that due to their lighter build they were unable to fight in battles in any useful way. We should not forget that, unlike today when in the age of the drones one can command deadly force while remaining thousand miles away from the battlefield, battles in the ancient world were very physical pursuits. Simply put, the strongest won. And in a culture where in spite of its intellectual achievements – "something of a tour de force, a triumph of intellectual effort between eras dominated by fear, guilt and unreason" (Dodds 1951) – the heroic conquest and the admiration of the warrior remained one of the most important cohesive forces, the inability of women to participate in battles seriously impacted the respect they received and the power they could wield.

Who is to Rule?

In the previous pages, I have tried to demonstrate how Ancient Greek ideas about the world contribute to our present understanding. However, there is one more – perhaps the most important – contribution to discuss: the idea of the democratic government, which underlined and facilitated everything in Greek society. If I strip it down to the basics, a democratic government was not a new idea, not even at the time democracy was tentatively first introduced in 600 BC. Essentially all tribal societies have the two main features of Athenian democracy: all ordinary citizens (usually meaning adult males) are eligible to participate and speak in the assembly that sets the "laws of the land", and all citizens are eligible to be elected to any leadership position. Some kind of participatory democracy was widely practised in nomadic tribes, but it was forgotten after the introduction of agriculture. As the tribes settled, the accumulation of wealth accelerated and self-governance dissipated into the past. This was the time for kings, tyrants (opportunist rulers), pharaohs, emperors and, at best, elected archons and oligarchies.

By the end of the 6th century BC, the continuous conflict between rival groups threatened the survival of Athens. At last Solon's (638–558 BC) reforms started to break the impasse. First, Solon freed many of the debt-bonded small-holders. The debt-ridden farmers, who were nothing more than serfs tottering at the edge of slavery, became debt-free landowners once again. Working for yourself and keeping the fruits of your labour can do miracles. To everyone's surprise, the farmers worked with renewed enthusiasm under the hot sun and squeezed sellable produce out of the rocky Athenian agricultural land, thus laying the economic foundations for a powerful, prosperous state. Solon also ruled that wealth, not birth, was the criterion for citizens to access public office. And, he published the Athenian laws so everyone could read and understand the rights and obligations of Athenian citizens. But forming a society that is capable of governing itself is a long, tedious process and it was only after more than a century of gradual changes that Cleisthenes, the demagogue (someone who intends to please the masses), announced reforms for "rule by the people" – what he called *demokratia*.

Again and again, tyrants, dictators, kings, or whatever we call them, at best thoroughly disappoint their followers, and at worst commit unimaginable crimes. Of course, democratically elected leaders are no better than the others, but most importantly they are elected and they can only remain in office as long as the majority supports them.

Democracy

The Peloponnesian Wars (431–404 BC) between Athens and Sparta were as much as about ideology as territorial disputes. It was longest war in the history of the Greek states and by the end it had exhausted both parties. Nominally Sparta and its oligarchic government won, with Persian help, but the end of the war marked the beginning of the end of Greek supremacy in the Mediterranean.

At the end of the first year of war, the Athenians held, as was their custom, an elaborate funeral for all those killed in the war. The brilliant and charismatic politician and general, Pericles, delivered the funeral oration for the dead. Pericles' funeral oration is the classic statement of Athenian ideology, containing practically in full the patriotic sentiment felt by most Athenians:

> "When it is a question of settling private disputes, everyone is equal before the law; when it is a question of putting one person before another in positions of public responsibility, what counts is not membership of a particular class, but the actual ability which the man possesses. No one, so long as he has it in him to be of service to the state, is kept in political obscurity because of poverty.

> We regard wealth as something properly to be used, rather than as something to boast about. As for poverty, no one need be ashamed to admit it: the real shame is in not taking practical measures to escape from it.

> Here each individual is interested not only in his own affairs but in the affairs of the state as well: even those who are mostly occupied with their own business are extremely well-informed on general politics – this is a peculiarity of ours: we do not say that a man who takes no interest in politics is a man who minds his own business; we say he has no business here at all.

> When we do kindnesses to others, we do not do them out of any calculations of profit and loss: we do them without afterthought, relying on our free liberality.

> What I would prefer is that you should fix your eyes every day on the greatness of Athens as she really is, and should fall in love with her. When you realize her greatness, then reflect that what made her great was men with a spirit of adventure, men who knew their duty, men who were ashamed to fall below a certain standard. If they ever failed in an enterprise, they made up their minds that at any rate the city should not find their courage lacking to her, and they gave to her the best contribution that they could.

> One's sense of honour is the only thing that does not grow old, and the last pleasure, when one is worn out with age, is not, as the poet said, making money, but having the respect of one's fellow men."

This speech is one of the pinnacles of describing the relationship between the state and individuals. He clearly states that a democratic state can only work if there is mutual respect between the state and citizens. There were echoes of Pericles' funeral oration in John F. Kennedy's inaugural address in 1961:

"And so, my fellow Americans: ask not what your country can do for you—ask what you can do for your country. My fellow citizens of the world: ask not what America will do for you, but what together we can do for the freedom of man."

This attitude is being forgotten by many in today's world, where "rights" without obligations have become a predominant feature of our societies. Rights are legal, social, ethical constructs that society decides to give to its citizens. And the emphasis should be on the citizen.

Ancient Spartan society decided that newborns with visible birth defects did not have the right to live and threw them off the Taygetos mountain. Had I been born in Ancient Sparta, as a premature baby I'd have most probably been thrown into the abyss from the mountain peak. Without ever gaining consciousness, I'd have never realised what happened; my parents probably would have been devastated by the loss of their first child until the arrival of my baby brother. Today's society has decided that, depending on your view, every conceived foetus (if you are a devoutly religious person) has the "right" to live, or, for those who are more liberal, that every newborn baby, including the most seriously handicapped, has the "right" to live. Neither the ancients, nor the religious devotees nor the liberals are right or wrong. It is simply a decision that a particular civilisation makes and its citizens agree to follow that rule. The important principle is that the citizens and the state cooperate. The death of the first ever documented "rebel", Socrates, clearly demonstrates the Greeks' thinking about the importance of honouring this "contract" between the state and its citizens, even if the price to pay was his own life. Although, he violently disagreed with the views of his fellow citizens, he accepted the jury's decision and drank the hemlock.

Today, many people talk about the breakdown of Western-style liberal, representative democracies. People are disappointed and sometimes disgusted with politicians. In many countries, no party can get a sufficient majority to govern and execute the programmes promised during the election campaigns. Countries limp along with coalition governments, formed from uneasy alliances, while the disappointed citizens riot, shouting about their rights.

Although Greek or Athenian democracy provided the model for present-day democratic societies, we tend to forget that there are significant differences between them. In Ancient Greece, a participatory democracy was practised that emphasised the citizens' participation in governing themselves. Only male citizens were allowed to participate in the democratic process, and citizenship, with few exceptions, could only acquired by birth. Thus, in spite of its cosmopolitan look, as far as governing was concerned, Athens was a homogeneous society. Although the citizens had rights, there was a vast array of responsibilities associated with citizenship, like compulsory military training, paying taxes, keeping your shop/house clean, respecting the laws and the property rights, and, most importantly, not only voting but also serving in the numerous democratic institutions. Due to the annual rotation of officials, every male citizen had a chance to serve in one of the democratic institutions of Athens at least once in 10 years. It looks quite chaotic, but somehow this system miraculously led to the emergence of capable leaders. But democracy has always had its doubters and rightly so. Not surprisingly, during the 4th century BC, Plato and his pupils trialled the model based on the idea of the "wise old men" and he and his pupils ran the philosophers' state in Syracuse. It was a complete failure. And this is where I despair: if Plato and Aristotle couldn't do it; What hope does humanity have?

In the 21st century, many people feel that democracy has been hijacked as many people refuse to cooperate with the state and accept the rules. Democracy cannot work in a society where individuals do not understand and/or are unwilling to respect the law of their country and do not fulfil their obligations towards their state. In some financially struggling US states, the state has agreed to four-day schooling rather than renegotiate teachers' lucrative salaries and working conditions. In this case, both the citizens' (the teachers) and the state (the political leaders) have failed to live up to the expectations put on them by democracy. Perhaps Sir Winston Churchill got it right when he said: "It has been said that democracy is the worst form of government except all the others that have been tried." So, our search for the perfect government continues.

EPILOGUE

We humans of course are no more than the result of a series of accidental events in the universe. After millions of years of evolution, we have acquired a unique consciousness that we use with so much enthusiasm to try to understand our surroundings. However, in spite of our haughtiness, we have remained selfish and interested mainly in ourselves. In short, we have remained hopelessly self-centred. The Greeks, perhaps unknowingly, recognised this primordial tendency. Putting man in the centre of their universe, they developed ideas that continue to satisfy our needs even 3,000 years later.

On top of that, the Ancient Greeks managed to devise the appropriate social structure to "cage the ape within" and guide people's behaviour without making a virtue of the idea of subordination of self-interest. The ever lasting present of the Ancient Greeks to humanity is the idea of individualism and rational thinking practised within the confines of a democratic state.

The answer to the question asked so many years ago by my children – "*Why Greece?*" – is complex. Nevertheless, I have attempted to summarise and reflect on what I found. It is not what the Greeks discovered – whether they were the first to do so or not – but rather their way of thinking about the world that made them fundamentally different from all other cultures. Their rational thinking led to the birth of the scientific discipline, which has become an crucial force in the history of humanity. It was no accident that the Industrial Revolution took place in Europe. The principles of Greek thought, woven into the European mind over thousands of years, were the driving force behind the technical and ultimately the social changes that have shaped the present world. Without the Industrial Revolution, the big cities of the world would be covered by metres of manure every day; the majority of new borns would die; trivial epidemics would continue to ravage the world; millions would work on the land with rudimentary equipment; most of mankind would be starving to death; and the abolition of slavery could never have taken place. In the history of mankind, feudal sophistication was achieved in many places, but it took the Europeans, brought up on Ancient Greek ideology, to take the crucial step to fire up the engines of the Industrial Revolution. I heard recently a slogan – "Modernisation without Westernisation". However, I have great doubts that progress is possible in the 21st century without accepting at least some of the tenets of Ancient Greek ideology. The Ancient Greeks put humans on a pedestal, harnessed their rational mind and made them think that – to use Barack Obama's phrase –"Yes, we can".

It is only this rational thinking and self-confidence, after so much delay now spreading all over the world, that can empower humanity to solve the problems of overpopulation, climate change, water, land and energy shortages, and all the other problems to come, in order to ensure the survival of humanity on this beautiful blue Planet Earth.

By writing this book, I also wanted to pay homage to the thousands of explorers who walked, climbed, sailed, flew and dived, risking it all to discover every nook and cranny of this planet.

Perhaps the Ancient Greeks discovered that the world only exists in human consciousness. Without human consciousness nothing exists as nothing matters. As human consciousness triumphs, understanding of the world unfolds and our understanding becomes us.

Johann Wolfgang von Goethe:

*"What the mind and the heart is for a human being,
Greece is for humanity."*

AFTERWORD

Our trips to Greece all happened before the global financial crisis was unleashed on the world. It turned out that the Greeks lived so well because the government had forged its financial reports to the European Union and that our observations about an indulgent, wasteful, badly managed society were all correct. The taxi drivers could afford to refuse fares and not to take customers' luggage as there were only limited numbers of taxi licences distributed, the unfinished projects and marinas around the towns were the result of embezzlement, the pompous little kingpins in the harbour masters' offices were members of the bloated, pampered public services, and the unhelpful restaurant and hotel owners were nothing but lifestyle retirees living on fat public service pensions from the age of 54. This was life in a country living on borrowed money and on borrowed time.

It has been almost ten years since I wrote these words. Unfortunately, the world has not become a better place. Rational thinking is in retreat; far-left, far-right and fundamentalist ideologies dominate politics. For the first time, I am really afraid for the future.

REFERENCES

Alighieri, D. (2008). Divine Comedy, Chartwell Books, Inc.

Apollonius and E. V. Rieu (1971). The voyage of Argo : the Argonautica. Harmondsworth, England, Penguin.

Atheneion. "Delos in Ancient Greek poetry." From http://stoa.wordpress.com/2007/02/18/delos-in-ancient-greek-poetry/.

Bittlestone, R., J. Diggle, et al. (2005). Odysseus unbound: the search for Homer's Ithaca. Cambridge ; New York, Cambridge University Press.

Byron, G. G. B. and J. J. McGann (2000). The major works. Oxford ; New York, Oxford University Press.

Cahill, T. (2004). Sailing the Wine-Dark Sea: Why the Greeks Matter, Anchor.

Chalcis, I. o. S. (2011). The Life of Pythagoras, Theophania Publishing.

Clift, C. (1956). Mermaid singing, pp. 320. Bobbs-Merrill Co.: Indianapolis, New York.

Dawkins, R. (2006). The God delusion. London, Bantam Press.

De Botton, A. (2000). The consolations of philosophy. Ringwood, Vic., Penguin.

Dodds, E. R. (1951). The Greeks and the Irrational, Cambridge Press.

Durrell, G. (1959). My family and other animals. Harmondsworth, Middlesex, Penguin Books.

Durrell, L. (1975). Prospero's cell : a guide to the landscape and manners of the island of Corcyra. London, Faber and Faber.

Encyclopedia Mythica (2012). "Phaedra." From: http://www.pantheon.org/articles/p/phaedra.html.

Fabre, J. W. (1997). The Hippocratic doctor : ancient lessons for the modern world. [London], The Royal Society of Medicine Press..

Fowles, J. (2001). The Magus, Back Bay Books.

Gardonyi, G. (1991). Eclipse of the crescent moon. Budapest, Corvina.

Gilson, E. (1964). Roman Catholics: The Case Against Celibacy. Time.

Hadingham, E. (2008). "Unlocking Mysteries of the Parthenon." Smithsonian Magazine, from http://www.smithsonianmag.com/history-archaeology/Unlocking-Mysteries-of-the-Parthenon.html.

Hanly, P. M. http://public.wsu.edu/~hanly/hum101/iliad_outline.html; http://public.wsu.edu/~hanly/hum101/odyssey_outline.html.

Hoare, F. R. (1991). Eight decisive books of antiquity. New York, Dorset Press.

Homer and R. Fagles (1990). The Illiad. New York, Penguin.

Homer and R. Fagles (1996). The Odyssey. New York ; London, Penguin.

Jong, E. (2004). Sappho's leap : a novel. London, Arcadia Books.

Kafka, F. and I. Parry (1994). The trial. London, Penguin Books.

Kazantzakis, N. (2000). Zorba the Greek. London, Faber.

Lette, K. (2007). How to Kill Your Husband, Pocket Books.

MacArthur, E. (2003). Taking on the world. London, Penguin.

Malouf, D. (2009). Ransom. North Sydney, N.S.W., Knopf.

New Oxford American Dictionary (2010). Oxford University Press, USA.

Papadopoulos, G. (2004). At the end of time: The eschatological Expectation, Holy Cross Orthodox Press, MA, USA.

Plato and B. Jowett (2000). The republic. Mineola, N.Y., Dover Publications.

Plato and D. Lee (1971). Timaeus and Critias. [Harmondsworth, Eng. ; Baltimore], Penguin Books.

Plutarch (1920). Plutarch Lives, IX, Demetrius and Antony. Pyrrhus and Gaius Marius, Loeb Classical Library.

Plutarch and I. Scott-Kilvert (1960). The rise and fall of Athens : nine Greek lives. Harmondsworth, Eng. ; Baltimore, Penguin Books.

Rushdie, S. (1991). Midnight's Children, Penguin Books.

Shakespeare, W. (1935). Julius Caesar. [s.l.], [s.n.].

Shakespeare, W. (1935). King Lear. London, N.Y.

Shakespeare, W. (1950). Antony and Cleopatra, Cambridge U.P.

Sophocles and R. Fagles, (1984). The three Theban plays. Harmondsworth, Middlesex, England ; New York, N.Y., Penguin Books.

Strabo, W. (2005). Geographica, Marix Verlag.

Thucydides, R. Warner, et al. (1972). The history of the Peloponnesian War, Penguin Books.

United Nations (1948). Charter of the United Nations and Statute of the International Court of Justice. U. Nations.

Verne, J. (1988). Around the world in eighty days. (United States), Aerie Books.

Virgil and D.A West. (1990). The Aeneid. London, England; New York, N.Y., USA, Penguin Books.

Wikipedia, c. (2012). Carpet, Wikimedia Foundation, Inc.

Wikipedia, c. (2012). Kombolói, Wikimedia Foundation, Inc.

Wikipedia, c. (2012). Liberalism, Wikimedia Foundation, Inc.